The Nine Symphonies of Beethoven

For David and Sara

By the Same Author

Talking About Symphonies
Talking About Concertos
Talking About Sonatas

The Nine Symphonies of
BEETHOVEN

Antony Hopkins

Heinemann
LONDON

University of Washington Press
SEATTLE

Heinemann Educational Books Ltd
22 Bedford Square, London WC1B 3HH

LONDON EDINBURGH MELBOURNE AUCKLAND
HONG KONG SINGAPORE KUALA LUMPUR NEW DELHI
IBADAN NAIROBI JOHANNESBURG KINGSTON
EXETER NH PORT OF SPAIN

Published in the USA by the University of Washington Press, Seattle

© Antony Hopkins 1981
First published 1981

Music examples executed by Dr Malcolm Lipkin

British Library Cataloguing in Publication Data

Hopkins, Antony
  The nine symphonies of Beethoven.
  1. Beethoven, Ludwig van. Symphonies
  I. Title
  785.1′1′0924   ML410.B4

  ISBN 0-435-81427-3

Library of Congress Cataloging in Publication Data

Hopkins, Antony, 1921–
  The nine symphonies of Beethoven.
  Bibliography: p.
  Includes index.
  1. Beethoven, Ludwig van, 1770–1827. Symphonies.
  I. Title.
  MT130.B43H6   785.1′1′0924   80-27053

  ISBN 0-295-95823-5

Filmset and printed in Great Britain by
BAS Printers Limited, Over Wallop, Hampshire

Contents

Preface

To add to the already immense stock of Beethoven literature is a daunting task; can anything new be said, anything be added to the millions of words already written? Scholars have worked so assiduously over every scrap of material that there is little research to be done. What I have tried to do within these pages is to approach the symphonies with the enthusiasm of a fresh explorer while taking account of the latest scholarship. The studies are more detailed than those to be found in various symposia but not so specialised as those of the true musicologists. Though not essential, miniature scores will prove a valuable aid—hence the numbering of bars in the music examples.

A.H.

I

Beethoven's Inheritance

Symphonies were not invented; as a musical form they evolved over a long period. Fundamentally the word symphony simply means 'sounding together'; it was thus a useful term to describe music for several instruments as opposed to music for a single performer. However it was by no means unacceptable to apply the word to compositions for solo instruments as Bach does in some of his keyboard works; in such a context symphony (or its German and Italian equivalents sinfonie or sinfonia) may be taken to mean the combination of several strands of music rather than a form. Even by the notoriously inexact standards of musical terminology the word symphony must stand unequalled in its vagueness. Consider for a moment something of the variety of compositions to which it has been attached; sacred works for choir and orchestra by Giovanni Gabrieli, instrumental interludes in Monteverdi operas, Purcell 'curtain-tunes', the introduction to Italian operatic arias (or indeed quite popular songs), the 'Pastoral Symphony' in Handel's Messiah, the first movement of a Bach Partita for solo harpsichord, Haydn's 'Surprise', Mozart's 'Jupiter', Beethoven's 'Eroica', Tchaikovsky's 'Pathétique', Mahler's 'Symphony of a thousand', Stravinsky's 'Symphony of Psalms', to say nothing of a massive four-movement piano work by Alkan, or six organ symphonies by Vierne. Truly the term might be described as all-embracing; yet one meaning has become predominant in all our minds—a substantial work for orchestra, usually in several movements, designed to reveal a wide range of mood ranging from the intellectual challenge of first movements through the intervening charms of a slow movement and a dance of sorts to the gaiety or possibly the apotheosis of a finale. Such was the pattern that emerged over a period of several decades in the first half of the eighteenth century. The initial prototype was the so-called Italian Overture, the 'symphony before the opera', whose function was not only to prepare the audience emotionally for events to come but also, more practically, to cover the arrival of late-comers. Catering for the need to capture the attention of restless audiences with a disposition to be entertained, such overtures were usually planned in contrasting sections, a lively introduction being followed by a seductive slow dance which in turn gave way to a quick movement to round things off. An alternative plan, the French Overture, began with a slow portentous introduction which was followed by a quick movement in fugal style. (Handel, a German composer, began his English oratorio 'Messiah' with a French overture.) Both types of overture acknowledged the need for contrasts of mood and tempo. In due course music of this nature acquired sufficient importance to cast off its operatic association and to develop an independent existence. Needless to say such a development could not begin to take place unless there were orchestras to play the music; where were they to be found? Not in city halls nor in the pump-rooms of spas but in the sumptuous homes of the aristocracy. Nowadays it is fashionable to decry the wealthy and the well-born as social parasites, yet their influence on the development of the arts was incalculable. Painters, sculptors, architects, landscape-designers, furniture-makers, couturiers, coach-builders and musicians were all members of a vast army of creative talents whose artistic potential was only realised through aristocratic patronage. A composer who failed to become attached to a nobleman's household would have had little chance of hearing his orchestral work performed since, apart from a few notable exceptions, municipal professional orchestras were a nineteenth-century development. Of nearly sixty orchestras of any permanence during the eighteenth century, four were attached to theatres, six to opera-houses, eight to churches, chapels or the private households of the church dignitaries; five only might be classified as independent or 'professional'—the Leipzig Concert-Gesellschaft, the London Foundling Hospital, the London Salomon Concert orchestra, the Paris Concert Spirituel and the orchestra 'La Pouplinière' from the same city;[1] the remainder were dependent on royal or aristocratic patronage, part of a princely establishment to be regarded with much the same pride as might be accorded to a string of racehorses or a herd of pedigree cattle today. If Haydn, who was ultimately to write over 100 symphonies, refrained from composing one until he was twenty-five (some say twenty-seven) it was because he would have regarded the operation as pointless until such time as he acquired a patron; unquestionably he would have known *how* to write a symphony since he had closely studied the music of such predecessors as C. P. E. Bach, Wagenseil and Gassmann, each of whom had explored the form. Perhaps the most important composer of symphonies before Haydn (though not necessarily an influence upon his work) was Johann Stamitz (1717–1757), a Czech who had something like fifty symphonies to his credit, written for what was reputedly the finest orchestra in Europe at the court of Mannheim. The English musicologist Burney heard the Mannheim orchestra and described it as 'deservedly celebrated. There are more solo players and good composers in this than perhaps in any other orchestra in Europe; it is an army of generals, equally fit to plan a battle as to fight it.'

[1] This information taken from Adam Carse, *The Orchestra in the Eighteenth Century*, I. W. Heffer, 1940.

2

This mention of composers as members of an orchestra is intriguing; how did Burney know that the players had this additional skill? Presumably because whatever programmes he heard consisted largely of music written by Stamitz and members of the orchestra; it underlines the contention that the availability of an orchestra was the first prerequisite for the emergence of an orchestral repertoire. The constitution of the Mannheim orchestra can be accurately charted over a period of more than sixty years (1720–1782). At its most sumptuous it had twenty-two violins divided equally into first and second, four violas, four cellos, four double-basses, two each of flutes, oboes and clarinets, four bassoons, two horns, timpani and (if required) no fewer than twelve trumpets, presumably part of the small private armies which flourished even as late as the 1770s. By comparison the orchestra which Haydn had at his disposal when he was at Esterhaz was pathetically small—eleven violins, one being Haydn himself acting as leader, two violas, two cellos, two double-basses, two oboes, two bassoons, two horns. This little band, only twenty-three strong, was nevertheless sufficient to inspire a seemingly endless flow of symphonies from Haydn's fertile pen. If flutes, clarinets, trumpets or drums were needed they were probably pressed into service from village bands, or alternatively 'doubled' by players already in the orchestra. The practise of doubling was very prevalent, flute and oboe normally being in the hands of the same player. For this reason we usually find flutes *or* oboes in the early symphonies of both Mozart and Haydn, seldom flutes *and* oboes. Clarinets, first appearing around 1750, were not generally available for some time; these too seem to have been doubled by the versatile oboists who at times must have wondered which instrument to pick up. As for the trumpets and drums they were so coupled together that like as not the drummer would look over the trumpeter's shoulder and improvise a part by matching him blow for blow. Trumpet parts were amazingly simple considering the remarkable virtuosity that had been called for in the Baroque era. When we see the demands Bach made on his trumpeters in the B minor Mass, the Magnificat or in many of the cantatas, it is hard to comprehend how a race of true virtuoso players could have become virtually extinct in less than a lifetime. It is thought to have been due to the jealous guarding of what might be termed a trade secret, the few players capable of playing such awesomely difficult parts being over-reluctant to pass on their ability to a new generation. Whatever the reason, the sad fact remains that the trumpet parts in scores by Mozart, Haydn and even Beethoven himself are relatively pedestrian, largely consisting of reinforcements of the tonic or dominant while adding emphasis to the rhythm. Duplicating these almost primitive patterns would not have been beyond the wit of any musically competent timpanist. Horn-parts were more enterprising, and Haydn in particular uses horns with enterprise and courage, sometimes demanding dangerously high but exhilaratingly effective notes.

Let us try to imagine what it must have been like to eavesdrop on the first read-through of a Haydn symphony, supposing that with the aid of some magical time-machine we could be transported back to the Esterhazy residence without losing our twentieth-century preconceptions. The first thing that would strike us would be the sheer lack of numbers; three desks of first violins, two of seconds and one only of violas, cellos and basses would seem barely adequate for a rather poorly supported school orchestra by our standards. Haydn himself would be standing by the front desk of violins, his own fiddle in hand. (Later, in London, he was to direct his symphonies from a centrally placed piano or harpsichord, but prior to that triumphant experience he would have led the violins himself.) At the first wind chords we would doubtless wince since all authorities agreed that intonation was a perpetual problem. Burney's frequent criticism of even the most admired orchestras of the day was faulty intonation: 'I know it is natural to those [wind] instruments to be out of tune,' he wrote, more in resignation than in anger. (Even Quantz (1697–1773), composer of about 300 flute concertos and its most renowned exponent, admitted that the flute had a natural fault in that some of the sharpened notes were never in tune.) Since large rooms with little furniture tend to have an excess of resonance, the impact of horns, trumpets and drums would seem positively coarse, even overwhelming, especially as the brass players were probably more accustomed to playing out-of-doors.

One advantage Haydn did have; his orchestra was in residence and had little else to do but play. Over the years he must have drilled into the players some sense of style and discipline so that at least their familiarity with his work ensured that he did not perpetually have to go over the same ground. But when after Prince Nicolaus' death Haydn became a free agent, able to travel to London, he must have been intoxicated with the excitement of witnessing the impression his music made on popular audiences, so different from the enclosed society to which he was used. Even so, the Salomon orchestra was still puny in numbers, a maximum of sixteen violins, four violas, three cellos, four double-basses, two each of the woodwind family, a pair of horns, a pair of trumpets and a timpanist. It would have been the largest orchestra Haydn would ever have experienced, but it was substantially smaller than the 'Concert de la Loge Olympique' for which he had written the so-called Paris symphonies of 1785–1786. Not only did the French orchestra have forty violins and ten double-basses; they also had a uniform—pale blue dress-coats, lace cuffs and decorative swords which the cellists may well have found something of an impediment.

Haydn's first visit to London took place in 1791, when Beethoven would have been in his twenty-first year. He returned to Austria in 1792, passing through Bonn and it was there that the two composers met and became acquainted. Beethoven showed Haydn a cantata[1] as a specimen of his work, creating a favourable enough impression to be accepted as a pupil. At the expense of the Elector of Bonn, Beethoven soon set off for Vienna to begin studies with the sixty-year-old composer. The fact that Haydn by then had written ninety-eight symphonies while Beethoven had written none does not seem to have abashed the young man. As might have been expected, he was a difficult pupil. Haydn put him on to a course of strict counterpoint, a discipline so unacceptable that Beethoven persuaded another teacher called Johann Schenk to help him with the exercises. Thus it was that unwittingly Haydn was gulled into correcting Schenk's work believing it to be Beethoven's. Even the discovery (after a year) of how he had been duped did not lessen Haydn's regard for his unruly pupil; he lent him money and interceded most generously on his behalf with the Elector Max Franz. When he returned to London for a second visit, Haydn arranged for Beethoven to continue his studies under the tutelage of Albrechtsberger.

It is futile to pretend that Beethoven was other than arrogant and boorish in his behaviour towards his teachers. Already established as a masterly pianist and a brilliant improviser, he was not likely to take kindly to criticism. His admiration for Haydn as a *fellow*-composer was unbounded; to accept him as a *master* was a different matter for it implied an inferiority in himself which this archetypal Angry Young Man was unable to come to terms with. It seems that he never forgave Haydn for criticising the third of his Op.1 piano trios, a work which he himself regarded with favour.

Clearly Beethoven was virtually unteachable and his three principal teachers, Salieri, Albrechtsberger and Haydn all seem to have had somewhat mixed feelings about the responsibility of directing his undoubted genius into the most productive channels. Of the three, Haydn would unquestionably have been the most helpful, a fact acknowledged by Beethoven with the dedication of the Op.2 piano sonatas (1796). If Beethoven, like all too many students, was not interested in doing studies in counterpoint for his distinguished master, there must yet have been many conversations of infinite value to him, discussions about orchestration, explorations of recently completed scores; no musician had a greater wealth of practical experience than Haydn, and Beethoven cannot have been so foolish as not to derive some benefit from it.

Curiously enough the bulk of the music written by Beethoven in his formative years gives very little evidence of his formidable genius. At times it may show flashes of eccentricity, but for the most part it is rather shallow imitative stuff based on conventional models. As a twenty-year-old he was positively inept by comparison with Mozart, Schubert or Mendelssohn. With

---

[1] Probably the funeral cantata discussed later in this chapter.

hindsight it is possible to detect an occasional suggestion of a theme that was to flower into something memorable in later years, but that is hardly surprising since so much thematic material is based on the notes of the common chord. Yet beneath an almost bland surface of musical triviality a huge creative force was slowly stirring, biding its time—perhaps because in his innermost heart, Beethoven knew that he had not as yet the power to give shape and substance to such immensities. One work alone stands far above the others at this time, a work which ironically he was never to hear performed. It is the 'Funeral Cantata on the death of the Emperor Joseph II' composed in 1790. Although it is possible for musical scholars to pinpoint the sort of influences one might expect in a young man's music—a touch of Gluck here, a trace of Mozart there—the fact remains that this score, unperformed until 1884, is the first work to reveal the true stature of the composer. Though it was apparently deemed unplayable by those who first saw the orchestral parts, the scoring shows the hand of a master, totally confident that every note would achieve its effect. Presumably because of the unco-operative attitude of the players projected performances of the work were twice cancelled, a fate which also befell the companion cantata which Beethoven wrote to celebrate the accession of Joseph II's successor Leopold II. Surprisingly we have no record of Beethoven's reaction to this considerable setback at a crucial period in his life. He must have realised that the funeral cantata in particular represented an enormous step forward towards artistic maturity; in fact he was to utilise some of the material in the second finale of *Fidelio*, a sure acknowledgement that he realised its worth.

I have not seen it suggested elsewhere, but I suspect that this double blow brought a psychological trauma in its wake. The effective rejection of two substantial works in a single year must have hurt Beethoven's self-esteem; certainly he continued to compose, but not for orchestra. Apart from the first two piano concertos, a form in which his mastery of the keyboard assured him of success, all the works written during the remaining ten years of the century were sonatas or chamber music of some kind. It seems quite probable that he had suffered a shock comparable to that experienced by Brahms after the 'failure' of his great piano concerto in D minor; the reaction was certainly similar—a marked reluctance to embark on anything so daunting as a symphony. Judging from his impetuous nature one would have expected the young Beethoven to have welcomed the challenge, indeed to have hurled himself at it with the enthusiasm of a mountaineer confronted with a spectacular climb. Instead, he was to wait a further ten years before producing his first symphony.[1] Whatever seeds the lessons with Haydn had implanted lay

---

[1] Sketches for one dating from approximately 1795 exist, but they are insubstantial.

dormant for seven winters; with apt timing they were to flower with the dawn of a new century in the year 1800.

The game of 'If only . . .' is perpetually fascinating in spite of its futility. We usually play it with regard to a hypothetical future—if only Mozart had lived to be sixty, if only Beethoven had not been deaf, if only we could win the pools. For once let us play it retrospectively and suppose that Beethoven and Mozart had been born in the same year (1756) and shared the same brief life-span of thirty-five years; how would we regard them then? Obviously they would have shared a common musical language since to a large extent all composers (except extreme eccentrics such as Gesualdo) are prisoners of the period in which they live. Mozart was singularly unfortunate in his search for aristocratic patronage, being treated abominably by the Archbishop of Salzburg. Beethoven would undoubtedly have fared even worse since his temperament would have precluded the sycophancy that was essential if a composer wished to progress. Without a court orchestra at his disposal Beethoven would have had some difficulty in achieving performances of his works; it should be understood that eighteenth-century composers seldom wrote for posterity. The unflagging industry showed by Mozart, Haydn and their equally productive contemporaries was designed to meet a continual demand for new music; whether it was an opera, a symphony, a concerto, a quartet or a sonata Mozart always had an immediate performance in mind whether by other hands or his own. In earlier days Bach poured out a flood of cantatas and organ music, not to be performed on the radio in the twentieth century but to be played on Sunday fortnight—sooner if the parts could be copied in time. Handel's prolific output of opera was largely prompted by the need to go one better than his commercial rivals, to provide new attractions for a notoriously fickle public. The sheer facility with which such composers met these demands is hard to accept; it was only made possible by the use of formulae, repeated quaver chords in accompaniments, running figures based on scales, conventional arpeggio figuration and the like. Bach wrote fugues in great numbers not because they were cerebral or difficult, but because it was a style that came very easily to him. The groundwork of a fugue takes care of itself; one can plot the various entries almost without thought.

Beethoven's creative processes were such that he would have been unlikely to survive in a comparable climate. Certainly he could (and did) write trivial music using the slick formulae of a musical production line; but when we come to the masterworks their birth pangs were slow and arduous. Mozart could write three superb symphonies in a matter of six weeks;[1] sketches for a Beethoven symphony extend over several years. According to Mozart's

---

[1] 'Expert' opinions range between two and eight!

librettist, Da Ponte, the composition of *The Marriage of Figaro* took Mozart a mere six weeks, whereas Beethoven mulled over *Fidelio* (or *Leonore* as it was originally called) from 1803–1806, the final version not actually being produced until 1814. Handel reputedly wrote his 'Messiah' in twenty-one days, though admittedly drawing freely on previous compositions as was his wont; Beethoven spread the composition of the 'Missa Solemnis' over a period extending from 1818–1823. One could argue from such comparisons that temperamentally Bach, Handel, Haydn and Mozart were sprinters where Beethoven was a long-distance runner. However long-distance runners put in a tremendous amount of roadwork to build stamina; if Beethoven's creative processes seem slow they were also remorseless. His sketchbooks show an extraordinary capacity for painstaking improvement, the original ideas often seeming so banal as to demand instant dismissal. Yet paradoxically the manuscripts often appear to have been written in feverish haste as though the vision, once realised, had to be captured before it disappeared. Though we may marvel at the prodigious output of Bach, Handel, Mozart, Haydn or Schubert, Beethoven's sheer productivity seems even more remarkable since all the evidence goes to show that composition for him was an arduous process. It is tempting to ascribe this to his deafness, but the sketchbooks predate the onset of deafness by a substantial period.

With all this in mind we return to the question 'how would Beethoven have fared had he been an exact contemporary of Mozart?' Would he have developed the symphony in the same way? Certainly not since orchestras were not available to scale such heights. Would he have achieved a similar revolution in the piano sonatas? Again the answer must be negative since the instruments were not yet made that could cope with such demands. It is highly unlikely that he would have stretched musical resources any further than Mozart did, whether in harmony, orchestral invention, dramatic content or sheer scale of vision. The dissonances that Mozart piles up in the closing bars of the introduction to the Symphony No. 39 are not matched in Beethoven until the 'Eroica'. The breath-taking beautiful moment in *Fidelio* when the prisoners emerge from their dark cells into the sunlight was anticipated musically by Mozart in the slow movement of his very first symphony, written at the age of eight; to simplify comparison I have transposed the Mozart example down a fourth.

Ex. 1. (Beethoven)

etc.

Ex. 2. (Mozart)

(It is a nice coincidence that Mozart uses the same Doh-ray-fah-mé pattern in the finale of his last symphony, the 'Jupiter'.) Obviously Beethoven's operatic treatment is more expansive, the vision more dramatic, but that is a matter of the use that is made of material rather than the quality of the material itself.

The fact remains that composers respond to the historical situation in which they find themselves, whether their name be Monteverdi, Mozart, Beethoven or Stockhausen. They may stretch the available resources to the utmost but the resources have to be there in the first place; Stockhausen would scarcely have conceived electronic music had some sort of apparatus, however 'primitive', not been available. The essential apparatus that Beethoven needed to realise his potential was an orchestra larger than any likely to be maintained in a royal household, a piano more powerful than any Mozart knew and a climate of opinion that would accept the artist as a leader rather than a servant. For all of these he had to wait though all were to come in due course. The world was ripe for change; the French Revolution of 1789 had proved to be more than a little local difficulty. If in the closing decade of the eighteenth century Napoleon was standing in the wings waiting to play the role of Ruler of the World, Beethoven was facing him on the other side just as ready to act out his own destiny as Liberator of Music.

2

Symphony No. 1 in C Major
Op. 21

Dedicated to Baron van Swieten

Orchestra: 2 flutes; 2 oboes; 2 clarinets; 2 bassoons; 2 horns; 2 trumpets;
2 timpani; strings

1. Adagio molto leading to Allegro con brio
2. Andante cantabile con moto
3. Menuetto e Trio
4. Finale: Adagio leading to Allegro molto e vivace.

First performance: 2 April 1800

Much has been written about the unorthodoxy of Beethoven's introductory bars in this symphony. The standard way of beginning any large-scale work, whether symphony, concerto, sonata or quartet, was to spell out a sequence of notes or harmonies that would establish the tonic or 'home' key. In an idiom in which tonality or the sense of key was so important, such a move was nearly as fundamental as setting out the pieces on a chess-board before the start of a game. Examine the start of all the Mozart symphonies and you will find that every single one begins with a clear and unequivocal declaration of tonality; if any doubt remains at the end of the first bar (for instance if it is a unison D with the options of D major or D minor still open) that doubt will be dispelled by the end of the first phrase. The same applies to the vast majority of the Haydn symphonies although occasionally he will begin a symphony in the tonic minor at a slow tempo before changing to the major for the ensuing allegro. While the idea of beginning a work in a foreign key was not unprecedented (C. P. E. Bach having begun an F major sonata with an opening phrase in C minor) it was nevertheless extremely unusual and Beethoven added to his abuse of convention by following his initial and misleading establishment of F major with a half-hearted trip to A minor followed by an extremely positive assertion of G major.

Ex. 3.

Just how positive Beethoven felt this chord of G to be is shown by his insertion of a theoretically unnecessary natural sign (♮) in front of the F quaver in bar 4. 'They'll never believe this,' he seems to be saying and anticipates an incredulous query from the violin section by meeting their objection in advance. Incidentally the scoring is highly individual, the impact of the sustained woodwind chords being intensified by *pizzicato* strings, launching the harmonies with a twang comparable to an archer's bowstring as it wings an arrow on its way.

Now so far each bar (1–3) has begun with the chord known as the dominant seventh. So important is this chord to the whole conception of this symphony that one might punningly refer to it as the Dominance of Dominants. Most commentaries on the symphony dismiss the introduction with a brief acknowledgement of its unorthodoxy without attempting in any way to explain its function—if indeed they see it as having one. Is it just a gesture designed to command attention or is there more to it than that? On closer examination one can see that this introduction far from being a mere gateway is a seminal source from which much of the subsequent Allegro is derived. The one 'proper' dominant seventh to establish the home key of C major is reserved for the final bar of the introduction:

Ex. 4.

Observe how even the first chord of bar 12, seemingly also a dominant seventh, is tainted by an alien F♯ in the ascending scale in the strings; only the very final chord before the double bar is uncorrupted. Linking that chord to its resolution at the start of the allegro produces this cadence:

which is an obvious parallel to the very first bar, though now behaving with propriety. This in itself is not a great discovery, but if we extend this line of reasoning into the Allegro we find that the main theme of the movement is nothing but a series of identical cadences, albeit disguised by being stated melodically rather than harmonically. Reduced to its essential *implied* harmony the theme becomes this:

Ex. 5.

This, it can be seen, is simply a number of reiterations of the very cadence that bridged the gap from the Introduction to the Allegro. However if we pursue the matter further we find another link of structural importance. The sustained woodwind chords in bars 17–18 (see Ex. 4) are rhythmically ambiguous; the first chord (bar 17) is a confirmation of what has gone before; the second chord (bar 18) is in fact comparable in function to the very first chord of the symphony in that it is destructive of the 'home' tonality of C as well as being yet another dominant seventh. Now it is musically sensible to assume that the allegro is what is known as *doppio movimento*—twice the speed. The semiquaver descent in bar 18

is clearly equivalent to the demisemiquaver descent in bar 12

Therefore the semibreve chords in the woodwind (bars 17–18) are equal in duration to the minim chords of the introduction. If then we take the last chord of bar 12 (slow tempo) and equate it with the woodwind chord in bar 18 (quick tempo), resolving both, we arrive at this sequence.

Ex. 6.

Assuming a common tempo I have had to change the notation of the second cadence from

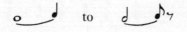

by doing so the relevance of the Introduction is made absolutely clear.

In case this seems to be a somewhat laborious way of making a debatable point, let us now turn to the Reprise. Having re-stated the main theme *ff* in unison lest any *dummkopf* in the audience should have forgotten it, Beethoven embarks on an extended sequence of dominant sevenths, each inevitably modulating to a new key which is no sooner established than it is cancelled out.

Ex. 7.

The first bar of this example (188) is exactly comparable to the D minor chord in bar 23 of the Exposition — or the final bar of Ex. 5. However, that initial venture away from C major is firmly rebuffed with an angry trill that re-establishes the tonality. Here, in the Recapitulation, it is the starting point for a series of flying visits to F major (bar 190), G major (192), A minor (193), B♭ major (194), C major (195) — 'sorry, no time to stay, must dash!' — D minor (196), F major (197) — 'what, back again?' — G major (198), at which point he keeps us firmly on a basic G (the dominant of C) for eight bars before consenting to return home to C. This entire sequence, perhaps the most thrilling moment in the whole symphony, is directly derived from the very first bar. Fully to understand the relevance of bar 1 we have had to explore bars 189–198!

This necessary excursion has forced us to abandon an orderly progress through the movement; let us return to the First Subject or main theme. Having started life as a scantily clad harmonic sequence (cf. Exx. 4–5) it soon blossoms into a much more solidly based theme, ambitious enough indeed to aspire towards the grandeur of the finale of the Fifth Symphony.

Ex. 8 Symphony 1

Symphony 5. (Finale)

With the neat *legerdemain* of an accomplished conjuror Beethoven fuses this idea with the initial one. It is a simple matter to decorate Ex. 8:

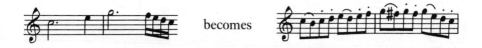

becomes

A quaver pattern such as this is not far removed from bar 3 of the Allegro (Ex. 4 bar 14); just six notes are enough to build a sequence with:

Ex. 9.

Here in embryo is an implied harmonic sequence clearly related to the spectacular development shown in Ex. 7. Place some flesh on its somewhat spiky bones and we arrive at this progression:

Ex. 10.

Whether consciously or not it is certainly a harbinger of the events already noted in bars 189–198, even arriving at precisely the same harmonic destination, albeit by a rather less tortuous route.

The Second Subject is sheer enchantment, not so much a theme as a quasi-operatic ensemble in which the 'voices' engage in a diverting colloquy initiated by the oboe and flute.

Ex. 11.

An ingenious and often unnoticed touch of craftsmanship is the sparsity of the accompanying figures, surely derived from the First Subject whose fourth and fifth bars,

are neatly transformed into a supporting pattern that minces along delightfully beneath the oboe's first phrase.

The ghost of Mozart hovers in the air, soon to be exorcised with peremptory rhythms that suggest the rattle of a side-drum, something not yet to be found in any respectable orchestra. Out of this brief clash of arms emerges a passage of mystery and magic; cellos and basses lead us into the shadows while the upper strings accompany with gently throbbing harmonies that offer intimations of minor keys as yet unvisited.

Ex. 12.

etc.

Compare the first two bars of this remarkable episode with bars 53–54 of Ex. 11 and it is easy enough to see how Beethoven arrived at it. For most composers this transformation alone would be enough; the touch of genius (as opposed to ingenious) is provided by a marvellously eloquent phrase on first oboe then oboe and bassoon, a phrase more characteristic of Schubert than Beethoven in its touching innocence.

Ex. 13.

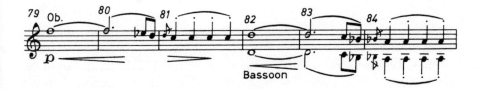

As if ashamed of this indulgence Beethoven gives us a firm reminder of the opening fragment of the First Subject, now in the dominant key of G—

before ending the Exposition with a brief Codetta whose most notable feature is an obliquely disguised reference to the Second Subject,

The Exposition having been duly repeated, thereby giving us a clear sense of the whereabouts of C major, Beethoven begins the Development with a rude shock, a loud chord based on C♯, the note best calculated to make us lose our bearings again. Three times he alternates tentative reminders of the First Subject with disturbing syncopations.

Ex. 14.

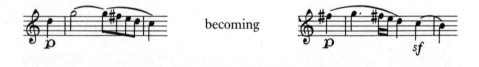

There follows a serious working out of the potential of the fourth bar of the main theme, those same few notes that were skilfully employed as an accompaniment to the Second Subject. As a Development it is a classic example of the way in which the smallest musical units are often the most useful. In one form or another that fragment of five rising crotchets appears eleven times between bars 122–135; an even smaller fragment of the First Subject

skips through the score nineteen times between bars 144–159. Towards the end of the Development quite a storm breaks out with angry unison strings placed in violent opposition to the full wind band. (Tovey points out the exceptionally full use Beethoven makes of wind instruments in this symphony.) It may be stretching the evidence but it seems to me that at the height of this storm the wind are presenting us with a somewhat tortured extension of the Second Subject. Perhaps a side-by-side comparison will clarify the issue.

Maybe?

At any rate the storm draws to an abrupt close; unison wind spell out the notes of a dominant seventh in measured tones and with a sudden snap, Beethoven whisks us into the Recapitulation. I have already quoted its most significant passage (Ex. 7); otherwise it follows the normal practice, the Second Subject appearing in the tonic key and due reference being made to any events of significance in the Exposition including the inspired excursion shown in Ex. 12. If there is rather too much unadulterated C major in the Coda (21 bars in all) Beethoven must have felt justified in confirming once and for all a tonality that he had originally approached by so devious a route.

The central two movements present a paradox; the slow movement is not so much a slow movement as an old-fashioned minuet pretending to be a fugue. The 'Minuet' on the other hand is certainly no such thing; it is Beethoven's first symphonic scherzo, a positive whirlwind of a movement whose label *Menuetto* can only have been attached to it as a Beethovenian joke, since the further instruction *Allegro molto e vivace* as well as Beethoven's own metronome mark of ♩ = 108 (added in 1817) forbids any tempo remotely comparable to the requirements of a minuet. While the slow movement is clearly the work of a Haydn pupil, the 'Minuet'-scherzo shows the pupil at his most headstrong, blowing convention to the winds.

The Andante begins with a demure theme given to the second violins alone.

Ex. 15.

Such unaccustomed exposure is calculated to frighten the wits out of any insecure players who find themselves among the 'seconds' because of technical ineptitude, but Beethoven had to start thus as he needs his first violins for the fourth entry of his little 'fugue'. It is an interesting comment on the probable number of players that he had at his disposal that he gives the second entry to violas and cellos in unison (quite possibly only seven or eight players in all), while the third entry is played by double basses reinforced with two bassoons. It would seem prudent therefore in any modern performance to reduce the strength of the combined violas and cellos by at least half in order to preserve a proper balance with the second violins.

The first violins duly make their entrance with substantial support from the wind; all is ordered and graceful, the opening paragraph being rounded off with a distinctly Mozartean phrase whose changing emphases recall Susanna at her most bewitching.

Ex. 16.

Sforzandi such as these should never be treated as hard accents but rather as a loving stress.

For a moment or two Beethoven leaves the strings on their own with a phrase of extreme elegance that is subsequently silvered at the edge by flutes while the violins add the daintiest embroidery. A brief outburst of *forte* in characteristic eighteenth-century dotted rhythm again brings a potent suggestion of an operatic ensemble. In so gracious a context timpani might seem to be unwanted intruders, but Beethoven introduces them in the most imaginative manner. Very quietly the timpanist taps out a dotted rhythm (written as

but in this case almost certainly meant to be played as triplets)[1] while the first violins and a solo flute unwind a decorative thread of melody spun from a continuous pattern of triplets. The only sustained element in this translucent scoring comes from two discreet trumpets, while the lower strings and the remaining wind alternate in gentle cross accents that lend a delightful ambiguity to the rhythm. Mozart himself was never more enchanting.

The second half of the movement begins with a mysterious modulation which may well have inspired the nineteen-year-old Schubert when he composed his Fifth Symphony in 1816. Here first is Beethoven:

Ex. 17.

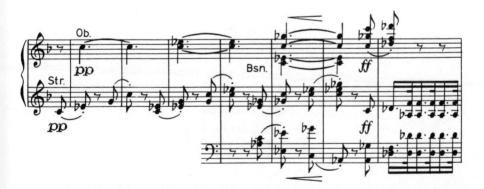

[1] The eighteenth-century custom being for dotted rhythms to be affected by their context.

At an exactly comparable place in his slow movement, Schubert has this more lyrical version of a markedly similar progression.

Ex. 18.

Change Beethoven's dotted rhythms to Schubert's equal semiquavers and the resemblance is more apparent; moreover if we pursue the comparison we find a duet-dialogue in Beethoven between oboe/bassoon and flute, a duet-dialogue in Schubert between violins and oboe/bassoon; Beethoven's phrases are initially concerned with rising sevenths which he presents unembellished:

Schubert also offers us rising sevenths, though his are lovingly disguised:

While similarities such as these do not render Schubert liable to prosecution for breach of copyright, they suggest at least a strong (even if unconscious) influence. He certainly would have heard Beethoven's symphony—it was popular and relatively often performed; an arrangement for piano quintet was published as early as 1802 without the composer's consent and it is quite likely that the young Schubert may have come across a copy some years later. His near-worship of Beethoven would have made him anxious to study every note he could get his hands on.

The dotted rhythm shown in Ex. 17 is not surprisingly appropriated by the timpanist who 'corrects' the tonality by establishing an often repeated C as a pedal-point, a note that refuses to give way whatever chromaticisms or dissonances may be piled on top of it. C is of course the dominant of F major, and only by fixing his course by it can Beethoven successfully navigate his way back to the tonic key. The rest of the orchestra, seemingly intoxicated by the heady delights of such exotic keys as Db major or Bb minor, shows a singular reluctance to go back to dull old F, postponing the return for twenty bars. At last the haven is reached and with it the original subject; once more it is given to the second violins but this time the cellos provide a delicate countertune which the first violins in turn find irresistible. Despite novelties such as this, the formal requirements of the movement dictate that all the salient features of the Exposition should be revisited, making the necessary transpositions to restore a tonal balance. However the dotted rhythm of Ex. 17 (last bar) loses its bite, only being allowed to take part in the final Coda if it agrees to behave. The last six bars are the nearest thing to a wink you could expect to find in music.

Ex. 19.

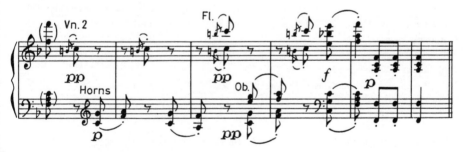

It is a joke he had already tried to delightful effect in the closing pages of the Piano Concerto in Bb. In that context it was the sort of humour one might expect, a display of irreverent high spirits; here it is much more private as though he was giving an impish smile to his closest friends.

The third movement, so often the least substantial, is here far and away the most original of the four, not only for its indecorous haste but also for the unconventionality of its modulations. It is the largest comparable movement he was to write for some time whether in sonatas or chamber music. Its initial theme covers a span of one-and-a-half octaves, though, as the brackets reveal, one could regard it as an octave phrase followed by a compressed version squeezed into a fifth.

Ex. 20.

An opening phrase of this kind, eight bars in length, should according to convention be followed by something of similar proportions, sixteen or at most thirty-two bars long. To show just how far he was prepared to discard the proprieties of the formal minuet, Beethoven gives us a second section of seventy-one bars whose breathless flight takes us through a number of remote keys. The springboard for this remarkable journey is the C♯–D rising semitone in bars 6–7 of the preceding example.

Blinded as we often are by the *appearance* of sharps and flats as opposed to their function, we can easily fail to see the connection between this interval and the ensuing phrase.

Ex. 21

They may not look the same, but if one plays them in this way,

their relationship immediately becomes apparent. Adherents to the school of Functional Analysis may seize on this as proof that it all stems from bar 1 of the symphony (Ex. 3), but I regard that as stretching the evidence; because some rising semitones are related it does not mean that they all are.

The shred of material in Ex. 21 keeps Beethoven going for many a sequence, enabling him to move convincingly into the contradictory key of D♭ major—a procedure sufficiently unorthodox as to justify several stamps with his foot to show he really means it. On the well-known principle that 'if I'd wanted to go there I wouldn't've started from 'ere', he now has to find his way back. The rising semitone to which I have already drawn attention provides a key to unlock several doors.

Ex. 22.

In its much more nimble-footed way this section matches the mysterious quality to be found in Ex. 12 from the first movement though I doubt if Beethoven intended the relationship to be felt. Both passages plunge us into unexpectedly shadowy places, both emerge triumphantly into the light of day; the scoring is not dissimilar, the repeated crotchet chords are common to both.

Such diversions from the 'proper' key of C call for some reassurance once it has been regained and this Beethoven provides with fourteen bars of tonic-dominant harmony to round off the section. There follows the so-called Trio which the form traditionally demanded, an oasis of calm after the excitements we have just experienced. Oboes, clarinets, bassoons and horns provide curiously static harmonies—eight bars of C major, four bars of A minor, four bars of D minor and so on while the violins make gracefully flowing gestures of agreement. In the second part clarinets and horn keep us suspended on a dominant seventh for no fewer than fourteen bars, teasing the violins by delaying its inevitable resolution for so long. However once the tantalizingly deferred C major chord is regained, it is scored with the greatest ingenuity, the tone-colour augmenting and changing five times in as many bars.

	Bar 122	123	124	125	126
Flutes				*♩ ♩ ♩	♩
Oboes			*♩ ♩	♩ ♩	♩ ♩	♩
Clarinets	♩ ♩	♩ ♩	♩ ♩	♩ ♩	♩ ♩	♩
Bassoons		*♩ ♩	♩ ♩	♩ ♩	♩ ♩	♩
Horns	♩ ♩	♩ ♩	♩ ♩	♩ ♩	♩ ♩	♩
Trpts.				*♩ ♩	♩ ♩	♩
Timp.			*♩.	♩.	♩.
Vns. 1					*♩ ♩
Vns. 2					*♩ ♩
Vla.			*♩ ♩	♩ ♩	♩ ♩	♩
Vc.			*♩ ♩	♩ ♩	♩ ♩	♩
D. Bass			*♩ ♩	♩ ♩	♩ ♩	♩

Each entry (*) up to and including bar 125 is marked *p* followed by a *crescendo*; only the violins in bar 126 come in *ff*, but they need to since by then the accumulation of sound has been impressive.

Impressive is the word for the opening gesture of the finale, a giant unison G from the entire orchestra sustained with the fullest tone. After such an opening, great events must surely lie ahead. In fact the giant unison is a giant leg-pull; like a bevy of hesitant beginners clutching unfamiliar instruments, the first violins make abortive attempts to play a scale, progressing one note further each time.

Ex. 23.

26

The loss of confidence on the first note of bar 5 just when things were beginning to go better is delightfully human. It seems that one conductor[1] in Beethoven's time habitually omitted this passage because he felt it would make the audience laugh; he could not accept that such a game of peekaboo could belong in a symphony, yet Beethoven is clearly playing a game. Haydn would have appreciated the joke to the full, being much given to such musical pranks himself.

Now as I have already said (fn. p. 6) sketches for a symphony were made during the mid-1790s. For the most part they consist of single lines, unsupported by harmony; most of the material is feeble and Beethoven was quite proper to reject it. The one idea that crops up with increasing persistance leads directly to this finale, though intelligent guess-work tells us that in all probability he originally intended it to be the main subject of a *first* movement. Time after time he experiments with the idea of starting a theme with a swift rising scale, and it may well be that the violinists' tentative efforts to achieve the same object had a wryly humorous significance for the composer as he recalled his numerous struggles to find the theme. Here are some of the many 'false starts' he actually made during his search.

Ex. 24.

[1] Curiously named Türk.

27

When we are confronted with the final outcome of these clumsy fumblings we find it hard to believe that it did not spring to life in an instant. Every bar sparkles with humour and vitality; it has been criticised for being too much like Haydn, but it is nevertheless like Haydn at his very finest.

Ex. 25.

The initial scale proves to have astonishing potential, its first variant being in augmentation (notes of twice the duration) as a counterpoint to this bucolic phrase.

Ex. 26.

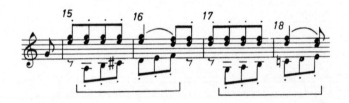

Beethoven makes extensive use of an inversion of the scale during the Bridge Passage that leads to the Second Subject. (The finale is in sonata form of the standard kind used for first movements, a fact which possibly supports my contention that the sketches quoted were intended for a first movement.) When the Second Subject materialises it proves to have the daintiness of a ballerina despite the discreet suggestion of a somewhat rustic oom-pah bass from the lower orders.

Ex. 27.

The rustic character becomes a good deal more evident between bars 78–86 when bouncing syncopations and rattling kettledrums conjure up visions of strapping peasants dancing their cares away. The Codetta to the Exposition contains what might be regarded as a rare miscalculation in the scoring when the second violins only are entrusted with important reminders of the initial scale. Against the full might of the rest of the orchestra they have little chance of making themselves heard; a friendly wave in their direction from the conductor will help to draw attention to their contribution, which may otherwise pass unnoticed.

The Development begins with further nimble scales, now leading to a spuriously pathetic phrase, spurious since it is merely a trap the better to catch us unawares with a sudden *fortissimo* outburst. This sudden roaring, such as Bottom might have emulated had he been allowed to play the Lion, gives way to a contrasting passage in which the cellos are given a chance to show that they too can play scales. Beethoven prudently suggests that the double-basses drop out at this point lest they prove unequal to his demands. In a passage whose delicacy Mendelssohn himself could not have excelled the little scales dart to and fro, now rising, now falling. Then, as if tiring of the game, they explode into a show of fury; two massive pauses lead us to a point where the least one expects is a mighty cadenza. Instead of fireworks, 'a mouse runs up the clock . . .' Timidly the little scale reappears, once, twice, three times, then tumbling over itself until at last it gets the tune back. Horns and oboes lead a joyous march through the closing pages decked with garlands of scales from flutes, clarinets and bassoons. Beethoven may well have been twenty-nine or so when he wrote it,[1] but this music is filled with the spontaneous happiness of children at play. Hindsight may easily lead us to regard it as less than representative of the Master; but if we share the joy he obviously felt in writing it the reward is rich indeed.

[1] The precise date cannot be ascertained but the score was probably completed early in 1800.

3

Interlude
A Private Despair

The way in which an individual reacts to personal disaster is rightly looked upon as a test of character. There are those who simply lie down and weep, whether by the waters of Babylon or a muddy canal being immaterial; there are those who blame others when in fact they are guilty of their own undoing; there are those who accept but who do nothing positive to fight back, and there are the rare and courageous souls for whom disaster is a challenge, a stimulus to greater effort. Such a one was Beethoven; indeed it could be argued that in the long run he became a better composer as a result of his deafness and the spiritual isolation it brought in its wake. At least its onset was sufficiently drawn-out to make it somewhat easier to come to terms with, however painful the process may have been. His own testimony is inconsistent concerning the precise date at which he realised his hearing was in danger. In an oft-quoted letter to a Dr Franz Wegeler dated 29 June 1801, he says, 'For almost two years I have ceased to attend any social functions, simply because I find it impossible to say to people: I am deaf'. On the other hand the *Heiligenstadt Testament* of October 1802[1] claims that 'for six years past I have fallen into an incurable condition . . . in the end compelled to contemplate a *lasting malady*, the cure of which may take years or even prove impossible'.

Now while every schoolchild, even if completely ignorant of his music, knows that Beethoven was deaf, he himself was at pains to keep it a secret as long as possible. Far from asking for sympathy he seems to have felt a sense of shame that so vital a faculty had become defective. He shunned society, unable to face the embarrassment of being incapable of sustaining conversation in a normal way. As a result of this wholly understandable reaction we now tend to assume that his affliction was more acute than it actually was; it suits our romantic conception to imagine him to have been *totally* deaf from the age of thirty or thereabouts. There is enough evidence to show that this view is needlessly dramatic; for one thing, his ability to hear seems to have been variable, almost normal at times even as late as 1808. Proof of this is to be found

---

[1]See pp. 32–34.

in a lengthy letter from a gifted young pianist called Wilhelm Rust who wrote to his sister (9 July 1808) describing a lesson he had had with Beethoven.

> He praised my playing, particularly in the Bach fugue, and said: 'You play that well,' which is much for him. Still he could not omit calling my attention to two mistakes. In a scherzo I had not played the notes crisply enough and at another time I had struck one note twice instead of binding it.[1]

This last detail is scarcely the sort of thing to have been noticed by a seriously deaf person; moreover at no point in the letter does Rust even mention the subject of deafness—surely the very first gem of personal news he would impart to his own sister. Czerny claims that Beethoven could hear both speech and music 'perfectly well' until nearly 1812, though the remark may have been coloured by loyalty. Beethoven's last public appearance as a pianist occurred as late as 1814 when he played the piano part in the 'Archduke' Trio, Op. 97. It seems that his co-performers had much to put up with and there is a painful description of a rehearsal written by Spohr, certainly a reliable witness.

> It was not a treat, for, in the first place, the pianoforte was badly out of tune, which Beethoven minded little since he did not hear it; secondly, there was scarcely anything left of the virtuosity of the artist which had formerly been so greatly admired. In *forte* passages the poor deaf man pounded on the keys till the strings jangled, and in *piano* he played so softly that whole groups of notes were omitted, so that the music was unintelligible unless one could look into the pianoforte part. I was deeply saddened at so hard a fate . . . Beethoven's continual melancholy was no longer a riddle to me.[2]

A second performance of the Trio was Beethoven's swansong as a performer, but that he could even have contemplated playing shows that he had not lost all hope.

By 1816 he had recourse to an ear trumpet for the first time while the first conversation books date from 1818, an indication that normal communication had become impossible. Yet even as late as 1822 he was still attempting to conduct, although the disastrous rehearsal of *Fidelio* in November of that year was one of the most humiliating experiences of his life. Though the overture went well enough, the orchestra being familiar with it, as soon as the singers began it was clear that Beethoven heard them not at all. The music ground to a halt; dismayed, Beethoven looked to left and right trying to determine what had happened. A dreadful silence ensued as he handed a notebook to his devoted disciple Anton Schindler so that he could write down what the trouble was. 'Please do not go on; will tell you more at home,' the unhappy man wrote. 'Out, quick!' said Beethoven and literally ran out into the street. Once he

---

[1] Thayer, *Life of Beethoven*. Vol II, Centaur Press, 1960, p. 117.
[2] Thayer, op. cit., p. 269.

reached his lodgings he threw himself down on the settee, covering his face with his hands like a tearful child. This shattering experience took place in 1822, twenty years after the historic document known as the *Heiligenstadt Testament*.

Now much as a rejected lover may feel that there is nothing left to live for and yet recover, so Beethoven seems to have suffered more at the onset of his deafness than in later years. His catalogue of ill-health was such that deafness was only one of many afflictions, one that he had perforce to learn to accept as best as he could. The most intense spiritual crisis seems to have occurred as early as 1802, a little over two years after the first performance of the Symphony No. 1. During the summer of that year he had, on his doctor's recommendation, moved to the country to the village of Heiligenstadt where the rural quiet would rest his ears and bring peace to his troubled mind. He suffered from buzzing or whistling noises in the head, the harder to endure for being inescapable; though quiet sounds were mostly inaudible, anything loud caused acute physical pain. It was a situation calculated literally to drive a man mad.

Having no such person as a psychiatrist in whom he might confide and reluctant to discuss the matter even with close friends, Beethoven seems to have hit intuitively upon a way of exorcising the demon that was tormenting him. He committed his innermost fears to paper in the form of a remarkable letter to his brothers Carl and Johann, though his relationship with them was far from cordial, so much so that he had a psychological block about actually putting Johann's name on to the page. In the circumstances it is all the stranger that he should confide so openly to them the very secret he had tried so hard to conceal from everyone else except his doctors. It is for this reason that I believe the letter to have served a deeper unconscious need that makes it directly comparable to the 'confessions' that are nowadays delivered from the psychiatrist's couch. Such corrosive fears as are revealed here must be brought out into the open before they can be effectively conquered.

TESTAMENT

For my Brothers Carl and   Beethoven

O you my fellow-men, who take me or denounce me for morose, crabbed, or misanthropical, how you do me wrong! you know not the secret cause of what seems thus to you. My heart and my disposition were from childhood up inclined to the tender feeling of goodwill, I was always minded to perform even great actions; but only consider that for six years past I have fallen into an incurable condition, aggravated by senseless physicians, year after year deceived in the hope of recovery, and in the end compelled to contemplate a *lasting malady*, the cure of which may take years or even prove impossible. Born with a fiery lively temperament, inclined even for the amusements of society, I was early forced to isolate myself to lead a solitary life. If now and again I tried for once to give the go-by to all this, O how rudely was I repulsed by the redoubled mournful experience of my defective hearing; but not yet could I bring myself to say to people 'Speak louder, shout, for I am deaf.' O how should I then bring myself to admit the weakness of *a sense* which ought to be more perfect in me than in others, a sense which I once possessed in the greatest perfection, a perfection such as few assuredly in my profession have yet possessed it in—O I cannot do it! forgive me then, if you see me shrink away when I would fain mingle among you. Double pain does my misfortune give me, in making me misunderstood. Recreation in human society, the more delicate passages of conversation, confidential outpourings, none of these are for me; all alone, almost only so much as the sheerest necessity demands can I bring myself to venture into society; I must live like an exile; if I venture into company a burning dread falls on me, the dreadful risk of letting my condition be perceived. So it was these last six months which I passed in the country, being ordered by my sensible physician to spare my hearing as much as possible. He fell in with what has now become almost my natural disposition, though sometimes, carried away by the craving for society, I let myself be misled into it; but what humiliation when someone stood by me and heard a flute in the distance, and *I* heard *nothing*, or when someone heard *the herd-boy singing*, and I again heard nothing. Such occurrences brought me nigh to despair, a little more and I had put an end to my own life—only it, *my art*, held me back. O it seemed to me impossible to quit the world until I had produced all I felt it in me to produce; and so I reprieved this wretched life— truly wretched, a body so sensitive that a change of any rapidity may alter my state from very good to very bad. Patience—that's the word, she it is I must take for my guide; I have done so—lasting I hope shall be my resolve to endure, till it please the inexorable Parcæ to sever the thread. It may be things will go better, may be not; I am prepared—already in my twenty-eighth[1] year forced—to turn philosopher: it is not easy, for an artist harder than for anyone. O God, Thou seest into my inward part, Thou art acquainted with it, Thou knowest that love to man and the inclination to beneficience dwell therein. O my fellow-men, when hereafter you read this, think that you have done me wrong; and the unfortunate, let him console himself by finding a companion in misfortune, who, despite all natural obstacles, has yet done everything in his power to take rank amongst good artists and good men.—You, my brothers Carl and   , as soon as I am dead, if Professor Schmidt is still alive, beg him in my name to describe my illness, and append this present document to his account in order that the world may at least as far as possible be reconciled with me after my death.—At the same time I appoint you both heirs to my little fortune (if so it may be styled); divide it fairly, and agree and help one another; what you have done against me has been,

[1]Beethoven was born in December 1770, and was therefore at this date nearly at the end of his thirty-second year. It was one of his little weaknesses to wish to be taken for younger than he was; and he occasionally spoke of himself accordingly (Grove's note).

you well know, long since forgiven. You, brother Carl, I especially thank for the attachment you have shown me in this latter time. My wish is that you may have a better life with fewer cares than I have had; exhort your children to *virtue*, that alone can give happiness—not money, I speak from experience; that it was which upheld me even in misery, to that and to my art my thanks are due, that I did not end my life by suicide.—Farewell, and love each other. I send thanks to all my friends, especially *Prince Lichnowski* and *Professor Schmidt*. I want Prince L.'s instruments to remain in the safe keeping of one of you, but don't let there be any strife between you about it; only whenever they can help you to something more useful, sell them by all means. How glad am I if even under the sod I can be of use to you—so may it prove! With joy I hasten to meet death face to face. If he come before I have had opportunity to unfold all my artistic capabilities, he will, despite my hard fate, yet come too soon, and I no doubt should wish him later; but even then I am content; does he not free me from a state of ceaseless suffering? Come when thou wilt, I shall face thee with courage. Farewell, and do not quite forget me in death, I have deserved it of you, who in my life had often thought for you, for your happiness; may it be yours!

LUDWIG VAN BEETHOVEN.

Heiligenstadt,
  6th October, 1802.

For my brothers
Carl and
to be read and to execute after my death.

Heiligenstadt, 10th October, 1802. So I take leave of thee[1] —sad leave. Yes, the beloved hope that I brought here with me—at least in some degree to be cured—that hope must now altogether desert me. As the autumn leaves fall withered, so this hope too is for me withered up; almost as I came here, I go away. Even the lofty courage, which often in the lovely summer days animated me, has vanished. O Providence, let for once a pure day *of joy*[2] be mine—so long already is true joy's inward resonance a stranger to me. O when, O when, O God, can I in the temple of Nature and of Humanity feel it once again. Never? No—O that were too cruel!

[1] Theresa Brunswick, to whom he was betrothed in 1806, or some other lady (Grove's note).
[2] *Der Freude.* The italics are his own.

34

Such eloquence needs little comment; the 'someone' who stood near Beethoven listening to the shepherd's pipe was a favourite student, Ferdinand Ries, who described the incident independently. The letter was never sent, although Beethoven not only made a fair copy but also preserved it to the end of his days. (It was found among his papers after his death.) These two facts seem to me to support the idea that the prime purpose of this heart-cry was to serve as a sort of therapy; but there was another more potent medicine to hand— composition. Once immersed in the task of committing a major work to paper, Beethoven's concentration was intense enough to drive all other thoughts out of his mind. It is almost impossible to reconcile the evident despair betrayed in the *Testament* with the energy and good humour to be found in the Second Symphony; even more remarkable is the serene beauty of the slow movement whose lyrical quality seems to reveal a mind completely at ease. The score was completed in the closing months of 1802, a period that synchronises uncannily with the spiritual and emotional crisis of which the *Testament* is undeniable evidence; yet only in the Introduction to the symphony do we find traces of despair; as soon as the Allegro gets under way, personal misery is swept away by the momentum of the music.

4

Symphony No. 2 in D Major, Op. 36

Dedicated to Prince Carl Lichnowsky

Orchestra: 2 flutes; 2 oboes; 2 clarinets; 2 bassoons; 2 trumpets; 2 horns; 2 timpani; strings

1. Adagio molto: leading to Allegro con brio
2. Larghetto
3. Scherzo and Trio: Allegro
4. Allegro molto

First performance: 5 April 1803

Accustomed as we now are to the laborious birthpangs experienced by Beethoven during the composition of his major works, it comes as no surprise to find that sketches for this symphony exist from as early as 1800. So far as can be deduced the seeds of the first movement were sown in that year, while much preliminary work on the finale (in which he breaks the newest ground) dates from 1801. The initial sketches are often so far removed from the final version as to be almost unrecognizable but he did manage to get very close to the introductory theme at quite an early stage as this fragment reveals.

Ex. 28.

The first attempts at the Allegro bear more resemblance to a bugle-call than a symphony.

Ex. 29.

One wonders why he bothered to commit such banalities to paper at all but it seems to have been an essential part of his creative procedure; at least it leaves evidence of the importance that he attached to tonality for a more blatant proclamation of D major would be hard to find. The next step brings us towards something faintly recognisable as the genuine article, though there is still a lot of refining to be done.

Ex. 30.

The significance of the third bar can only be appreciated in the very final stages (see p. 39); meanwhile bar 1 showed that he was moving on the right lines. In due course an approximation to the theme as we know it emerged.

Ex. 31.

Bars 3–6 here are of considerable value in establishing the sort of tempo Beethoven appears to have had in mind, probably a little slower than what we are used to. The sketches give plentiful evidence of the labour entailed, so different from the facility with which Mozart had clearly worked. Cipriani Potter (1792–1871), an English musician who knew Beethoven personally, claimed that he had made three full scores of the symphony before being satisfied, but no trace of what would therefore have been very substantial manuscripts exists.

The symphony begins with what Haydn would have called a *coup d'archet*, a stroke-of-the-bow, calculated to impress the listeners with its forcefulness. As an immediate foil to this strongly masculine gesture a quartet of oboes and bassoons offers a phrase whose expressive tenderness has more the character of an introduction to an operatic aria than a symphony. A descending scale in thirds from the remaining woodwind leads to a repetition of the opening gesture; this time it is the strings who offer the response, their harmonisation of the theme being more chromatic (and hence more expressive) than the original. Six repeated F♯s from the horns lead us into a mysterious sequence of modulations, via B minor, C major, then D minor to the quite unexpected key of B♭ major. It is a key that is in direct opposition to the 'home' tonality of D since it cancels out the vital attributes F♯ and C♯. It gives a very real impression of a breakthrough into a different world, a Dante-esque world of echoing caverns through which great winds seem to blow; any temptation to dismiss its rapid scales as mere decoration should be quelled by the eerie horn notes which stab through the darkness. A sudden and massive *crescendo* leads to a tremendous unison powerfully supported by timpani. To anyone familiar with both works the anticipation of a comparable moment in the Ninth Symphony is uncanny.

No. 2   No. 9

It may not be so apparent to the eye as it is to the ear and needless to say it is a coincidence not to be over-valued.

It is at this moment in the Second Symphony (bar 24) that we find a rare intimation of Beethoven's deep sorrow with the use of a falling diminished seventh, that classically eloquent interval which Handel used memorably in his 'Messiah' to the words 'And with His stripes . . .'. Against this hallowed gesture of anguish, Beethoven puts a passage in triplets whose effect is extraordinarily different from a seemingly not dissimilar passage in the slow movement of the First Symphony; there all was sweetness and light; here we have pain and darkness.

Ex. 32.

The *staccato* here should have weight rather than delicacy; horns double the sustained notes in the double-basses whose deep tones add an individually sombre colour. Roles are reversed, the violins taking over the cello theme, the cellos and violas lending their darker hue to the triplets. Strong first-beat accents alternate with fluttering trills on flute or first violins as one has the feeling of great forces gathering. Clear as a lighthouse beam a long sustained A sounds out from the first violins, duly to plunge down a scale of ten notes to the opening bar of the Allegro. It is a device notably similar in conception to the bridge between Introduction and opening movement proper in the First Symphony, but here the scale (in both senses) is so much grander.

No. 1   No. 2

To an accompaniment of excited reiterations of the 'tonic' note D, violas and cellos give us the first statement of the main theme, whose derivation from the sketch shown in Ex. 31 is clear enough.

Ex. 33.

But what of the previous sketch (Ex. 30)? It bears fruit in the subtlest of ways, its somewhat pedestrian third bar being transformed into a mercurial flash of light from the first violins, a recurring feature of the symphony.

Ex. 33a.

The second stanza of the theme also shows some influence from Ex. 30 bar 4 in that it begins on the same note, G, the sub-dominant or fourth degree of the scale. With a characteristic avoidance of the obvious, Beethoven changes the final note of the phrase by sharpening it (G♯), briefly allowing the woodwind to take over with a new and expressive tune before bringing back the main theme with the full pomp of trumpets and drums. Paradoxically, at the very moment when the tonality of D major thus seems most firmly established it is severely at risk; Beethoven introduces a dramatically alien note, C *natural* (the flattened seventh), one of the two notes most likely to deprive D major of its very essence. (The other is the major third, F♯; they are the two notes indicated by the two-sharp key signature.) This is how he arrives at this disturbing moment:

Ex. 34.

Reduced to its bare bones this is simply a D major triad followed by a flattened seventh:

Ex. 34a.

I have put in a C♮ at the lower octave since one can then perceive that here is a basically similar procedure to the one employed at the start of the Third Symphony; a simple transposition makes the point clear.

Ex. 34b.

The procedure may be similar; the effect is totally different. While Ex. 34a is an eminently Classical device that might be found in virtually any symphony by Haydn, Mozart or their numerous lesser contemporaries, Ex. 34b is essentially a Romantic conception, mysterious and enigmatic, since instead of paving the way for a standard modulation to the closely related sub-dominant key it steps momentarily aside into a harmonic limbo. Allowing for the transposition I have made for purposes of comparison, the 'Eroica' fragment should not be written with a C♮ in the third bar but with a B♯—the same note but with quite different harmonic implications.

Ex. 34c.

To the layman this may seem nothing but academic nit-picking; if the phrases *sound* the same they surely must *be* the same. To a musician, perhaps especially to a composer, the difference is full of significance. The C♮ of Exx. 34a and 34b opens the door to the nearby key of G major:

Ex. 34d.

In other words, the C♮ is susceptible to what might be thought of as a gravitational pull downwards. The B♯ of Ex. 34c is subject to a different impulse; its tonal pull is *upwards*, probably to the more distant key of C♯ minor.

Ex. 34e.

I make no apology for this brief diversion into harmonic theory since excursions from one key to another are a fundamental aspect of musical structures. Certainly the powerful C♮ in bar 49 (Ex. 34) has a profoundly disturbing effect on the tonality. Its first 'attack' on the home key is repulsed by a restoration of C sharps a couple of bars later; but the assault is renewed with greater intensity (B naturals are dragged down to B flats), and the music shifts dramatically through D minor, B♮ major to the dominant of A minor. This chord sequence, skeleton though it may be, should make these transitions clear.

Ex. 35.

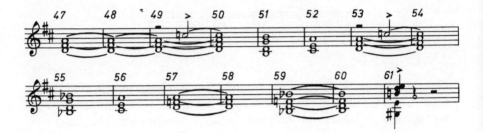

Notice that when the break-out does come in bar 61 the harmony chosen is an abrupt contradiction of the one immediately preceding it, a gesture as dramatic as the breaking of shackles.

We are now embarked upon what is traditionally known as the Bridge Passage, that necessary link between First and Second Subject material. If we glance back at the initial sketch shown in Ex. 30 we can see that Beethoven was ultimately to change the original rhythm

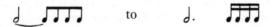

however, the first version did bear some fruit since its rhythm acts as a springboard for the whole of this next section.

Ex. 36.

This phrase, whose angular contours extend over more than two octaves with many chromatic notes thrown in, engenders a considerable turbulence with the music flying off in opposing directions until the disparate elements converge in a mighty unison.

We have arrived at the Second Subject, an almost Mozartean little march were it not for the raucous acclamation with which the full orchestra greets its first phrase.

Ex. 37.

Notice that in bar 80 not only is the volume suppressed but also there is a little scurry in the violins very comparable to their comment on the First Subject (Ex. 33a). The excitement this conveys is carried on into a shimmering trill, written out in full—

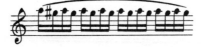

and imparting a wonderful glitter as the woodwind proceed with their crisp march. A brief patch of fairly strenuous counterpoint (the upper instruments chasing after the lower) leads to some abrupt chords whose function is to stop the music in its tracks.

One can try an interesting experiment here that admirably demonstrates the difference between orthodoxy and genius. It makes perfectly good musical sense to cut from bar 99 to bar 120.

Ex. 38.

A perfectly acceptable formula, but a formula none the less despite the emphasised dissonances. Instead, at the very brink of such a resolution, Beethoven interrupts the cadence dramatically:

There follows a moment's silence (whose effect I venture to suggest will be made more apparent to twentieth-century audiences if the conductor is courageous enough to make a slight pause),[1] whereupon Beethoven produces a stroke of pure genius, a whispered reminder of a fragment of the main theme, whose very existence has by now almost been forgotten.

---

[1] In a resonant hall the acoustic demands it; anyway unorthodoxy deserves unorthodox treatment!

Ex. 39.

It would be nice to be able to assume that there was some significant relationship between the bold resolution of this diversion and the poignant phrase in bars 24–25 of the Introduction:

but the interval was in such common usage at the time that I doubt if Beethoven was even aware of the coincidence.

The function of Ex. 39 apart from its pure drama has been to recall the main theme of the Exposition; in the subsequent bars (the Codetta) it is subjected to considerable stress until a number of jarring cadences (see Ex. 38) finally establish not only the dominant key but the conclusion of the Exposition.

The Development is largely influenced by two factors, the transposition of the main theme into the minor and its fragmentation on the lines suggested during the strange interpolation we have seen in Ex. 39. A further link with past events is an echo of the violin trill that originally glittered against the Second Subject. It is a handy enough device to be usable in almost any context and it is a simple matter for Beethoven to harness it to the First Subject by way of a change.

Ex. 40.

45

The change of context plus some added dissonances charge this apparently neutral figure with an almost sinister significance, the flight of a kestrel rather than a kingfisher. It leads to a considerable storm (see Ex. 51a) in which the innocent little semiquaver group from the First Subject becomes a veritable shriek in the woodwind, while trumpets and horns make a notable contribution considering how elementary the actual notes are. However the storm blows itself out and after a tiny pause for breath a deft development of the Second Subject ensues, nimble triplets in the violins adding a new element. Gradually the tonality shifts further away from keys closely related to D until the music finds itself apparently locked inextricably in F♯ minor.

Ex. 41.

For fourteen bars the harmony rocks between F♯ minor and its dominant (C♯), creating an impasse that literally brings everything to a halt. For two bars a unison C♯ holds us in suspense; 'where do we go from here?' Like helpful policemen, the two horns point the way by superimposing an A, thereby breaking the deadlock by creating the dominant of D. One triumphant affirmation of the Lost Chord leads us back to D major and the Recapitulation.

Initially this all goes according to plan; however the final pages reveal the increasing importance Beethoven was beginning to attach to the Coda, an importance which was to become enormously significant in the 'Eroica'. One passage in particular stands out when, after some dramatic alternations of blustering fortissimos and somewhat disheartened references to the main theme, he launches the cellos and basses on a majestic chromatic ascent (bars 326–335) which inevitably recalls the climax of 'The Heavens are Telling' from Haydn's 'Creation'. It was a work Beethoven much admired and the tribute may well have been intended as an act of homage.

If the names of Haydn and Mozart seem to have made an undue number of appearances so far, as though Beethoven was perpetually looking over his shoulder at his great predecessors, it is only right at this moment to bring in Schubert, since the idyllic Larghetto of this symphony might aptly be described as prophetic in its Schubertian manner. Indeed Schubert himself responded to it by lifting clearly recognisable extracts and transplanting them into his Grand Duo for Piano. The relaxed serenity of this movement is almost impossible to reconcile with the spiritual anguish revealed in the *Heiligenstadt*

Testament with which it appears to be exactly contemporary. The date of any preliminary sketches seems here to be irrelevant since the full working out of the material must have been accomplished during the period of spiritual crisis—the more so if Cipriani Potter's story of three complete versions of the whole symphony is true.

Some authorities attribute the derivation of the opening theme to this sketch:

Ex. 42.

Beethoven jotted down his intention to score this for two horns. Now while it is true that the sections I have bracketed do bear some resemblance to the proper theme, the fact is that nowhere in this very lengthy movement does he give the tune to the horns. Indications of specific orchestration and tempo are a rarity in the sketchbooks and I cannot help feeling that in this case theme and instrumentation are so integral that it is a mistake to assume a relationship between Ex. 42 and this symphony. Is it not far more probable that it refers to the theme given to horns (and trumpets) in the slow movement—incidentally an *andante*—of the Fifth Symphony?

Ex. 43.

Much more convincing as the seed from which the sublime melody of the Larghetto flowered is another more fragmentary sketch that lacks both clef and key signature; nevertheless, if we read it in the treble clef and as though in A major we come very near to the theme Beethoven ultimately found, as this comparison clearly shows.

47

Ex. 44.

Ex. 44a.

The relevance of the sketch is confirmed on the final page of the movement when bars 5–8 of Ex. 44 appear virtually note for note in bars 268–271.

Apart from a prodigal wealth of material one of the principal delights of this movement is the felicitous scoring. Trumpets and drums are omitted; it is the clarinets and bassoons in particular that lend the music its special colour. Although the strings are given the first presentation of the opening theme, their function is often purely decorative. As is so often the case in Mozart's instrumental writing, there are moments that seem to cry out for the human voice; apart from the impracticality of the pitch a 'duet' such as this is perfect opera.

Ex. 45.

It is even followed by a miniature 'ensemble', after which the violins, standing in for an imaginary soprano, begin an aria calculated to melt the most villainous heart.

Less obvious are numerous subtleties of orchestration including delicate effects of pointillism such as this treatment of an utterly insignificant figure.

Ex. 46.

It is merely a supporting background to some elegantly decorative passage-work for the first violins, yet such touches of craftsmanship give real distinction to the music.

To catalogue every theme and happening in this extensive movement would be unnecessarily wearisome since the appeal of the music is immediate; there is one moment though that should be mentioned, not only for its enchanting good humour, but because Schubert found it literally irresistible;

Ex. 47.

he could not refrain from using it as a prototype in his Grand Duo in C.

The comment that the horns make on this argues a touching faith in the ability of the performers; twice the first horn player is expected to tackle a dreaded top C (sounding E at concert pitch), and red faces have been acquired from more than one cause in the process.

Beethoven's invention never flags for a moment in the 'heavenly length' of this movement. Particularly magical is the use he makes of the second, third and fourth notes of the initial theme. The simple doh-ray-me is transformed by being put into the minor and then used as the basis for a ghostly dialogue between the lowest strings and plangent woodwind.

Ex. 48.

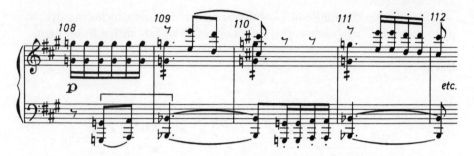

This evocative passage builds into a substantial climax in which the opening phrase (all four notes now) is made into an impassioned duet against a relentlessly hammering rhythm from the inner strings. It is a tough central core that is needed lest the movement should become over-indulgent in sentiment. The emotional heart lies in a passage of extraordinary intensity whose throbbing chords high in the strings are a remarkable prevision of the ultimate climax in the finale of the 'Pastoral' Symphony. A side-by-side comparison would take undue space within the confines of a book, but those who are sufficiently interested should compare bars 148–154 of this movement with bars 219–237 from the finale of the Sixth Symphony. These figures speak for themselves in revealing the larger span of the later work but there is clearly a marked resemblance, especially in the eloquent exploitation of flattened sevenths (C♮s in No. 2, E♭s in No. 6).

After one of his longest symphonic slow movements Beethoven seems to have felt that the more compact the Scherzo was the better. (Note that it is here called a scherzo not a minuet.) It may well be that the doh-ray-me so liberally used in the slow movement left so deep an imprint in his mind that he could not escape its influence, for the Scherzo is dominated by a rising pattern of three notes.

Ex. 49.

The scoring, a bar of this followed by a bar of that, is virtually unique, and one can visualise chaos reigning at the first rehearsal when many a player must have been caught unprepared. The dynamics too are capricious with the sudden alternations between loud and soft. After the first sixteen-bar section, duly repeated, the strings introduce a slightly more coherent tune, though it too has its eccentricities.

Ex. 50.

Sir George Grove in his classic book on the symphonies draws our attention to 'the rushing fiddles', that hallmark of the first movement. However he fails to mention what seems to me a far more intriguing correspondence that follows immediately afterwards. Consider these three bars from the Scherzo:

Ex. 51.

The exact resemblance of the top-line to one of the most important motifs of the first movement might be dismissed as coincidence; but when we couple it to the chromatic descent in the bass we find coincidence stretched far enough to make us ask seriously whether this is not a true cross-reference.

Ex. 51a.

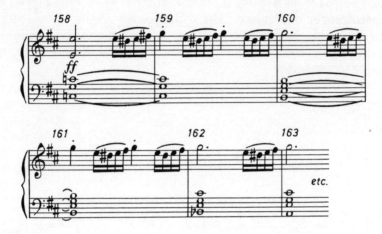

Such speculations can never be satisfactorily resolved; but whether by accident or design family resemblances of this type must help to give unity overall.

The Trio introduces a neat little theme scored for a quartet of oboes and bassoons which, in a later version, acquires a running bass in the lower strings, *pizzicato*. For reasons that will become apparent, Ex. 52 combines the two presentations of the theme.

Ex. 52.

More than twenty years later a markedly similar idea was to turn up in the Ninth Symphony at precisely the same structural moment—the Trio of the Scherzo. As it is in the Second Symphony, the theme is introduced by the woodwind; of course the scale of the later work is immeasurably larger but the link is worth mentioning. Even more fascinating is the possibility that herein lies the embryo from which the 'Song of Joy' was developed. The key is the same, the outline intriguingly similar; here first is the relevant quotation from the Ninth Symphony Trio.

Ex. 52a.

One doesn't have to rig the evidence too dishonestly to arrive at this possible sequence of events.

Ex. 52b. Symphony 2.

Symphony 9.

Symphony 9 (Finale).

Though I am not suggesting for one moment that such a link was conscious, it is worth bearing in mind that Beethoven had first expressed his intention to set Schiller's 'Ode to Joy' to music as early as 1793 when he was still in his early twenties. There is documentary evidence to that effect in a letter to the poet's sister Charlotte by one Fischenich, a lecturer on human rights (!) at Bonn University.

Let us put conjecture aside and return to the Trio of the Second Symphony. After that first innocent phrase on the woodwind (Ex. 52) the strings catch us unawares with an extraordinary excursion into F♯ major; since nobody seems to wish to argue with such inexplicable behaviour, they settle contentedly on to this new tonic (F♯), so much so that they seem to be in danger of going to sleep, like chickens who, having flapped their wings aggressively, settle on a new perch and doze off. A rude awakening follows as all the rest of the orchestra, trumpets, horns, timpani and woodwind bellow a huge unison A so as to put things back into the proper tonality. It is a typical Beethoven joke whose sense of fun needs to be conveyed in performance; for instance, conductors should not spoil the surprise impact of the sudden *fortissimo* by telegraphing its imminent arrival with some histrionic gesture.

The finale is full of such jokes, from its initial hiccup to the tiptoe games in the closing pages. The F♯ to which the strings were so unexpectedly and compulsively drawn during the Trio of the Scherzo proves to be the first note of the finale; it would be hard to find a more unconventional way of beginning a movement than this.

Ex. 53.

The mood is both explosive and exuberant; as a demure contrast, Beethoven introduces a bland theme in the cellos which he handles with eminent propriety, no doubt recalling weary hours spent on exercises in counterpoint.

Ex. 54.

It is merely an episode in an elaborate Rondo, its almost unctuous phrases soon being overwhelmed by fizzing arpeggios in the violins. Against their excited chatter, the Second Subject[1] appears, the sheer pace of the movement dictating that it should consist of semibreves and minims if it is to provide any real contrast. Sudden spurts from the violins do their utmost to disturb its poise.

Ex. 55.

The tune continues with pleasing modulations through A minor and C major until at last the dominant seventh of the home key (D major) is forcefully established. Here again Beethoven shows a great sense of fun since the somewhat blustering assertion of the dominant in the cellos and basses is carried on by a lone bassoon, while the violin section is seized by a paroxysm of 'hiccups'. (Beethoven's digestive and abdominal ills plagued him all his life . . .) A reprise of the opening theme is neatly attained, whereupon Beethoven pretends to take it seriously for a little while; I say 'pretends' since, though the lower strings may hack this out with a show of aggression,

flutes and oboes refuse to take them seriously, parodying their gestures irreverently like children baiting an angry adult. With our instinctive feeling that symphonies are a Serious Matter it may be hard to accept that even a

---

[1] The movement is in what is called 'sonata-rondo' form.

substantial outburst of orchestral fury proves to be a hoax, but Beethoven's deflation of his own rhetoric is unmistakable.

Ex. 56.

It is a moment of pure comedy which however makes a perfect link back to the initial theme. After a substantial Recapitulation the music builds to a huge climactic chord, a dominant seventh majestically proclaimed by the full orchestra and long sustained. What is going to happen? One expects a Handelian coda, a sort of orchestral Amen, perhaps combining some of the main features of the movement in some such manner as this.

Ex. 57.

Good stirring stuff, but by 1802 a played-out cliché. Instead of this all too predictable gambit Beethoven gives us a chord veiled in mystery.

a chord that seems to come from nowhere. Soft-footed, cellos and basses start on a downward scale which ideally should descend through an octave and a half; sadly, such a descent goes out of the cellists' range, but the thought is there. If Beethoven had ever wanted to write music for *A Midsummer Night's Dream* he had the material here, for this is the music of fairies, an entry into a magical world where even the incessant cheep of birds is hushed as night falls. (It looks towards the very closing bars of the storm in the 'Pastoral' Symphony in its evocation of calm stillness.) In a shimmering haze it seems as though the sun sinks slowly below the horizon; every listening soul is enraptured by the beauty of the scene.

It is one of the cruellest confidence tricks ever played on an audience; with a huge *fortissimo* blare of sound Beethoven jolts us out of all our poetic reveries and rhapsodies and whips the movement on to its conclusion. Its conclusion? There is still another surprise to come, another pause, more tiptoeing and whispering, more incredulous cheeps and more raucous laughter from the composer as we are gulled once more. It is an ending whose originality can never have been excelled.[1]

Before we leave this symphony, often dismissed by commentators as of little moment, let us think back briefly to two points that have emerged. First it is seen to be a nursery for great events to come, a harbinger of clearly identifiable episodes in both the Sixth and Ninth symphonies. Secondly it has a singular unity of themes; what I have called the 'doh-ray-me' element occurs with remarkable frequency. Even the very first bar shows us its inversion (me-ray-doh), while the main subject of the first and last movements are in effect decorations of the same idea.

Ex. 58.

cf.

<hr />

[1]For further discussion of the finale see pp. 191–192.

Whether such relationships are intentional or not seems to me almost irrelevant; what matters is that the symphony emerges as a true entity, no longer four independent movements derived originally from a suite but an organic whole. The *scale* of the symphony as a form was ripe for development; the huge expansion this brought about is to be seen in the 'Eroica'.

5

Interlude
Liberté, Égalité, Fraternité

It is only natural to think of Beethoven as a spiritual and intellectual Rock, pursuing his path with unswerving integrity, his eyes for ever fixed upon the goal of artistic truth. Admirable though the image may be with regard to his music it is scarcely true of anything else. As might be expected of someone who nowadays would be described as manic-depressive, his attitudes were susceptible to considerable fluctuation. Though he disapproved of the concept of aristocracy, he liked to mingle with the nobility and valued the patronage of princes; though he condemned Mozart's *Don Giovanni* as immoral in its subject -matter (yet admiring the music) he himself had an eye for any attractive woman and was described as being 'very frequently in love, but usually only for a very short time' (Ries). While he was obsessive about washing himself he paid so little heed to his clothes that he was on one occasion arrested as a tramp and detained in a police cell overnight. He was violent and inconsiderate enough to empty a dish of stew over an unfortunate waiter, yet filled with enlightened idealism about the brotherhood of man. Nowhere was his ambivalence more significant than in his attitude to Napoleon.

In an age when satellite pictures flash instant news on to our television screens and when every political event is remorselessly discussed by commentators, it is hard to appreciate how slowly news appears to have travelled in the early years of the nineteenth century. For instance, in October 1799, Napoleon had made a triumphant progress from the south of France to Paris applauded by a populace who had no idea that he had suffered a crushing defeat at the hands of Nelson *two months* previously.

Since he had become First Consul of France, Napoleon had grown into a demigod; to the eyes of an astonished world it seemed as if such legendary figures as Tamburlaine or Alexander the Great had been reincarnated. The French Revolution spread its repercussions throughout Europe; the rise of a leader who held his position not by right of birth but by popular acclaim was a concept so radical as to appeal to all lovers of freedom. (I doubt if Beethoven knew of the incident during the Parisian insurrection of 1795 when Napoleon was in command of the artillery detachment whose fire raked the streets surrounding the Tuileries, or he might have viewed him with more sceptical

59

eyes.) If the idol proved to have feet of clay they were nevertheless clad in field-boots, and soon the tramp of the French infantry echoed far beyond the borders of France. Campaigns against Italy and Austria were brilliantly successful; a myth of invincibility was born. It is at this point that we must pause to ask a pertinent question. While it is easy enough to appreciate that the god-like figure of Napoleon captured admiration from afar, how was it possible that such adulation could continue even in the very countries that were the victims of his military ambitions? If Beethoven looked upon Napoleon as a great man even while his armies were invading Austria, was he then a Quisling at heart? There is no great evidence of a country groaning under some awful tyranny; indeed Joseph II, on whose death Beethoven had composed the remarkable cantata I have already mentioned (p. 6), seems to have been a relatively enlightened monarch, under whose benevolent despotism a number of reforms had been introduced. Napoleon's hold on Beethoven's imagination seems therefore to have been not so much as a man (certainly not as a conqueror) but as a symbol of Liberty, Equality and Brotherhood, that resounding slogan that had fired men's hearts in Europe and America. That conquering armies seldom bring freedom in their wake was a lesson still to be learned.

Possibly drawn by a vision of Paris as a Fountain of Liberty from which all should drink Beethoven appears to have resolved to leave his native Vienna and make for the French capital in 1802, this despite an explicit denunciation of Napoleon in a letter to a publisher who had suggested that he should write a sonata to celebrate the hero of the hour. (It is interesting that although far from being an orthodox Christian, he was deeply upset by Napoleon's pact with the Vatican, which he regarded as a betrayal of revolutionary principles.) Doubtless remembering the prior examples of Haydn and Mozart, both of whom had made notable foreign conquests with symphonies as ammunition, he could well have decided that a new symphony —especially if it was a tribute to Bonaparte—would be a useful item of luggage. Now so much has been written about the pictorial-cum-biographical nature of the 'Eroica' that I do not wish to add greatly to the total. The facts are all peripheral to an authentic anecdote told by Ries.

In this symphony Beethoven had Buonaparte [sic] in mind, but as he was when he was First Consul. Beethoven esteemed him greatly at the time and likened him to the greatest Roman consuls. I as well as several of his more intimate friends saw a copy of the score lying upon his table with the word 'Buonaparte' at the extreme top of the title page, and at the extreme bottom 'Luigi van Beethoven', but not another word. Whether and with what the space between was to be filled out, I do not know. I was the first to bring him the intelligence that Buonaparte had proclaimed himself Emperor, whereupon he flew into a rage and cried out: 'Is he then, too, nothing more than an ordinary human being? Now he, too, will trample on the rights of man and indulge only his ambition. He will exalt himself above all others, become a tyrant!' Beethoven went to the table, took hold of the title page by the top, tore it in two, and threw it on the floor. The first page was rewritten and only then did the symphony receive the title Sinfonia Eroica.

This mute relic of Beethoven's tantrum has been preserved to vouch for the truth of the story, though Ries is misleading in his suggestion that the title Sinfonia Eroica was an instant choice; it was not used until two years after the incident. Two further facts need to be taken into consideration; in a letter to the publishers, Breitkopf and Härtel (26 August 1804), Beethoven mentions 'a new grand symphony . . . The title of the symphony is really Bonaparte'; even more significant are the words 'Geschrieben auf Bonaparte', written in pencil by the composer on his own copy of the score (though never erased!). Here is the gateway through which all the idiotic speculation about the programmatic context of the 'Eroica' has slipped. Spellbound by that little phrase, 'Written on Bonaparte', even critics as normally perceptive as Berlioz could perpetrate misjudgements so crass as to describe the symphony as 'the hero's *funeral rites*' (his italics, not mine). Even in the Scherzo he sees 'play of a funereal kind, at every instant clouded by thoughts of mourning—a kind of play, in fact, recalling that which the warriors of the Iliad celebrated round the tombs of their chiefs'. Another writer, Ambros, in his *Über di Grenzen der Poesie und Musik* supposes the Finale to represent 'a procession of many generations of men towards the hero's tumulies, formed by a huge pile of roughly hewn stone blocks, which they decorate with leaves and flowers, concluding the ceremony with the festive solemnity expressed in the poco andante, and the joyful festivities of the final presto.' In a desperate search for 'meaning', one critic pronounced that the oboe tune in E minor (first movement, bars 284 et seq.) represented Napoleon's Egyptian adventure since it had a clearly Eastern flavour!

Knowing what we now do of Beethoven's method of composition, the pertinacious reworking of fragments, the slow process of assembly, it would seem that the last thing to be likely to be completed would be the title-page. If we couple this with his own remarks about the much more programmatic 'Pastoral' symphony—'a recollection of country life; more an expression of feeling than a painting'—it seems to me that we gain a considerable clarification of the problems surrounding the 'Eroica'. Like the 'Pastoral', that too was to acquire a sub-title—'*composta per festiggiare il souvenire d'un grand' Uomo*' (composed to celebrate the memory of a great man). Now it has always been assumed that the 'great man' was Napoleon, his 'greatness' sullied in Beethoven's eyes by his assumption of the title of Emperor. Suppose though that we venture to start from a different viewpoint, leaving Bonaparte out of it to begin with.

In 1800 Beethoven had written the ballet-score 'The Creatures of Prometheus', a substantial part of which was to reappear as the finale of the 'Eroica'. Most commentators have explained this rather unlikely transplant by suggesting that Beethoven equated the legendary figure with Napoleon. But although in mathematics equations can be read in both directions, in language there is a subtle difference if I submit as an alternative proposition that he equated Napoleon with the legendary figure. If Prometheus is seen as the *starting-point* rather than as a Handelian type of time-saver the outlook changes completely; the scenario would then read like this:

As he composes the ballet, and even more as he savours its success (twenty-three performances in 1801–1802), the idea of developing a symphony from its material comes into his mind, a symphony based on the concept of a truly legendary hero, Prometheus, the bringer of fire from Heaven. The symphony begins to take shape, still with no thought of Bonaparte in mind; then comes the decision to make for Paris, prompted perhaps by disillusionment with the political climate of Hapsburg Vienna. Why write a symphony in praise of Bonaparte when he had defeated Austria in 1800? (The Peace Treaty of Lunéville was signed in February, 1801.) Austria suffered more than any other country at Napoleon's hands, so much so that it would seem entirely proper to write a funeral march for the *Austrian dead* in a symphony concerned with heroic myth. The last movement would give the clue as to the Promethean identity of his hero-figure.

If we take Beethoven's proposed visit to France into account we can see how simple a matter it would have been for him to effect the mental substitution of an actual Bonaparte for a legendary Prometheus, if only for opportunistic reasons. It seems that he was prepared to go quite a long way to make his Austrian (and therefore 'enemy') persona acceptable to the French; on the title-page of his own copy of the score his name appears not as Ludwig but as 'Louis' van Beethoven, after the French manner. Why was the title-page that Ries saw him tear up so bare—just the two names, 'Buonaparte' and 'Luigi van Beethoven'? (Observe another attempt to disguise his Austrian background.) This extremely unusual title-page has never been adequately explained, but if my hypothesis is true it is just the sort of thing that might have happened. With the symphony already written, Beethoven speculates about calling it 'Buonaparte', tries out the look of it by writing a draft title, but, still uncertain, omits all the usual information about key, opus number, etc. Suddenly that sentence in the letter to Breitkopf takes on a new significance: 'The title of the symphony is really Bonaparte . . .'[1] Does not the word 'really' imply that there

---

[1] Or perhaps 'really is Bonaparte . . .'

had been some doubt in his mind? Moreover doesn't the addition of the words 'Geschrieben auf Bonaparte' *in pencil* suggest that it was an afterthought, added perhaps to give credence to an idea that the composer himself had secret cause to regard as unconvincing?

There remains the problem of the 'great man' in whose memory (according to Beethoven's own footnote) the symphony was written. It seems a very odd phrase to use about someone still living, even someone whose idealised image had been shattered by what Beethoven regarded as a betrayal of principles. Two possible explanations occur to me. Presumably by the time Beethoven added this postscript to the title 'Sinfonia Eroica' he had told quite a number of people that the symphony was to be known as 'Bonaparte'. Having changed his mind about this, he had to find a convincing explanation for the omission of Napoleon's name; to someone as given to self-dramatisation as Beethoven was, the phrase he chose has a fine ring — 'to celebrate the memory of a great man. . .' But Napoleon as we well know was not dead, and the funeral march seems inexplicable as an anti-Napoleonic gesture since it was written *before* the Ries anecdote concerning Napoleon's coronation. Suppose though that my hunch about the funeral march really being for the Austrian dead[1] is correct, we then have the possibility that the 'great man' is what we today would call the Unknown Warrior, the nameless war hero who stands for all who were killed in battle.[2] Such an interpretation accords perfectly to the concept of a 'Heroic Symphony'.

If, as has been repeatedly maintained, Beethoven's theatrical tearing-up of the title-page expressed such a bitter disillusionment with Napoleon, is it likely that in 1809 he would have given a cordial reception to his ambassador, the Baron de Trémont, at the very time that the French were bombarding Vienna? Would he in that same interview have given the impression that he would have been flattered to receive any mark of Napoleon's esteem? Would he have contemplated dedicating the Mass in C, Op. 86, to Napoleon in 1810? Intriguing questions all, tending to tilt the balance a little away from the usual interpretation given to Ries' story. I leave the matter there; let us examine the music.

---

[1] One of Beethoven's physicians (Bertolini) claimed that it was intended for the British General Abercrombie who died *fighting Napoleon* at the Battle of Alexandria (1801). But since he also claimed that it was prompted by the rumour of Nelson's death at Aboukir one wonders how reliable such evidence is.

[2] cf. '*Marcia funebre sulla morta* d'un eroe', in the Piano Sonata in A♭, Op. 26 (1800). What hero? A nameless one.

It's a pity I don't understand the art of war as well as I do the art of music; I would conquer him.

(Beethoven in conversation after Napoleon's victory at the Battle of Jena. 1806.)

6

Symphony No. 3 in E♭ Major, Op. 55

Dedicated to Prince Lobkowitz

SINFONIA EROICA composta per festiggiare il sovvenire di un grand'Uomo, e dedicata A Sua Altezza Serenissima il Principe di Lobkowitz da Luigi van Beethoven, Op. 55

Orchestra: 2 flutes; 2 oboes; 2 clarinets; 2 bassoons; 3 horns; 2 trumpets; 2 timpani; strings

1. Allegro con brio
2. Marcia funebre: Adagio assai
3. Scherzo and Trio: Allegro vivace. Alla breve
4. Finale: Allegro molto—Poco andante—Presto

First performance: 7 April 1805

Although nothing could sound more positive than the two abrupt chords of E♭ which begin the symphony, Beethoven did not arrive at them at once. The very first sketches show two abortive openings, both based on dominant seventh harmony.

Ex. 59.

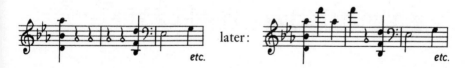

Both of these were properly rejected, although they do seem to have a suggestion of 'flight' about them that would bear out the idea of a Promethean descent from heaven. By changing them to two unchallengeable chords of E♭ major Beethoven stresses the importance of the fundamental tonality, an emphasis that is needed since the first theme seems to drift away from it in a curiously disturbing way.

Ex. 60.

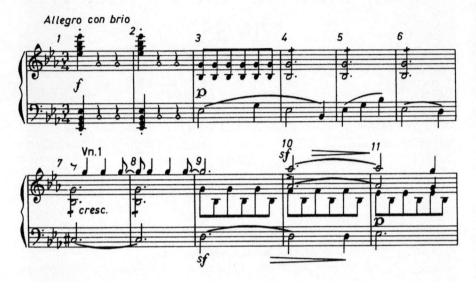

I have already discussed the significance of the C♯ in bars 7–8 (see pp. 40–41), but notice with what firmness Beethoven asserts its function—to rise, not fall—by accentuating the ensuing D, which in turn brings a responsive accent in the violins and violas in bar 10. Not surprisingly, since it is eminently suitable for the instrument, the theme is soon given to the first horn-player (who has the hitherto unprecedented experience of having *two* colleagues beside him). The beauty of thematic material based on common chords is that it is so easy to extend it in a convincing way, either by using sequences—

Ex. 61.

or by a simple process of stretching—

Ex. 61a.

(cf. the rhythm of bars 16–18).

Now up to this point, apart from the two opening chords and a momentary feeling of unease in the violins prompted by that alien C♯, the music has been almost bland, its rhythmic stress falling notably on the first beat of the bar. It is time to introduce a tougher element, strong accentuation that breaks the rhythmic pattern. Why? Because Beethoven wishes later to assert the theme more powerfully; the best way of asserting power is to overcome opposition. These rhythmic jolts and dissonances (bars 25–34) provide just such an opposition, a hostile force that is dramatically overcome by the *ff* restatement of the theme that follows (bars 37–40).

Conventional analysis falters in the face of this giant symphony since there is such a wealth of material. It is as futile to try to reduce the structure to the textbook props of First and Second Subjects as it would be to attempt to reduce *Hamlet* to a play with only the two characters, Hamlet and Ophelia. *Romeo and Juliet* gives us a more fruitful analogy since the protagonists at least belong to opposing *families*, and we are very aware of the conflict that permeates the drama as a result of the Montague-Capulet feud. Similarly in the 'Eroica' it is a simpler task to detect families of themes (having kinship though not necessarily compatibility) than it is to provide them with the name-tags beloved of examiners.

The word kinship leads me to the next idea to surface. It appears to have cost the composer a lot of thought; the first signs of it in the sketches look distinctly unpromising, Three Blind Mice without much of a future.

Ex. 62.

In due course a considerable development of this appears, covering a wide span, though, as is usual in the sketchbooks, still laid out on one stave, manuscript paper being precious.

Ex. 63.

67

The interesting thing about this evolution is that Beethoven himself seems to have been unaware of what his subconscious was telling him. If we think of that disturbing C♯ in the opening theme and the way it was approached (see Ex. 60 bars 6–7), it is easy enough to see an explicit 'kinship' between the original theme and the newcomer. Transpose this brief fragment

to a higher register, and it becomes

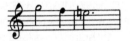

which, at exactly double speed is

I would be prepared to accept this as special pleading were it not for the fact that this fragmentary but productive idea appears so closely to the triumphant reprise of the opening theme. Whether consciously or not Beethoven himself suggests the relationship in the bar immediately before the newcomer's appearance. Second violins, violas and three wind instruments are given this decorative turn,

which is merely a roundabout way of saying this:

68

If its provenance is only of peripheral interest, the idea itself is certainly important; from bars 45–54 it is the sole topic of conversation between oboe, clarinet, flute and violins, bars 55–57 being a massive agreement from the whole orchestra that the discussion has been well worthwhile. A new character glides on to the scene, seductively voiced for clarinets and oboes.

Ex. 64.

This is immediately taken up in a varied form by the violins; but any expectation that it will behave with the gentle charm of properly behaved Second Subjects is quickly dashed by a sudden outburst in G minor whose emphatic ♩♪♪ rhythm is reinforced by massive chords each side of the bar-lines (bars 65–70). Inevitably the generation of so much energy leads to a substantial climax. The section ends with a nice demonstration of Beethoven's structural instinct, matching the unison descent in bars 55–57 with a comparable though more rapid unison in bars 81–83.

Ex. 65.

Ex. 65a.

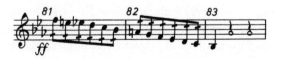

While not thematically related, the two phrases serve an identical function — to modulate into (or to confirm) the dominant key of B♭ by the strongest possible means.

Bar 83 sees the advent of another important character in the drama, a 'heroine', perhaps to give comfort to the 'hero'. The harmonies show a quality of tenderness that has so far been absent; indeed, it is as well to consider it as a sequence of harmonies rather than a tune.

Ex. 66.

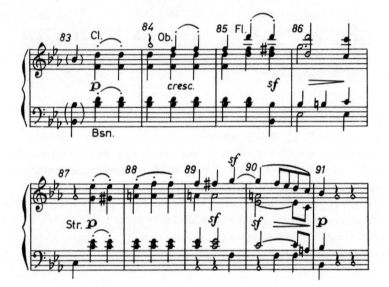

The modulations that follow as a result of putting this into the minor are such that Schubert himself could not have rivalled them in beauty. It is an oasis of calm out of which, delicately and two steps at a time, the strings hesitantly drag us. A climax follows, brief and to the point with disguised references to the initial themes poised over reiterated low Fs—which can confusingly be called the dominant of the dominant. For a few bars the music seems to be thrown into a maelstrom of wildly tossing harmonies; massive chords break through the turbulence, grimly distorted reminders of the monolithic opening bars. It is a relationship of which we are at first unaware, but which Beethoven forces us to accept shortly before the end of the Exposition. The original two explosive tonic chords are extended into no less than seven dominant B flats, at times rocked by savage dissonance.

Ex. 67.

Notice how the initial theme, emerging out of harmonic chaos (147) is instantly discoloured by the chromaticisms of bar 150. We are about to arrive at the double-bar, the traditional point for a repeat sign, repeats being made so that the audience might have a better chance to absorb the material. Having at first agreed that the convention might be dispensed with in view of the exceptional length of the movement, Beethoven had second thoughts and asked that it should be observed in order to produce a better balance. The point is sound, for in a movement whose Coda is over 140 bars long there is a danger of the tail wagging the dog. Moreover, despite the rich profusion of ideas in the Exposition there has been a strong bias towards the dominant key of B♭; from bars 45–149 the music deserts the home-key of E♭ entirely, while standing out like mountain peaks are three heavily reinforced cadences into the dominant (see Exx. 65, 65a and 67). Since many other excursions away from the home-key are ahead, it is not surprising that Beethoven felt the need to re-establish his base.

The Development begins with mysterious gropings which lead us ultimately into the clear daylight of C major, a key so far unvisited. Though the tonality is new, the material is the same little phrase that had been so elegantly discussed in bars 45–54 (see pp. 68–69). These pretty pleasantries are stopped in their tracks by the appearance of a ghost. Accompanied by the melodramatic *tremolando* beloved of film-composers of the twenties, the initial theme makes a spectral entrance in cellos and basses. The chromatic distortion first essayed in the second violins and violas in bars 150–151 (see Ex. 67) has born sour fruit by making it possible for the theme to appear in the minor, a truly disturbing change of character.

Now I have already mentioned the feeling for balance and proportion which Beethoven exhibits as musical architect. All commentators on this symphony are bound to mention an unforgettable moment that occurs at the start of the Coda (bars 551–565). Having finally re-established E♭ major with apparent finality, Beethoven subjects us to the abrupt shock of plunging us without warning into the contradictory key of D♭; no sooner have we taken this in when he thrusts us even more brutally into C major. Reduced to its essentials the sequence reads like this:

Ex. 68.

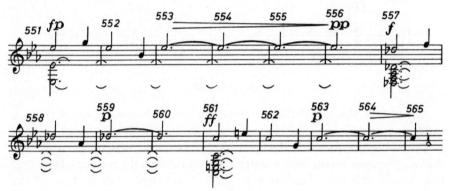

As if the shifts of tonality were not alarming enough, the dynamics (*pp*, *f*, *p*, *ff*, *p*) are also extremely unsettling; small wonder that a contemporary critic called it 'a daring, wild fantasia . . .'. But while this point is so obvious that it cannot be missed, it has been anticipated with extraordinary subtlety by an almost identical *reverse* procedure at the start of the development, the essential difference being that he is now concerned with minor keys rather than major ones. Let us reduce Ex. 68 still further to its three fundamental harmonies:

Now start to think in terms of minor keys with the inevitable contraction of intervals that that involves. Surely one can see a distorted mirror image in this sequence:

Change the second chord's notation to C♯ minor for convenience and one now has the framework of the crucial bars which start the Development of the main theme.

Ex. 69.

A gulf of some 370 bars is fixed between these two points and yet they are surely complementary to each other.

Bar 186 (see above) is the signal for Beethoven to reintroduce the rhythm which originally appeared at bar 65. At the time it seemed a random episode, dramatic enough in its own right but having no real relationship to what had gone before. We are now shown the error of such an assumption as this dynamic rhythm is combined with the intense D minor version of the opening theme.

Ex. 70.

Tonal relationships of the greatest subtlety are revealed here. Turn back to Ex. 60 and notice the reaction the mysterious C♯ (bars 7–8) created in the violins above, agitated syncopations on a reiterated G. Now C♯ is what is called the 'leading note' in the key of D minor; in this orthodox cadence it 'leads' into that key.

Therefore one of the possible implications of the C♯, even in the initial context, is that it should 'lead' us into D minor; it is very easily done.

Ex. 71.

Not until bar 186 is this potential realised, but when D minor *is* attained what do we find in the violin parts? Identical syncopations, except that they are now on the 'proper' note, the dominant of D minor. At the start of the symphony the functions of both the C♯ and the syncopated notes were an enigma; now they have found their place.

For some time the storm rages, although, as in nature, there are momentary lulls in the tension. At last we find relief in what I have called the conversation-piece (bars 45–54, pp. 68–69), now in the *sub*-dominant key of A♭ whereas originally it had been in the dominant (B♭). This new tonality makes for easy access to yet another key, F minor; the 'conversation' takes a much more serious turn as Beethoven launches us into a fugue (bar 235). Strictly speaking it should be called a 'fugato' since it is given little time to develop; such labels are easy enough to attach *post facto*, though I see little value in them. The point is that we are meant to *believe* it is going to be a fugue, since only then will we fully appreciate the brutality with which it is cut off. The subsequent denial of expectation forms not only one of the most remarkable passages in the whole symphony but is surely the most rugged and monumental ever to have been written up to the time of its composition. Its genesis is easy enough to comprehend since it clearly springs from the cross-accentuations in bars

25–34, that first flexing of symphonic muscle in the early stages of the movement. Apart from the extreme dissonances at the end of the sequence the actual harmonies are part of a vocabulary so familiar that it might as easily have been used by Handel or his contemporaries. A passage such as this would occasion no surprise in a Handelian prelude.

Ex. 72.

The sheer magnitude of the 'Eroica' has often been the subject of comment, and it would be harder to find a better example of the expanding scale of Beethoven's thought than this passage. Bar 1 of my pseudo-Handelian exercise becomes six bars of intensely dramatic conflict, with the dissonant qualities of the harmony heavily underlined and a rhythmic pattern that rides roughshod over the properties of a normal three-in-a-bar.

Ex. 73.

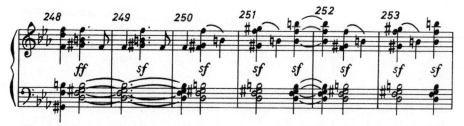

This sets the pattern for what is to follow; bar 2 of my hypothetical Ex. 72 is also extended to a comparable six bars, as are bars 3 and 4. To increase the

75

tension still further, a compression now takes place; the harmony shown in bar 5 is hammered out explosively for two bars

bar 6 being treated in the same way. Only in bar 7 does Beethoven add a dissonance that would have been really unacceptable to eighteenth-century ears, the E♮ wherein lies the rub in this chord:

This proves to be the ultimate turn of the screw, and bar 8 of Ex. 72 becomes, in Beethoven's hands, a resolution taking four more bars, the first two still affected by the overpowering dissonance of the preceding harmony, the remainder allowing the tension to slacken. Eight bars of reasonably conventional harmony (as shown in Ex. 72) are stretched to thirty-six bars of thunder, as the following table clearly shows.

Pseudo-Handel (Ex. 72)		'Eroica': bars 248–284
bar 1	becomes	6 bars
bar 2	,,	6 bars
bar 3	,,	6 bars
bar 4	,,	6 bars
bar 5	,,	2 bars
bar 6	,,	2 bars
bar 7	,,	4 bars
bar 8	,,	4 bars
(bar 9	,,	2 bars)

There follows an episode that has had musical analysts scratching their heads for many years. Even so perceptive a musician as Charles Rosen in his admirable book *The Classical Style*[1] seems to me to have lost his head at this point. Speaking of the inherent unity of the symphony he described it as 'so intense that a cello-oboe duet which is almost always called a new theme in the

---

[1] Faber, 1971: the passage quoted is on p. 393.

development is directly derived from the main theme. It is the oboe line that is later dropped, and the cello's motif remains and is transferred to the winds. The relation between the cello line and the main theme is very close':

Ex. 74.

I see no point in applying the methods of Procrustes to this passage when it responds so much better to more gentle treatment. Beethoven himself has already given us a clue in the turbulent D minor passage sketched in Ex. 70 (p. 73). Both there and in the ensuing G minor section (bars 188–203) he alternates the minor version of the theme with an extension based on its own dominant. If we apply exactly the same principle to the passage we have now reached we find that the oboe tune in question makes a perfect counterpoint.

Ex. 74a.

There is no need for so close a relationship to be underlined in this way, hence Beethoven's expressive new cello part shown in Ex. 74 (the upper line), a clever disguise for what otherwise might be too obvious a variation. The fact that he later chooses to develop the cello tune further requires no defence since it has enough attractive features of its own to warrant it.

As though to make the relevance of this 'obscure' passage perfectly clear, Beethoven returns to the main theme, now back in the major for the first time in the Development—though not for long! C major gives way to C minor; for a few bars it even seems as though the original tonality of E♭ major is within grasp. Indeed, by the normal proportions of previous first movements the Recapitulation would probably have arrived at bar 320 as is suggested here.

Ex. 75.

A perfectly acceptable solution, though too conventional for Beethoven's taste; wishing to approach the Recapitulation by a much more devious route, he creates a diversion by turning towards the contradictory key of E♭ *minor* at bar 320. A further exploration of the possibilities of Ex. 74 follows, and it is here that he sees the melodic potential of the cello phrase discussed by Charles Rosen. It is at bar 338 that our destination truly comes in sight as the first bassoon and first clarinet begin to discuss the opening theme, toying with different tonalities, but at least starting from the proper signpost, the dominant. Meanwhile the lower strings begin to climb relentlessly in ever widening strides towards a common goal.

Ex. 76.

Notice that the music still keeps drifting towards E♭ *minor*, so much so that in the end Beethoven is driven to make a harmonic pun; the crucial notes E♭–G♭, the basic minor third in E♭ minor are given new significance by having C flats thrust beneath them.

We are at the tonal epicentre where flats and sharps converge, for this chord is better known as B major; out of the context of a flat key it would certainly be written thus:

—same sound, different implications. Four times oboes and bassoons proclaim this chord with the greatest confidence; even the strings are convinced, spelling out the notes C♭–E♭–G♭ in unison. And then, as though Beethoven himself was saying, 'This can't be right', doubts creep in; the wind chords grow less and less confident, the string phrases become little sighs and then isolated *pizzicato* notes. The music seems about to disintegrate. Irresolute, the harmonies alternate around the notes C♭ and B♭, feeling for some secure footing. At last nothing is left but an almost inaudible rustle; we feel that we are literally 'trembling on the brink', but on the brink of what? Somebody must find the courage to make a move and it is the second horn-player who tentatively offers a way out of the impasse.

Ex. 77.

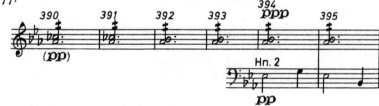

The direction *ppp* is exceptional for 1805 but not so exceptional as the conjunction of tonic and dominant harmony in bars 394–5 nor the atmospheric character of the orchestral colouring. It is a moment that never loses its magic, a magic that was spoiled for Beethoven at the first rehearsal when the ever-helpful Ries suggested that the 'damned horn player had come in wrong', narrowly escaping a box on the ear for his pains.

However tentative the horn-part may seem, its suggestion that what everyone is looking for is the main theme serves as a proper tonic in both senses of the word; two jubilant bars proclaim a universal acceptance of the proposition. The way to the Recapitulation has been found. Knowledgeable listeners can sit back, confident that things will now go according to precedent for a few pages at least.

Needless to say they are wrong. Six bars precisely elapse before Beethoven departs from the dictates of convention. The always enigmatic C♯ in the bass (Ex. 60, bar 7) presses downwards to a C♮, opening the door to a tonality that Beethoven has skilfully kept in reserve for just such an eventuality. There is a radiance about these excursions into the more distant major keys that belongs especially to this period. By the mid-nineteenth century shifts of tonality were to become so frequent as to begin to lose their effectiveness, but in 1805 to go from E♭ to C major or F major was to enter a neighbour's garden in full flower. In due course E♭ major is re-established on a more solid foundation and something approaching a conventional Recapitulation materialises. For 120 bars (430–550) Beethoven maintains a predictable course, giving the tonality of E♭ a long deferred chance to establish its domain. Where in the Exposition the bulk of the material headed inexorably towards the dominant key (B♭), now it keeps returning with equal emphasis to the tonic. It is perhaps for this very reason that Beethoven felt the need for the drastic steps he took at the start of the Coda (see Ex. 68). With a bluntness that listeners of the day must have regarded as crude he jumps (one cannot call it modulation) to D♭ major and then to C. Although this has the appearance of sheer perversity there is a sort of logic to it; seeds have been planted earlier in the score. We have already seen how bars 6–7

by a process of transposition and diminution can become

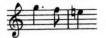

Whereas the original version consists of two falling semitones, the later variant has a falling *tone* followed by a semitone. Apply this second formula, using E♭ as a starting note, and you get

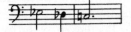

Now the potential of that C♮ has already been discovered by Beethoven; but while he has used diminution he has not tried augmentation. Such processes were standard techniques in contrapuntal studies and one can imagine Beethoven taking a certain delight in using a trick Albrechtsberger had taught him and turning it to revolutionary purpose. Thus

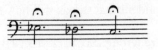

becomes those block-busting changes of key at the start of the Coda. (Augmentation indeed!)

The Coda might legitimately be described as a 'development of the Development'. The most important new factors to emerge are a delicate embroidery that serves to decorate the main theme;

Ex. 78.

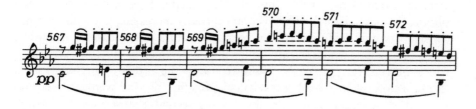

The first bar of this serves later as the basis for a delightful dialogue between the two ranks of violins (bars 595–602). In addition to this we are bound to notice a Mozartean phrase a single bar in length

whose repetition at different levels leads to a marked relaxation of mood. Evidence of this change of heart is offered by a new look at the rhythmic pattern which, up to this point, has always proved to be stormy. Compare Ex. 70 with the following Ex. 79 and you will see what a transformation has been wrought.

Ex. 79.

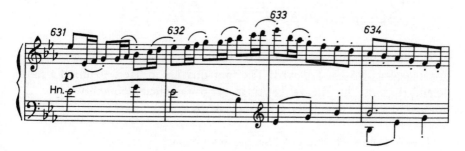

This development brings joy in its wake, gradually spreading through the orchestra until all hearts are united in a paean of triumph; it scarcely seems the appropriate moment to go to a funeral. . . .

Needless to say the presence of a funeral march in a symphony supposedly in praise of Napoleon proved to be a contentious point for musical commentators. Berlioz took refuge in four lines of Virgil, which can hardly be called constructive analysis. Wagner saw in the first movement—all the emotions of a richly endowed personality (himself?) in a state of restless agitation—in a phrase, 'manly vigour'. This vigour appears increasingly as an 'intense concentration of destructive force' whose crushing power hastens towards a tragic catastrophe whose solemn significance is revealed in the slow movement. More perceptively, J. W. N. Sullivan[1] sees the whole symphony as 'a transcription of personal experience'. In the first movement we find Beethoven's courage in defying fate, in the second a lapse into the despair brought on by deafness; the scherzo celebrates the emergence out of that private hell into a new outburst of creative energy ('From today on I will take a new path': Beethoven, 1801) while the variation form of the finale symbolises the range of achievement now open to his newly-fired 'Promethean' spirit. This seems psychologically convincing, certainly more so than the supposition that the Funeral March is a musical equivalent to the famous line, 'I come to bury Caesar, not to praise him.'

Scorning anything by way of introduction Beethoven begins the movement with a solemn theme, accompanied not by muffled drums as one might expect, but by a far deeper *drum-like sound* from the double-basses. No drum can pitch accurately notes as deep as these, but their low rumble evocatively suggests the tread of many feet stepping forward at a cruelly slow tempo. In its earliest stages, Beethoven conceived the tune in four-four time, a point worth bearing in mind when deciding upon the proper tempo.

Ex. 80.

The first phrase was to remain virtually unchanged, but he was rightly dissatisfied with what followed. The four quavers in bar 3 acquired a more doleful rhythm; the interval D–A♮ in bar 6 was filled eloquently. Here, the product of much labour, is the finished article.

[1] J. W. N. Sullivan, *Beethoven*, William Brown & Co., 1927.

Ex. 80a.

The tune is at once taken up by a solo oboe with *all* the strings providing a drum-roll rhythm

Since timpani are now involved, though only playing single notes on the beat, one cannot help wondering why the rhythm is not given entire to the drums; the answer must be that Beethoven felt that the sound would become muddy and indistinct as a result. It sheds interesting light on attitudes to percussion at the time; although it was used on occasion (Haydn's 'Military' Symphony, Mozart's sleigh-bells in K. 605, sundry 'Turkish' marches, etc.) symphony orchestras as such had no percussion players other than a timpanist. Not until the Ninth Symphony does Beethoven employ bass-drum, cymbals and triangle, and then only in the finale.[1] (His use of a harp in the Prometheus music, something unique for him, was presumably dictated by the fact that one was available in the pit-orchestra at the theatre.) All the same, the absence of a side-drum in the Funeral March is surprising, the more so when we think how often its sound is represented by other means.

After the oboist has given us his version of the tune, modifying it so as to end in E♭, the strings introduce a broad melody whose early promise of lyrical fulfilment is soon nipped in the bud.

Ex. 81.

[1] This applies to the symphonies: exceptions are the 'Ruins of Athens' (1812) and the 'Battle of Vittoria' (1813).

Although this seems to come to nothing at the time, it needs to be borne in mind, for reasons which will become clear. For the moment it merely leads us back to a reprise of the initial theme, now in the sub dominant key of F minor. Logically enough, the plan continues with the oboe-player in turn taking over Ex. 81. Together with its Codetta this huge opening paragraph extends for no less than 68 bars. The lower strings provide an inspired link into the contrasting section which is to follow by transforming the opening rumble

into a measured tread:

The oboe, clearly the leader of the woodwind in this movement, introduces a marvellously consoling theme such as Haydn (a true believer) might have used to symbolise redemption. Whether Beethoven had so specifically religious a connotation in mind I doubt, though the combination of C major and the clear tones of the flute's reply suggests a ray of light 'amidst th' encircling gloom'.

Ex. 82.

As though fearful of sentimentality, Beethoven interrupts this idyllic moment with a thunderous outburst on the dominant chord of G; then, again relenting, he allows the strings to extend the oboe's theme, introducing an expressive new element, the flattened seventh:

Ex. 83.

The innocent looking triplets in bar 84—the sort of figure Mozart would use to express tears—lead to increasing tension until, in a great explosion of sound from the full orchestra, the section ends in C major. It is a paradox that though this has an air of finality one senses that it could not possibly be the end of the movement, even though a hundred bars may have passed. A mysterious unison descent in the strings leads us remorselessly back to the opening theme whose course again leads us towards F minor. It is at this point that a significant new episode begins.

You will remember that I said that Ex. 81 needed to be borne in mind; it is the second violins who first reveal the possibility of inverting it so that

can be transformed into

Against a counter-subject whose accented minims suggest the tolling of bells, an expressive fugue[1] begins.

Ex. 84.

[1] Strictly speaking it is a 'double' fugue, but that is needlessly confusing.

(For the benefit of those who find such a texture bewildering to the eye, the entries of the 'subject' are marked with an asterisk.)

The fugue builds majestically, scales spreading across the page with increasing frequency, like raindrops falling on the cortège. At its most intense climax the opening notes of the fugue subject are not only doubled in speed but rocked to and fro in a vivid depiction of one of the instinctive gestures of grief, the head swaying from side to side as though incredulous in the face of death.

Ex. 85.

Forlorn, the first violins, unsupported, offer us a reminder of the opening theme; it breaks off despairingly on a lone A♭. This pathetic note is followed by a hugely dramatic *low* A♭ on cellos and basses, *fortissimo*; its impact is almost melodrama, comparable to Florestan's great cry of '*Gott!*' at the start of Act II of *Fidelio*. Stark but massive fanfares ring out on unison brass; is it a vision of the Last Judgement? It could well be, for soon afterwards the cellos and basses have a climbing motif that might be intended to describe the laborious ascent from the grave upon that Day when the trumpet shall sound.

Ex. 86.

The accents on the second and fourth quavers give an extraordinary heaviness to this figure against which the initial theme (on oboe and clarinet) seems curiously wan. In fact we are embarked on a recapitulation of sorts, albeit more elaborate in figuration than in the original presentation. In effect it is a reprise without repeats, the original 69 bars being reduced to 36. At the very moment when a potentially 'final' cadence seems to have arrived (bar 208), Beethoven interrupts it by the classic device of moving the dominant bass up a semitone. It seems that we are to be diverted into A♭ major; this proves to be an illusion since A♭ turns out to be not the new tonality but its dominant. With melting tenderness the violins introduce a variant of Ex. 83, the faltering syncopations adding a pathos near to tears.

Ex. 87.

It is the beginning of a disintegration which is so to affect the original theme as to rend it apart. Beethoven was a master of the eloquence of silence as he had already shown in the introduction to the G minor Cello Sonata Op. 5 or the slow movement of the Piano Sonata Op. 7. An early sketch for the funeral march shows his preoccupation with the emotional power of silences.

Ex. 88 (cf. Ex. 81).

It was a technique he was to apply most effectively at the very end of the movement, recalling Lear's great cry—

'Break heart, I prithee, break!'

The Scherzo which follows could scarcely be a greater contrast, bustling along without a care in the world, its rhythmic vitality unflagging. Excitedly the strings set the rhythm ticking; after six bars of *pianissimo staccato* chords, the oboe offers us a quirky little tune beginning with seven repetitions of the same note.

Ex. 89.

Now although the strings seem to have made every effort to begin the movement in E♭ major, even if in suppressed tones, this tune is clearly in B♭. Part of the elusive charm of this movement is due to the teasing way in which Beethoven puts off a positive confirmation of its tonality. Ninety-two bars pass fleetly by before E♭ is allowed to assert itself as the home key, an affirmation which is clearly recognisable when it comes, even though the unknowing ear may not realise how the effect is achieved.

After Ex. 89 has appeared a couple of times, the strings seem to become a little uneasy at the refusal of the tonic to establish itself properly. Speculatively they move up to D flats; not surprisingly there are no bids and so they move on up to F. The flute takes a fancy to this and tries out Ex. 89 in F major (the dominant of the oboe's B♭ major). The strings decide for the moment to make the best use they can of the last few bars of the cheerful little tune; perhaps a corrective dose of contrapuntal imitation will lead an air of respectability to these frivolous antics.

Ex. 90.

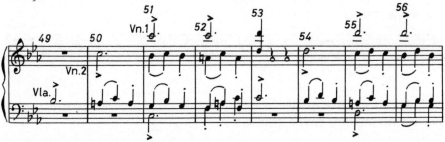

These chatterings only lead us further astray to G minor, on whose dominant (D) the violas find themselves stuck with nothing to do but mark time. More constructively the cellos suggest a B♭; it is at least the dominant of the 'proper' key and with a bit of luck should lead to it. The other strings and then a majority of the wind follow suit; all is set for a safe arrival but once more the irresistible pull towards B♭ exerts itself. Brute force seems to offer the only solution and with a sudden *crescendo* the deadlock is broken. In full voice the whole orchestra hammers out E♭ major, the lower strings alone being a bit slow to realise what has happened.

Ex. 91.

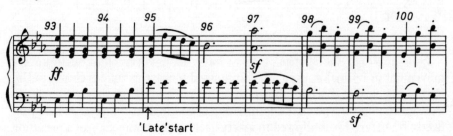

'Late' start

The discovery of the correct tonality after so long a search fills everyone with exuberance, so much so that a few rowdy spirits knock it off its perch again with some irreverent D flats; these need be no cause for alarm since they present no real threat. E♭ major has been well and truly established as this splendid new theme proclaims.

Ex. 92.

Inevitably this has given rise to a considerable amount of speculation; is it intended to be an oblique reference to the main theme of the first movement? Obviously bars 115–116 only need a reversal of their rhythm to produce a direct resemblance to bars 3–4 of the whole symphony.

For what it is worth, my own opinion is that such relationships can be given an importance that they do not merit. There are only three notes in that very 'common' chord, the major triad—doh-me-soh. The number of permutations available are severely limited and it would not be hard to prove that virtually every classical symphony was related at some point to the Blue Danube. The Eroica Symphony is full of apparent cross-references about which we can only conjecture; for instance the theme of the Scherzo bears a notable resemblance to the theme shown in Ex. 66 (p. 70), an accumulation of repeated notes and a segment of a falling scale (bar 90). It is a resemblance that carries more significance to the eye than to the ear and I cannot believe that Beethoven intended it. On the other hand it is clear that when he was working on a symphony he did not start on page 1 and compose it straight through. Scores of ideas would have been milling around in his brain at the same time and it would be amazing if they never became infected by each other's presence. When he does intend cross-references from one movement to another he usually makes them abundantly clear as he does for example in the Fifth and Ninth Symphonies or in the Op. 101 Piano Sonata.

In due course he brings us to the central Trio, a term that is a good deal more apt than usual since it is initially scored for three horns. Several sketches exist, the first of which does bear quite a strong resemblance to the original cello tune from the first movement.

Ex. 93.

His firm rejection of the opening bars in particular confirms that he certainly didn't wish to establish any noticeable relationship between the movements. Instead, after several attempts, he finally arrived at the theme as we now know it.

Ex. 94.

Even today first horn-players can grow pale at the thought of the dizzy ascent in bars 180–181; the absence of any dynamic at the start of the Trio (apart from the *sf* in bar 167) suggests that Beethoven felt that he should be grateful for what he got, let alone asking for any refinements. However despite the probable crudity of the playing in the original performances, he does ask for some truly poetic effects towards the end of the Trio, when a hushed dialogue between horns and strings establishes a twilight mood that is different from anything else in the symphony. Here, one feels, the spirit of German Romanticism was born.

The quiet ending of the Trio makes the transition back to the beginning of the Scherzo an easy matter; but while it seems that Beethoven is simply going to observe a hallowed convention by such a reprise he has other things in store for us. Just when we are really in danger of believing that 'as it was in the beginning is now' and is likely to continue to be so, he breaks loose with a remarkable gesture. Ex. 92, having reappeared in normal guise, suddenly takes off in a new rhythm.

Ex. 95.

Each pair of minims should be played in the time of three crotchets so that although the fundamental pulse remains the same, the effect is disturbing and exhilarating. Order is restored, yet one surprise still remains. It is a short Coda initiated by the timpanist, in which a strange sequence D♭–D♮–E♭ appears. To my ears it sounds like a backhanded reference to the E♭–D–C♯ (=D♭) that had been such a significant factor in the first movement, though it may be wishful thinking on my part to assume as much. The whole Scherzo is roughly twice the size of any comparable movement by Haydn, not that direct comparisons can be made so unique is its conception. Yet despite its size and ingenuity it does follow in a tradition; the same cannot be said of the finale which is a true curiosity.

In April 1827 a performance of the 'Eroica' was billed in London. It was given (according to a critic of the day) with the first two movements only, 'omitting the other parts which are entirely inconsistent with the avowed design of the composition'. One could not ask for a better demonstration of the folly of trying to force music to fit—or not fit—a preconceived programme.

The theme of the finale had already been used by Beethoven on three occasions, briefly as one of a set of dances, extensively as the finale of the Prometheus ballet Op. 43, and even more enterprisingly in a fine set of variations for piano, Op. 35. (The opus numbers are misleading in that they suggest that the piano work preceded the ballet. The variations were probably written to follow up the success of the ballet, perhaps at the suggestion of a publisher; however their seriousness of content and technical difficulty preclude the possibility of their being an attempt to 'cash in' on a popular success.) For whatever reason, it was obviously a theme that had a special appeal for the composer; having started its life as an innocuous little *contredanse*, it was to have all the resources of his great intellect lavished on it in works of increasing scope and complexity. Now it is always hard for the ordinary person to accept that intellectual forms such as variations or fugues can be leavened with humour. Even if we do agree that university professors might make jokes we have a suspicious feeling that they might be in Latin. The first precept I would urge on anyone who finds this movement puzzling is that they should try to share in the obvious sense of fun that Beethoven experienced in writing it. The second is that they should cast out all thoughts of the word 'Eroica', a word which is indeed 'entirely inconsistent with the avowed design' of *this part* of the composition.

The opening bars, impressive though they may sound, are frankly a hoax, roughly comparable to the late and lovable Tony Hancock giving us a few lines of *King Lear* by way of a warm-up. 'This should impress the natives,' Beethoven seems to say as he lets loose a torrent of semiquavers in the strings—and in G minor too, a good key for tragedy. Eight massive chords from the full orchestra such as might be used to usher in a faded Hollywood star at the London Palladium lead us to expect a Grand Entrance. The subsequent anticlimax must have set Beethoven laughing out loud as he penned it; all that dramatic preparation and look what comes in!

Ex. 96.

In case anyone still doesn't see the joke he follows this with a well-tried music-hall routine in which two partners try to get in step with each other as they mince across the stage. Ex. 96 is repeated with the woodwind 'a beat out' until the last two bars. (It was a joke Beethoven played even more cruelly in the Scherzo of the 'Kreutzer' Sonata in which, if the violinist plays 'right' it will invariably seem to be 'wrong'.)

There is a silence.

'Knock-knock-knock!' say wind, brass and timpani as loud as they can. Another silence.

'Sorry, didn't mean it—' comes the apology.

The strings resume their tiptoe march.

Ex. 97.

'Did you say KNOCK-KNOCK-KNOCK?' ask the strings incredulously.

'YES WE DID!' reply the other instruments.

Strings: 'Oh . . .' (*quietly*)

Wind and brass: 'Hum . . .' (*pensive*)

Once more they tiptoe through the tulips, the wind as out of step as ever.

Now I am fully aware that this scarcely conforms to the normal procedures of musical analysis, but abnormal music demands an abnormal approach. As the great Donald Tovey says in his *Essays in Musical Analysis*,[1] 'we can almost see Beethoven laughing at our mystified faces ...'. If it is 'funny' to see 'KNOCK-KNOCK-KNOCK' in a supposedly serious book on the Beethoven symphonies, it is every bit as 'funny' to find a passage such as this *in* one of the symphonies. The really disconcerting thing about it is not its humour but its *slapstick* humour.

Beethoven now begins to explain what's going on. The second violins, possibly more sober-minded than their exhibitionist colleagues, proffer a more sustained version of Ex. 96. Even so there is nothing they can do about the inexplicable second half so they keep it as it is, hoping perhaps that the rather sketchy counterpoint supplied by the other strings will cover their embarrassment.

Ex. 98.

[1] Oxford University Press, Vol. I, p. 33.

'Ever hopeful' (though far from sure) the first violins now take over the second violin line from Ex. 98, transposing it up an octave to see if it sounds any better. The violas, who have been rather left out of things, embark on a busy little finger-exercise in triplet quavers which is taken up by second violins and cellos in turn. The riddle of the second part of the 'theme', if theme it is, is still unexplained.

At last the secret is revealed; it *isn't* a theme at all—it's the *bass* of a theme, a servant wearing the master's clothes. What does one do with such an upstart? Put him in his place, and that is precisely what Beethoven now does; the proper place for this enigmatic tune is the cello and bass part,[1] while above it should float an elegant tune. The mysterious silences are filled, the strange 'knocks' and the even stranger 'apology' make sense at last.

Ex. 99.

The mystery once solved, the violins appear to be in such good humour that they begin a little dance-tune based on the semiquaver run that filled in those gaps. Beethoven doesn't allow this to go far; as though saying to himself 'Nobody will take me seriously if I carry on like this', he settles down to developing the fugal possibilities initially suggested in Ex. 98. Proof of his new seriousness of purpose is manifest in the omission of the laughable second part of the original, as well as a transposition into the minor. In later years his fugues were often to seem a real struggle as he wrestled with intractable material. Here the counterpoint seems unusually well-oiled.

[1] Also the horns who sustain the principal notes.

Ex. 100.

With what masterly logic the irreverent little scale from Ex. 99 (bars 84–85) is now compressed and fitted into this new serious context (124–125).

The fugal entries proceed with academic propriety until, just at the point when we begin to reel with the complexity of it all, the Tune makes a plaintive appearance, as though to ask if it has been forgotten. Its rather wan character as it reappears is caused by an ingenious twist to the harmony; the first violin part is clearly in D major, but the supporting figures are just as clearly in B minor until, after four bars, they see the error of their ways and accept the verdict of the violins. D major it is, and this rather unlikely key is greeted with a sparkling variation on the Tune from the woodwind, while the first violins have a quick session of scale-practise. The slapstick humour of the opening has given way to intellectual wit as Beethoven changes course from writing a respectable fugue to composing light-hearted variations.

Now part of the ingenuity of these variations lies in the fact that Beethoven has given himself two very different strands of material to work with, the Bass, serious in character at least in its first eight bars, and the Tune, essentially frivolous. Since despite this discrepancy of character they actually fit together (see Ex. 99), a variation on one can easily be transformed into a variation on the other. This ambivalence can lead to problems for the listener; the fugue was obviously serious, the D major variation in the woodwind was clearly flippant. But what of the march in G minor which soon ensues? Nineteenth-century listeners hoping to see Napoleon pop round the corner at any moment must have heaved a sigh of relief when this martial music began.

Ex. 101.

If this is Napoleon's army I am ready to swear that they have been turned into toy soldiers. I cannot accept that Beethoven meant this Battle of Bakerloo to be taken seriously—not within the context of this movement. He tells us as much at its conclusion when the Glorious Victory of General Hooizit over Field-Marshal Watcys-Nayme is appropriately celebrated with this noble refrain.

Ex. 102.

This intrusion is both comic and delightful, but having effectively deflated the military Beethoven begins to take things seriously again. A new fugue begins; while its structural function within the movement is to balance the earlier one with a comparable patch of counterpoint, it is notably different in character. Fugue I (Ex. 100) is essentially 'proper', something that one could submit as an academic exercise with every confidence of good marks. Fugue II gives an impression of suppressed irreverence, like choirboys whispering during the sermon. For twelve bars Beethoven tries out the possibility of combining the opening notes of Fugue I with a minor version of the Tune.

Ex. 103.

Though this may present a solemn appearance of rectitude, it is prevented from making a suitably serious impression by what I can only describe as a giggling motif in the first violins, a ripple of stifled merriment that makes me think of Maria and her cronies observing Malvolio rehearsing his amorous advances. (See p. 43) for a similar pattern in the Second Symphony.) In a topsy-turvy world such as we find in this movement it seems only natural to turn a serious fugue subject on its head; and that is precisely what Beethoven now does. The sheer fun of it in no way detracts from its skill as his ever-fertile brain finds new uses for the material. For instance he takes a fresh look at the little scale passage from the Tune (Ex. 99, bars 84–85); dispensing with the final 'knocks' he turns it into a ribbon of notes so that this fragment,

is transformed into an ingenious counterpoint to the now inverted fugue-subject.

Ex. 104.

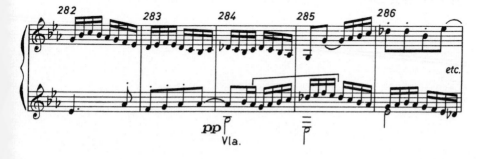

At the third entry of the subject (cellos) the flutes cannot resist putting in a particularly skittish version of the Tune, just in case anybody should be taking this all too seriously.

Fugues by their nature must be cumulative: it is no surprise then that this builds up to a substantial climax with the full brass reinforcing the *rhythm* of the subject in those places where they are incapable of playing the actual notes. At last there is a general convergence upon a climactic chord, the very same dominant seventh that in bar 11 had originally heralded the comic first appearance of what we now know to be the essential fugue subject, though at the time it seemed to be an imposter.

The tempo changes to *Poco Andante* and a divinely beautiful variation ensues; initiated by a choir of woodwind instruments, its relationship to the tune is too clear to need illustration here. It is taken up by the strings who extend its expressive line in a positively operatic manner. The orchestra takes on the semblance of a great cathedral organ, the Tune transferred to the pedals while the organist improvises an elaborate postlude. After an immense climax the sound gradually begins to die down over an oft-repeated G in the bass. (Did not the movement begin in G minor, something we need to be reminded of at this point?) Then with a sudden memory of the very opening flourish, Beethoven whips us into a final *Presto* in which the horns present a 'hunting' version of the tune.

The last pages have provided material for many a comic sketch for musicians with their seemingly superfluous repetitions of an E♭ chord. Are so many statements of an obvious truth really necessary? Beethoven obviously felt that they were. Here he was at the end of a giant achievement, his longest symphony apart from the Ninth, and the largest-scale orchestral composition that had ever been written up to that time. In its course he had modulated to many remote keys and explored a number of extremely novel ideas; of all the movements the last is the most unorthodox in construction, the most adventurous in concept. He needed to establish a firm and rock-like stability at the end. It is easy enough for us now to say 'we know it's in E♭'; he seems to have felt that such reassurance should be made doubly sure.

A conversation between Christian Kuffner, a poet, and Beethoven:
Kuffner: 'Tell me frankly, which is your favourite among your symphonies?'
Beethoven: 'Eh! Eh! The Eroica.'

(Summer, 1817)

7

Symphony No. 4 in B♮ Major, Op. 60

Dedicated to Count Oppersdorf

Orchestra: 2 flutes; 2 oboes; 2 clarinets; 2 bassoons; 2 horns; 2 trumpets; 2 timpani; strings

1. Adagio: leading to Allegro vivace
2. Adagio
3. Menuetto: Allegro vivace. Trio: un poco meno Allegro
4. Allegro, ma non troppo

First performance: March 1807

During the summer and autumn of 1806 Beethoven stayed as an honoured guest at Prince Lichnowsky's summer castle near Troppau. There he would have been given the facilities he needed to get on with his work, a quiet room with a piano and a writing desk. In comparison to the habitual squalor in which Beethoven tended to live, conditions must have seemed luxurious indeed. He cannot have been an easy guest; the deterioration in his hearing made him extremely anti-social, while his total preoccupation with composition caused him to behave with alarming eccentricity. Contemporary reports tell of him hurrying bare-headed round the castle grounds even when rain was teeming down. He would sing or shout raucously as he wrestled with the profusion of ideas that flocked into his mind. At times he would shut himself in his room for days and nights on end, his food brought to him by servants who looked on him as a madman. It was at this castle that the famous incident occurred when Beethoven refused point-blank to play to a French General, commander of the occupying troops. (The French had taken over the area after their victory at Austerlitz in 1805.) A *soirée* had been arranged in the General's honour, but Beethoven, upset by tactless remarks made by a French staff officer at dinner, gathered up his things and quit the castle, walking through a heavy rain-storm to the nearest town, where he stayed overnight with a friendly doctor.[1]

It seems though that one visitor to the castle did manage to get on well with Beethoven; Count Oppersdorf had a summer residence nearby and often called on his princely neighbour. On one such occasion he heard a private performance of the Second Symphony and was very much taken with it, so much so that he commissioned Beethoven to write another, offering him a fee of 350 florins. At the time Beethoven had already made substantial progress with the C minor symphony that we know as No. 5; spurred by the incentive of some real money he decided to meet the commission with the nearly completed work. Not for the first time in his life he then changed his mind, possibly because his host (a valued patron) had expressed enough interest in the work in hand to feel that it should rightfully be dedicated to him. An alternative explanation could be that in conversation Count Oppersdorf might have expressed a wish for a symphony of the same character as No. 2. At any rate, for whatever reason, Beethoven interrupted work on the C minor symphony and wrote No. 4 in B♭. As we shall see there are relationships between the Fourth and Fifth Symphonies which give clear evidence that both were in his mind at the same time. The first such clue appears in the very opening bars.

On the face of it there could hardly be more difference between two works, the Fourth beginning in veiled mystery, the Fifth magnificent in defiance from the first bar. But the substance of music is not the same thing as its sound and in substance both works are initially concerned with the same concept, falling thirds. Romantically-minded listeners long for great compositions to be 'about' events in the composer's life, preferably unhappy love affairs. To learn that symphonies can be written about such abstractions as a falling third or a rhythmic pattern distresses their sensibilities. Yet however different they may be in effect there is surely a relationship between these two patterns.

No. 4   No. 5

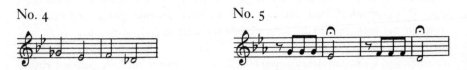

(For purposes of comparison I have simplified the notation in the second example but the sound would be unaffected.)

If the difference between a *pianissimo Adagio* and a *fortissimo Allegro con brio* seems to be too great to be bridged by a visual comparison of this sort, what about passages such as this from the Allegro of the Fourth Symphony?

---

[1] The rain-splashed MS of the Appassionata bears witness to the journey.

Ex. 105.

Change the rhythm throughout to ♪ ♩♩♩ | ♩ and you are immediately transported to the territory of the Fifth Symphony. Even in the Minuet/Scherzo there are shadows of the Fifth Symphony; many passages are based on this and similar patterns.

Ex. 106.

It is quite a revelation to change the rhythm:

Ex. 106a.

It is ironic that no sketches for the Fourth Symphony seem to have survived; it seems possible that by using materials that shared so much in common Beethoven was able to shorten his usual laborious approach to a new project so that in effect the uncompleted C minor symphony gave him all the stimulus he needed. (It was often his practice to work on several compositions at once.)

While the similarities may not be immediately apparent, the differences need no emphasis. The two symphonies are a world apart in emotional significance, so much so that the Fourth has always tended to be overshadowed by its mighty neighbours. Certainly after the 'Eroica', the B♭ symphony must seem something of a lightweight, though if we are to assess it fairly we should approach it free from the odium of comparison. Seen thus it is a magical work, perhaps the best orchestrated of all the nine. Even the opening bars of the Ninth Symphony are not more atmospheric in tone-colour; the material may be more impressive, the overall plan of the movement palpably larger, yet the opening of the Fourth is unforgettable for the beauty of its sound.

Remembering a trick from the First Symphony, the 'archer's bowstring' effect of a plucked note launching a sustained sound, Beethoven begins with a long-held B♭ on wind and horns that is brought into being by a *pizzicato* unison from the strings. If the analogy were not too modern I would say the sound is 'switched on' in this way; perhaps the suggestion of a magic wand will serve as well. Against the sustained B♭ the strings begin their mysterious opening phrase, perhaps the first time in music that a composer captured the mysticism of Whitman's lines, 'Darest thou now O soul walk out with me towards the unknown region'.

Ex. 107.

The *crescendo-diminuendo* in bar 5 is like a great sigh from a sleeping giant. The separate quavers from bar 6 onwards give an impression of dreadful isolation, an isolation that is racked by painful sobs—witness the eloquent despair of the G♭–E♮–F phrase on a solo bassoon echoed in the darkest tones of cellos and basses. Once more the great B♭ tolls out from the woodwind; this time the G♭ in bar 5 (now bar 17) is destined to serve a different function. Instead of falling a semitone, as in bar 6, it holds firm. Treating it for the moment as an F♯ (its enharmonic equivalent) Beethoven is able to open up new vistas, tonalities that are far removed from B♭ major; admittedly the introductory phrases have not given us the smallest hint that B♭ major is to be the proper key of the movement. Because of the awkward fingerings it involves for wind and strings alike B♭ minor is one of the least used keys for symphonies; it would therefore have seemed unlikely to any perceptive listener of the time that the music would stay in such an obscure tonality. Haydn had already revealed the possibilities of starting a symphony in a major key with an introduction in the minor. Hearing the work without prior knowledge, one could make an intelligent guess that B♭ major is the ultimate destination; but how is Beethoven going to reach it? The approach is cunningly devised, drawing out the suspense so that we are never sure where the harmonic progressions are leading us. The chord-chart below reduces the passage to the barest bones while giving us an idea of how many keys are touched on.

Bars 18–24 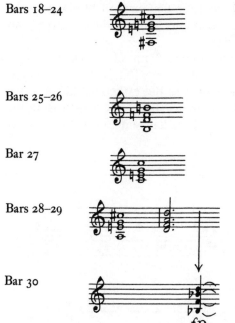 Chord of 'dominant ninth' implied for seven bars in spite of bass being disturbed by G♮ or E♯. Should ultimately resolve on to B minor, BUT . . .

Bars 25–26 cadence is interrupted by dominant seventh on G. Expected resolution would be C minor, BUT . . .

Bar 27 we find instead one bar of C major, then . . .

Bars 28–29 a transition to D minor,

Bar 30 immediately interrupted by B♭ on an unexpected beat.

Have we reached the destination? No; it is a glimpse of it but does not attain it. A setback ensues:

Bar 31 a dominant seventh expected to lead to A minor, BUT . . .

Bars 32–35  it turns out to be not A *major* but the dominant of D minor as the second half of the bar reveals.

B♭ still seems a long way away; but suppose we change the function of the A in bars 32–35 . . . Four times Beethoven 'weighs' this note, repeating it like a shot-putter toying with his missile before throwing it. Then with a convulsive effort comes the heave and the throw:

Bar 36

The new look at the note A turns it from the dominant of D minor to the leading-note of B♭ major; the change of harmony in bar 36 does the trick, and with a further heave B♭ is finally achieved.

As in the First and Second Symphonies, both of which had slow introductions, the final break into the Allegro comes from a dominant chord whose hold is broken by a scale, descending in the earlier symphonies (see p. 39) but ascending here. With some positive yelps of excitement from the violins, a pack let off the leash, we are rushed headlong into the first movement proper.

Ex. 108.

Notice how in bar 50 the top note (B♭ on an oboe) lingers for what seems like a bar too long before resolving on to the A, and how the violins seem to say 'Get on with it!' with their entry at the end of the bar. The whole of the main theme (bars 43–49) is taken up joyously by the full orchestra giving an invigorating feeling of emerging into bright sunlight after the extreme darkness of the introductory bars. After a few playful slaps at the closely related harmonies adjacent to B♭ major, a Rossini-like *crescendo* begins, starting *pianissimo* and building up progressively by means of a disguised scale, four bars of B♭, four bars of C, two of D, one of E♮, one of G, four of A and thus back home again to B♭ and the third statement of the main theme, now in the lower strings as a contrast to the delicate and transparent texture of the original version. This leads to a bold sequence founded on a splendidly solid bass; compared to the 'Eroica' it may seem a retrogression since there is nothing here that Haydn might not have done.

Ex. 109.

Restless syncopations ensue, though they have none of the rugged force we found in the first movement of the 'Eroica'; they are simply a rough passage designed to enhance the smoothness of what follows. Quiet sustained chords on the strings serve as an accompaniment to a perky little theme on the woodwind, not dissimilar from the village-band episode in the Scherzo of the 'Pastoral' Symphony. It cannot be described as *the* second subject since there are other themes as important, but it is certainly the leader of a new thematic group.

Ex. 110.

It is a potent demonstration of the mysterious musical alchemy by whose magic a composer can so change the content of a pattern of notes. Consider bars 2–3 of the symphony, that slow ghostly progression of minims:

change the notation to sharps for reasons that will disclose themselves:

now drop the third note down a semitone to E♮. The pattern will now be in B major; quicken it up by a factor of four (♩ = ♪) and hey presto! we have the cheerful little tune which on its arrival had seemed entirely new.

Ex. 111.

The thematic relevance of the introduction is consequently greater than we at first realise.

Now I have already shown something of the relationships which seem to exist between the Fourth and Fifth Symphonies. Unison strings soon present us with an unusual passage which shares something in common with a memorable sequence in the C minor symphony. In Op. 60 there are no harmonies, although through duplication at the proper pitches for violins, violas, cellos and basses, the sound is spread over a range of three octaves.

Ex. 112.

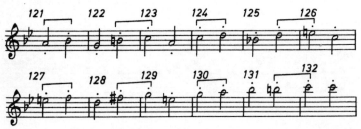

Only at bar 132 does some harmonic support arrive. For purposes of comparison I have bracketed a number of pairs of notes which consistently rise. If we turn now to the first movement of the Fifth symphony we find a very similar concept, pairs of notes with an upward progression; admittedly the dynamics are reversed, *crescendo* in No. 4, *diminuendo* in No. 5; granted also that the later work has substantial harmonies. Nevertheless the passages surely have a family likeness.

Ex. 112a.

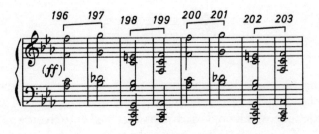

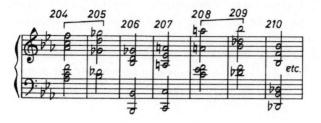

Now intriguing though this may be it should not blind us to the absolute 'rightness' of both passages within their proper context. The progressive march of those minims in the Fourth Symphony (Ex. 112) stems from the immediately preceding passage in crotchets which Beethoven not only augments () but turns back to front and upside-down as he wills. For example, bar 120,

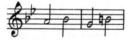

by a process of inversion and augmentation becomes bars 121–122,

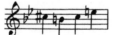

while bar 119

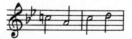

backwards, inverted and augmented becomes bars 123–124

As for the extract from the Fifth Symphony it is simply a huge extension of two notes taken from this seminal phrase

Thus may two acorns grow into two oaks, two trees whose branches differ in number, whose trunks differ in girth and whose outlines differ to the eye; yet they are clearly of the same species.

After this arboreal diversion it is time to return to the symphony under discussion. After a conventionally classic cadence into the dominant key of F, clarinet and bassoon introduce a delightfully naive canon, seemingly a new theme.

Ex. 113.

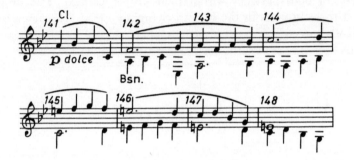

On closer examination this proves to be a subtle variation on Ex. 110, as we can see by combining them in this way.

Ex. 113a.

The canon (Ex. 113) is taken up boisterously by wind and strings, though the oboes and bassoons stay rooted to the dominant for eight bars, as though walking a chalk-line in a test of their sobriety. Then, for several bars, Beethoven plays games with us, alternating between whispering *pianissimi* and loudly banging *fortissimi*. It all proves to be too much for the violins who, in the closing bars of the Codetta (177–186), find it impossible to play on the beat.

The Development begins in an orthodox manner with the main theme of the movement (Ex. 108, bars 43 onward) transposed into the dominant. The harmonic pulse is slow, one chord to every four bars to begin with, and then one to each pair. As is so often the case a conventional formula is used to put us off our guard. With a sudden suppression of tone Beethoven switches to an unexpected and contradictory chord based on C♯. (Academically it would be described as the first inversion of the dominant of D, though it is more important to savour the surprise than to give it the correct label.) This harmony is sustained by implication for no fewer than fourteen bars while the violins repeat a little five-note ascent a number of times. It is the flute that finds the way out of this impasse, flicking the music delightfully into the long-deferred D major, a decision endorsed by the bassoon five bars later.

Now although I have several times referred to the main 'theme' it should be understood that it is, like the main themes of the three earlier symphonies, not just a tune but an implied sequence of harmony. Bars 43–47 of Ex. 108 are presented to us 'horizontally', but their 'vertical' implications would be just as significant to Beethoven; in fact they yield three chords:

The beauty of using material as basic as this is that it makes development so simple; anything that 'fits' this chord-progression will inevitably 'fit' the main theme. If Beethoven seems to produce a ravishing new theme from nowhere, we may be tempted to marvel at his skill in finding a smoothly flowing melody that will serve as counterpoint to the darting quavers of the main theme. He would smile at our naiveté, for his 'smoothly flowing melody' is child's-play to find if we use the chord-sequence above as starting-point.

Ex. 114.

Lovingly he extends this idea through some twenty bars, its serene progress unaffected by the tic-toc of quavers or *staccato* crotchets in the background. Suddenly there is a blast of sound from the full orchestra, a stentorian chord of E♭ major. It is a rhetorical gesture that is so familiar from the eighteenth century that we scarcely listen and yet even here there is subtlety. Suppose that I take Ex. 114 as it appears in bars 237–240; it would be quite logical to follow it up in this way:

Ex. 115.

But Beethoven has already used this type of sequence five times; to continue for yet another would be positively trite. The *ff* interruption is fully justified as a way of breaking out of a seductive circle; the genius lies in the choice of notes, for what I described as a rhetorical gesture proves to be a compression of exactly the sequence I proposed. The melodic phrase

is crumpled up like a piece of waste paper and becomes

Needless to say this is closely related to the final triplet of bar 42 (Ex. 108); what seemed like a charming but somewhat irrelevant decoration is shown to be an integral part of the whole conception.

Although the pace of the movement remains undiminished Beethoven now expands the time-scale by prolonging individual harmonies for a considerable span. The process is disguised by skilfully contrasted dynamics, usually between the full orchestra (less timpani) playing *fortissimo* and the two ranks of violins ticking along with quiet *staccato* crotchets. From bar 241 onwards the plan is:

241–248	E♭ major:	4 bars *ff*: 4 bars *p*.
249–256	G major:	4 bars *ff*: 4 bars *p*.
257–280 (!)	Diminished seventh:	8 bars *fff/f*: 2 bars *dim*:
		2 bars *p*: 12 bars *pp*.

This extreme prolongation of one harmony, and an irresolute one at that, creates a strange feeling of suspense (see Ex. 105, p. 101 for a quotation). Finally the music is reduced to just two notes, D♭–B♭, which are changed for harmonic convenience to C♯–A♯. 'Where can this be leading to?' At last a solution to the riddle is found. As quietly as possible the strings suggest the dominant of B major.

Ex. 116.

Now B major is theoretically just about the last key that is wanted at this point; we should be making for B *flat* which, according to strictly grammatical notation has not a single note in common with B major. I like to think that the quiet rumble on the timpani is an admonition to the strings to think again, a reminder that B♭ is their proper goal. Again they persist in their folly, again the timpani growl a warning. In a moment that is truly inspired, Beethoven gives the first violins *for the first time in the symphony* that portion of the main theme that initially appeared in the woodwind (see Ex. 108, bars 47–49). As yet it is little more than a memory, disguised as it is by the 'wrong' tonality and a lack of any harmonic support.

Ex. 117.

Several abortive attempts are made to use this, both by the violins and the lower strings. Employing the principle that if you have lost your way you should try to get back to the place where you went wrong, the players return to that same diminished seventh which had been sustained for some twenty-four bars. As though throwing a beam of light from a torch, a solo flute leads them out of the maze by showing them a different way of resolving the chord. It is a moment of sheer magic.

Ex. 118.

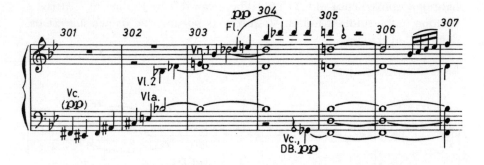

This time the timpani murmur an approving B♮; over a long-held drum-roll the strings proffer a number of tiny flickers of sound, all leading to fundamental notes of the B♭ major chord. It is an orchestral parallel to a passage near the end of the development of the 'Waldstein' Sonata Op. 53 which had been written in 1804,[1] a way of giving a sense of immense relief when at last the Recapitulation is 'delivered'.

The Recapitulation begins with substantial changes of texture; instead of the delicate initial statement from first violins we have an orchestral *tutti*, *ff*, followed by a reversal of roles, with a solo oboe taking over on the repetition of the phrase, while a blend of strings and wind gives new colour to the smooth descending scale which had at first been allotted to the wind alone. The material shown in Ex. 109 (p. 105) is considerably extended before the reappearance of the delightful Second Subject group of themes whose rustic character is in no way altered by the necessary transposition to the home key of B♭. Since the proportions of the movement do not demand a lengthy coda, Beethoven rightly resisted any temptation he may have felt to extend things further. Eight bars confirm that B♭ is the 'proper' key; we await the next movement.

[1] Op. 53, I, bars 146–156.

The danger of associating music too closely with outside events was never better illustrated than in Sir George Grove's admirable book on the Beethoven symphonies[1] which for many years was a musicological landmark. In it he proposes that the reason for the geniality of this symphony's quick movements and the 'celestial beauty' of the Adagio is that the composer had recently become engaged to Therese von Brunsvik, a young Countess who was sister to one of his friends and patrons. 'His heart must have been swelling with his new happiness,' says Grove, little thinking that he had been deceived by fraudulent evidence. Beethoven's most detailed biographer in the nineteenth century was the American Alexander Wheelock Thayer. Like many other writers, Thayer devoted much thought to the identity of the mysterious woman in Beethoven's life known as the 'Immortal Beloved', a title bestowed on her as the result of three letters couched in extravagant and passionate language which were discovered in Beethoven's desk after his death. In 1890 a book was published called *Beethovens unsterbliche Geliebte, Nach persönlichen Erinnerungen* (Beethoven's Immortal Beloved, from personal reminiscences). It purported to be a true account given by the ageing Countess of her love affair with Beethoven, including the engagement in 1806. Naturally the book was read avidly in much the same way that daring disclosures of the love-life of our popular idols today are devoured in the spicier Sunday papers. The second edition was even graced with an endorsement from Thayer expressing his belief that the mystery had now been solved. In the following year the book was exposed as a fiction, but by then the myth had taken hold and even Grove was taken in by it. His entire thesis concerning the emotional content of the Fourth (and Fifth) Symphonies in relation to Beethoven's private life was built upon an elaborate hoax which he had welcomed unwittingly as a happy solution. It was a human error that is easy to forgive when put beside the immense scholarship he brought to all fields of music; that his name has become synonymous with the world's greatest dictionary of music (even long after his death) is proof enough of our debt to him.

The slow movement, in the subdominant key of E♭ major, begins with a measured repetition of the tonic and dominant of that key.

In establishing such a pattern Beethoven was dealing with the fundamentals of music and it is worth noting that Schubert planned to use a similar figure,

[1] *Beethoven and his Nine Symphonies*, Novello, 1896.

although to very different effect, in the first Allegro of his great C major symphony. In Schubert's notation, at a much quicker tempo, it looked like this:

but having written the whole of the first movement using this as the main theme, he felt the need to modify its relentless insistence on two notes and laboriously changed it throughout to

In Beethoven's case the danger does not arise since the figure is not even used consistently as an accompaniment; it is nearer to a distant horn-call, a 'signal' in the military sense that prepares us for the arrival of the serenely beautiful melody, a princess royal indeed.

Ex. 119.

Loud and near, with trumpets horns and drums, the signal sounds out again before the theme is repeated in the woodwind. The simplicity of the theme is deceptive for soon Beethoven is to embark on the most elaborately decorative passages that un-nerve the amateur player by their blackness on the page. Essentially they are based on straightforward ideas, but even a simple scale can look bewildering when it is as heavily disguised as it is here.

It needs a clear head to disentangle this and see that it is simply a busier version of this elementary phrase.

Beethoven was to become an absolute master of the technique of combining tranquillity of the spirit with activity of the fingers as the late piano sonatas demonstrate particularly well. It is essential in a movement of this kind to maintain the sustained breadth of the melodic conception and not to distract the listener with too fussy an exposure of detail. When we look at a mosaic we do not examine each individual stone though each may well have a beauty of its own.

After the first of these decorative episodes a new theme appears; given to a solo clarinet its initial ascent seems designed to counterbalance the descending melody of the opening.

Ex. 120.

Under its calming influence the business of the immediately preceding bars is stilled, while *pizzicato* strings in the background suggest a nocturnal serenade. The theme swells up through the full woodwind choir before the double-basses reintroduce the 'signal' motif. At once a ripple of activity stirs in the cellos followed in turn by violas and violins. The woodwind continue their serenade, but the force beneath is not to be denied and after four slow bars (six beats to each bar) the martial rhythm takes command. A tremendous unison leads us back to a reprise of the opening theme, this time considerably embellished. Yet again the signal sounds out, leading to an astonishingly dramatic descent, each note heavily accented with explosive cannon-shots from the timpanist and aggressive *tremolandi* in the lower strings. Quite how Grove reconciled this passage with his image of the happy lover is hard to see; it was a nettle he was reluctant to grasp, dismissing it casually as 'six bars of the same subject, but in E♭ minor', without so much as a word about its startlingly dramatic scoring or its evident toughness.

It is normally useless to seek extra-musical explanations of such outbursts; music has a mysterious way of creating its own inner demands. The ancient cliché 'one thing leads to another' contains much truth, and to a composer it is quite logical to suppose that if one puts a trite but relevant passage in a full-blooded unison in one bar it will create a spontaneous energy that leads to a ferocious outburst in the next. It may seem absurd to the layman, since the composer holds the pen that puts down the notes and would therefore seem to be in complete control; yet the effort involved in breaking out of the stranglehold of the tonic key could be enough to generate the violent gesture we find in bar 50.

Ex. 121.

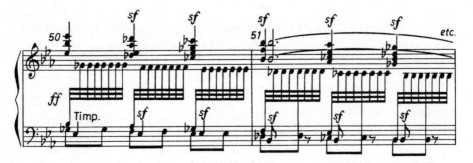

If the prime purpose is indeed to demolish the nexus of E♭ major it succeeds admirably for out of its violence emerges the gentlest of phrases elegantly traced by first and second violins as they coil sinuously around the dominant seventh of G♭ major. Tovey, even in a somewhat perfunctory treatment of the symphony, describes this whole central episode as 'one of the most imaginative passages anywhere in Beethoven'. After the strings have found their way to the haven of G♭, we again hear the 'signal', imaginatively if daringly scored for a solo bassoon. Schumann found the effect humorous, though I suspect that his reaction was dictated by an inadequate performance. Bearing in mind the famous passage in the Fifth Symphony where, during the first movement reprise Beethoven was compelled to use bassoons instead of horns for a vital solo (owing to the limitations of the 'natural' horn), it strikes me as possible that he would have preferred a horn at this point, ideally 'stopped'. Certainly the bassoon tends to stand out a little too obtrusively within this context unless played with consummate artistry; a stopped horn would be a better match for the magical effect of the very quiet double-basses and then timpani that follow.

After this wonderfully evocative interlude, a delicately poised scale on the flute leads us back to the main theme once more. A formal Recapitulation follows, Ex. 120 duly appearing in the home key of E♭ while the closing bars of the phrase are given to the horns rather than the bassoons—a hint that my suggestion that Beethoven regarded them as interchangeable has some justification.

The Coda has a romantic beauty that is virtually unsurpassed in the whole canon of the nine symphonies. Quietly the cellos and basses repeat the 'signal' motif while woodwind and horns remind us of the tenderest of operatic ensembles. The decorative figuration in the violins suggests those gentle zephyrs beloved of the Arcadian poets; all is peace. Then, just as we are nearly awash with sentiment, there is a sudden huge *crescendo* to a brief *fortissimo*. Is it a heartfelt cry from Beethoven's inner self that such idylls are no longer for him? Or, as seems more likely to me, does it express anger with himself for indulging in a touch of self-pity? The questions are immaterial in the long run, since the movement is so profoundly satisfying as it stands.

Though Beethoven still uses the obsolete term Menuetto for the third movement it is far from being a minuet; scherzo is the only word to describe its jokey mixture of bluster and sly humour. Initially we are back in the main key of the symphony, B♭ major, but it is to be subject to continuous attack from foreign influences. Furthermore the rhythmic pulse is deliberately disturbed by violent cross-accents in some places and a complete *absence* of accentuation in others. The importance of this second point is not always understood.

Before we examine the music further let us imagine a stately minuet such as Haydn might have composed in his youth.

Ex. 122.

As music it is passable enough, the brief flirtation with the minor in bars 5–8 making a worthwhile contrast to the unadventurous opening. It was precisely such conventions that Beethoven was only too happy to blow apart, and I am tempted to think that he used the word Menuetto as a touch of sardonic humour. Much has been made of his gesture in tearing up the title-page of the 'Eroica', but musically this rude demolition of an antique form has far more significance. Compare the first two bars of Ex. 122 with what Beethoven actually wrote and you will see how ruthlessly he clubbed the minuet to death.

Ex. 122a.

Not content with pulverising the rhythm he immediately sets about destroying the tonality with a weird ribbon of notes divided between wind and strings and devoid of any supporting (and therefore explanatory) harmony.

Ex. 123.

A more devious route from tonic to dominant can seldom have been devised, and while it is easy enough for the academic mind to assess it as a juxtaposition of diminished sevenths, I believe that a contemporary audience would have found it as disturbing as a tone-row is to conservative listeners today, containing as it does nine of the available twelve chromatic notes (F G♭ A C E♭ D♭ E♮ G♮ B♭).

Perhaps feeling that there were shocks enough already, Beethoven had second thoughts about the tempo, changing it from *Allegro molto e vivace* to a mere *Allegro vivace*.

Having ended the first twenty-bar section (usually sixteen) securely in the dominant key of F, he immediately pitches us without warning into D♭ major. Surprise follows surprise; if we have a feeling for musical proportion we naturally expect anything corresponding to the first four bars to be followed by a parallel to bars five to eight. Not a bit of it; defying expectation, Beethoven extends the last four notes of the first phrase in a delightful game of 'pass-the-parcel'.

Ex. 124.

The game continues while cellos and bassoon try to inject a more serious tone with a long sequence of sustained notes falling through a sequence of descending fifths from high F to low D. The diversion over, the full orchestra recalls the opening bars, this time followed as before by the unisons of Ex. 123. As though aware that this phrase is a bit naked, Beethoven now clothes it in respectable harmony before bringing the section to a close.

The Trio that follows is delightfully whimsical, a tongue-in-cheek gesture towards the old-style minuet with a country band of wind-players interrupted by a bunch of self-taught violinists who can neither hit the note in the middle nor control their bows adequately. How else can one sensibly interpret passages such as this?

The first notes are clearly 'wrong' while the *sforzando* is uncalled for. Moreover when the violins essay a more melodic phrase they slide down chromatically as though playing with one finger. A further exhibition of insecure intonation comes in bars 130–138 where the strings grope about uncertainly trying to find the 'right' note until at last they settle in relief on B♭–A which they alternate happily for eleven bars.

Now I am fully aware that this is a heretical view, but why should Beethoven's only joke at the expense of musicians be confined to the 'Pastoral' Symphony? There is a great deal of evidence to show that he had a malicious sense of humour; his experiences with orchestras were far from happy and he had every justification for mocking them. It is all very well for Grove to describe this section as 'one of the tenderest and most refined things to be found anywhere' and to compare the chromatic descent in the violins

to a robin singing of the departed delights of summer. (Some robin!) I do not ask for the music to be made into an obvious caricature, nor that it should be played badly. I see no reason why great art should not be tinged with humour, though here the satire is affectionate rather than mordant. Within the context of this movement with its high-spirited 'scherzo' at beginning and end, I am convinced that the central 'minuet' stands as a symbol of the refined conventions that Beethoven had lost patience with.

The finale is as exuberant a movement as he ever wrote, almost a *moto perpetuo* in character. The first violins make an abortive attempt to start what might be called a theme,

Ex. 125.

but it is snatched away from them by the seconds and violas; three loud chords leave us wondering what has happened. Beethoven then appears to decide that it would be more fun to write an operatic overture than a symphony. Perhaps he remembered the closing pages of the overture to *The Marriage of Figaro*.

The bracketed figure corresponds very closely to the basic pattern that Beethoven uses, as does the quiet murmur of rapidly articulated notes. Out of this suppressed but excited chatter a wisp of tune emerges.

Ex. 125a.

It is instantly taken up by the woodwind who, by a process of simple decoration, manage to relate it to the very opening notes of the movement,

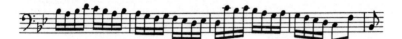

being transformed into

A strongly held B♮ in wind and brass provides a focus for the continuing activity in the strings. The double-basses have a particularly busy time in this movement and Beethoven shows them little pity. Back in 1799 the double-bass virtuoso Dragonetti had visited him and, to the composer's amazement and delight, had played the G minor *Cello* Sonata Op. 5 to perfection. From that day on Beethoven ceased to regard the double-bass as an instrument to be coddled with simplifications of the cello part. For many years there had been a tradition that bass-players could modify anything that looked like an unreasonable demand. Thus an experienced player would take one glance at a passage like this—

and reduce it to its essentials.

My reason for exposing this dubious practice will become clear at the end of the chapter.

After thirty-six bars the excitement dies down and an oboe, accompanied by a clarinet 'left-hand' introduces a second subject. The flute replies, whereupon the violins produce a chromatic and syncopated variation on their little duologue. A loud chord of F minor ushers in some rough treatment for the four-note fragment from bar 1, now distorted to

but the violins run away from a potentially nasty scene with a phrase of enchanting fleetness (bars 70–73 and 78–86). The Codetta simply establishes the dominant in a delightfully bustling manner whose busy figuration spills over into the Development.

Like Mozart and Haydn before him, Beethoven was a more than adequate violinist and there are passages in this symphony that suggest that he was recalling hours of technical practise spent in mastering the instrument. After eighteen bars of tortured fiddling the violins are rescued from a conveyor-belt of modulations by a resounding B♮. A splendid joke follows. Every musician in the orchestra must have been sure that such a note would prove to be the dominant of E major. Assuming that his next intention was to allude to Ex. 125a this would mean something on these lines:

Ex. 126.

Instead, Beethoven breaks all the rules of harmonic propriety, slips neatly up a semitone to a C♮ and gives us the substance of Ex. 126 in the 'wrong' key of G major.

It is unnecessary to catalogue every remaining event in this effervescent movement. One point that may of structural importance is a lengthy dwelling on one harmony from bars 165–181. Between great clanging chords, the strings twice repeat this figure:

Ex. 127.

It is tempting to say that here we have a fusion of the darting quavers from the first movement and the elusive unisons from the Scherzo-Menuetto. Certainly the latter relationship *looks* convincing enough:

Ex. 127a.

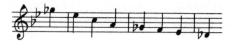

All the same I do not believe it to be more than a coincidence. The harmony spelt out by these notes, a dominant minor ninth, has been a significant feature of the symphony ever since the G♭–E♭ minims in its very second bar; it is suggested by the faltering quavers in the Introduction, by the unisons of Ex. 123, and now by emphatic repetition in Ex. 127. Most dramatically of all it appears as a sustained tension chord just before the final coda. This proves to be a sheer delight with the cellos and basses hard put to it to sustain the pace. (Was it for their sakes that Beethoven added a cautionary *ma non troppo* after his original direction *Allegro*?) Eleven bars from the end the violinists reach exhaustion-point; their weary fingers can only play at half-speed.

A tired bassoon[1] and equally fatigued second violins and violas agree that they are literally 'played out'; a pause, a rush for the exit, and the symphony is ended.

Before we move on it would be worth while to glance at a contemporary criticism written by Carl Maria von Weber, in his early twenties at the time and therefore one would have thought in sympathy with any new trend. Written in the form of a dialogue between the instruments of the orchestra it has the double-bass saying,

> I have just come from the rehearsal of a Symphony by one of our newest composers;[2] though I have a tolerably strong constitution, I could only just last out; five more minutes and my frame would have shattered . . . I was made to caper about like a wild goat.'

The cellist wet with sweat was too exhausted to speak. After more in the same vein the orchestra attendant suggests the latest formula for a symphony:

> First a slow movement full of disconnected ideas at the rate of three or four notes to each quarter-hour; then a mysterious drum-roll with something for the violas suitably seasoned with pauses and ritardandi; to end with, a furious finale whose only requirement is that there should be no recognisable ideas but an abundance of changes of key—never mind modulating, just jump on to another note when you like!

Beethoven suffered enough from imperceptive critics; he might have hoped for better understanding from a fellow-composer.

[1] There is a notoriously tricky solo for bassoon in bars 184–7.
[2] Beethoven would have been thirty-seven!

8

Symphony No. 5 in C Minor, Op. 67

Dedicated to Prince Lobkowitz and Count Razumowsky

Orchestra: 2 flutes; 1 piccolo; 2 oboes; 2 clarinets; 2 bassoons; 1 contra-bassoon; 2 horns; 2 trumpets; 3 trombones; 2 timpani; strings

1. Allegro con brio
2. Andante con moto—Piu moto
3. Allegro: leading into . . .
4. Allegro—(Reprise of part of 3)—Allegro—Presto

First performance: 22 December 1808

Ask that proverbial creature the 'man in the street' to sing or whistle the first notes of Beethoven that come into his mind and he will almost certainly proffer the opening bars of this symphony. Without question it is one of the most arresting openings ever written, immediate in its dramatic impact, memorable in its simplicity. It has become a musical symbol of the very image we carry in our minds of the composer, rugged and uncompromising. Yet the first performance does not seem to have made the overwhelming impression on the audience that one might have expected. In all fairness they had had a wearing evening; the programme consisted of the first performances of two symphonies (numbers 5 and 6[1]), two movements from the Mass in C major Op. 86, the Choral Fantasia Op. 80, with the Fourth Piano Concerto as the only previously performed work. The music was certainly inadequately rehearsed, while the temperature was freezing. 'There we sat from 6.30 until 10.30 in the most bitter cold,' wrote Reichardt, 'and found from experience that one could have too much even of a good thing, and still more of a loud . . .'. Originally it was planned to end this marathon concert with the C minor symphony, but Beethoven, perhaps thinking that the chorus was under-

---

[1] As a matter of interest they were numbered the reverse way, the 'Pastoral' as No. 5, the C minor as No. 6.

employed, decided to finish with the Choral Fantasia whose extensive piano introduction he improvised on the spot. During the performance the Fantasia ground to a halt owing to a misunderstanding about repeats in the wind parts; poor Beethoven had to get up from the piano and rush into the orchestra to sort out what had gone wrong. Some of the players wanted to walk out, though the audience seem to have taken it in good part. It seems likely however that a major contretemps of this nature might well have erased whatever good impressions the symphony might have made. It was not the immediate success one might have expected and the first London performance (given by the Philharmonic Society, 1816) was incomplete, the concert-master Salomon having declared the music to be rubbish. Some years later he recanted and told the orchestra at rehearsal that he now considered it to be one of the greatest compositions he had ever heard.

The first sketches of the symphony appear as early as 1804 in the same book that contains much of the initial working-out of the 'Eroica'. We have already seen that work on the Fifth Symphony was interrupted so that the Fourth could be written, but it appears that even after the Fourth had been completed, Beethoven was still unable to devote his energies exclusively to the C minor symphony. Strange though it may seem, work proceeded on the 'Pastoral' at the same time; thus the composition of the Fifth Symphony overlaps both its neighbours. As an instance of this, the link between the 'Storm' and the finale of the 'Pastoral' was apparently composed *before* the link between the last two movements of the Fifth Symphony, serving as a useful try-out for a new procedure.

Although there are aspects of the C minor symphony that must have seemed frighteningly novel to a contemporary audience, its form proves to be surprisingly conventional. Moreover, Beethoven was not making any special effort to cut himself off from the past; relationships can be found not only with works by his fellow-composers Cherubini and Méhul, but even with Mozart. Here is a fragment taken from the start of the finale of Mozart's great symphony in G minor, No. 40 (K. 550).

Ex. 128.

If we turn now to the Scherzo of Beethoven's Fifth and, for ease of comparison, transpose it into the same key, there is an evident similarity in the shape of the phrase.

Ex. 128a.

One might dismiss this as mere coincidence were it not for the fact that Beethoven actually copied out twenty-nine bars of the Mozart finale in the very same sketchbook he was using for the preliminary work on the Fifth Symphony! A similarly intriguing line of descent can be traced from the slow movement of Mozart's 'Jupiter' symphony —

Ex. 129.

to the finale of Beethoven's Fifth (again transposed for convenience).

Ex. 129a.

As is so often the case the first sketches are so banal that one can scarcely believe that they could be used so fruitfully. The ultimate pattern of three repeated notes followed by a drop of a third is there, but the triteness of the sequential repetition courts disaster.

Ex. 130.

The next stage in Beethoven's arduous progress towards the realisation of a goal as yet barely comprehended still suffers from the dreadful banality of its reiterated patterns, all too neatly packaged.

Ex. 131.

Ex. 131a.

The tempo indication *presto* gives us an indication of the inherent agitation of the sequence, but a tempo in itself is scarcely enough to redeem the ordinariness of the harmony. Nor is Ex. 131a which follows immediately after much more promising, being little more than a rather fussy chromatic scale; nevertheless, it was to prove to be a seed of some significance. Meanwhile, the possibility of treating these repeated notes in an altogether gentler fashion had caught Beethoven's fancy, and on the facing page of the manuscript we find a remarkably close approximation to the opening of the Fourth Piano Concerto.

Ex. 132.

The ease with which he seems to have 'found' this tune compares curiously with the travail which accompanied the birth of the symphony.

It was Beethoven's factotum Anton Schindler who recorded the remark 'Thus Fate knocks at the door . . .' supposedly made by Beethoven about the opening of this symphony. As a witness he is far from ideal, being prone to romantic fabrication. (Hans von Bulow scathingly referred to him as 'that strawhead'!) The phrase has caught on because it accords so admirably with what we want to believe; yet Beethoven did not make the remark until many years after the symphony had been written. Much nearer the time he offered a rather different attribution to Czerny, saying that the little pattern of notes had come to him from a yellow-hammer's song, heard as he walked in the Prater-park in Vienna. Needless to say, given the choice between a yellow-hammer and Fate-at-the-door the public has preferred the more dramatic myth, though Czerny's account is too unlikely to have been invented. In the long term the source of the material is irrelevant; what matters is what was made of it.

Although one could scarcely ask for a more positive or emphatic opening, the fact is that to a musician the first phrases are ambivalent in tonality.

Apart from any information the programme may give us there is nothing in the music that tells us that this is in C minor; it could as easily be in E♭ major, and had Beethoven elected to continue like this we would accept E♭ as the proper tonality without demur.

Ex. 133.

The difference in the emotional implications is enormous, the aggressive opening bars now becoming a jest rather than a gesture. All the same, though the symphony proves to be in C minor, the E♮ potential of the opening phrase should not be discounted as we shall discover later in the movement. For the moment let us reduce the music to a bare skeleton, deprived of the vital force of its rhythm.

Ex. 133a.

It is easy enough to see (or to hear) this as two falling thirds, but it is equally important to be aware of the *rising* tone between the second and third notes. As a piece of musical fabric it contains several possibilities; a four-note melody as shown above, a sequence of two *harmonies*,

Ex. 133b.

more likely to be in E♭ than C minor, and a possible rearrangement into a rising tone and a falling fourth.

Ex. 133c.

Add the dynamic forward impulse given by the repeated quavers and the idea is truly ripe for development.

Now there are certain types of music that make their meaning very clear, loud and quick, quiet and slow, rich or austere in texture, majestic or puckish and so on. Even the tone-deaf can surely distinguish between a funeral march and a charleston, a love-song and a war-cry. More subtle, and therefore ultimately more enduring, is the music that has an element of ambiguity; there can be few better examples than the first movement of this symphony. If we consider the opening bars to be a brief introduction that simply informs us in stentorian tones of the subject matter, the movement proper *begins* in bar 6. (In passing, notice how Beethoven is at pains to ensure that the second pause is longer than the first, the extra bar being more than mere caprice.) Thinking of bar 6 as the true beginning changes our entire conception of the movement, emphasising the pathos so that, like the sonata in the same key, it becomes a 'Symphonie Pathétique'. Part of the music, indeed its emotional heart, longs to indulge in self-pity of a truly forlorn character.

Ex. 134.

Here is what might be termed the melodic aspect of the music; but it is not allowed so open an expression of grief. Instead, it is driven on by a relentless rhythmic force so that two conflicting emotions are put in opposition to each other, pathetic and dynamic co-existing in an uneasy marriage. In such a conflict, the rhythm is likely to prove the victor, but there are occasions (most notably perhaps in the touching oboe cadenza) when pathos speaks out so eloquently that even the pitiless rhythm must halt its persistent onward drive. If there is any one quality that I would single out above all others as the hallmark of this movement it would have to be the almost continuous internal conflict between the cry for pity and the refusal to grant it. For instance take the sustained minim G that emerges in this cadence (bar 21):

Ex. 135.

Why is this note left unsupported if it is not to emphasise its isolation, a single arm raised from the abyss? And if one sees it not as a gesture of strength but as a cry for help, how cruelly is that cry swamped by the giant unisons that follow:

The essential pathos of a falling minor third is again revealed in the forlorn response this evokes; gradually the rhythm generates more and more force until it seems as though the whole orchestra is being pounded with battering quavers; the sound literally breaks apart, a single crack of a chord separated from its surroundings by silence. Horns in unison announce the imminent arrival of the Second Subject.

Ex. 136.

The phrase serves a dual purpose, preparing the way for what is to come, but also revealing the potentially *major* aspect of the very first bars. The harmonic version of bars 1–5 (Ex. 133b on p. 130) fits perfectly against Ex. 136 so that the horn-call, far from being new, turns out to be a different view of the opening material. Furthermore, when we look more closely at the Second Subject we find that it stems from the four-note call shown as Ex. 133c on p. 130. Of what did it consist? Intervals of a second and a fourth, precisely the intervals which comprise the Second Subject.

Ex. 137.

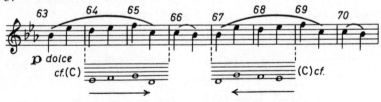

After so much agitation, one might expect this tune to create a pool of calm, but it is not to be. Once more the internal conflict of the movement manifests itself; the cellos and basses quietly but ruthlessly set out to destroy any peace of mind the Second Subject might bring. How easily Beethoven could have relented and allowed them a gracious gesture of acquiescence:

Ex. 138.

Such concessions are not to be found in this movement. Instead of the bland minims suggested above, we find muttered reminders of the all-pervading rhythm—

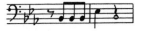

—mutterings that gather in strength until, like a tidal wave, they swamp the last plaintive cries of the Second Subject.

Ex. 139.

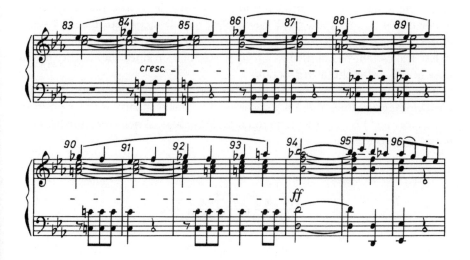

It is interesting to compare the chromatic ascent in the lower strings (bars 84–94) with the crude prototype shown in Ex. 131a; as for the almost meaningless sustained C in the upper part of the same example, it evolves into the anchor-note E♭ which continues as part of the harmony throughout bars 83–93 of Ex. 139.

The obliteration of the Second Subject shown above leads to a formidable Codetta which thumps E♭ major into our heads so forcefully that two bars' rest are called for. The obligatory repeat lends a new meaning to the famous opening phrase; it now becomes a *modulation* back into C minor, so that, by implication, we hear it as though harmonised in this way:

Ex. 140.

It may come as something of a surprise but the range of tonalities explored in this exposition is considerably more restricted than it is in any of the four preceding symphonies. Within the first 124 bars the music is entirely in C minor or E♭ major, apart from the briefest of side-steps into F minor (bars 75–78) and A♭ major (bars 79–82). The apparent brush with E♭ minor shown in Ex. 139 cannot be counted as a proper modulation since the tonality is in a state of flux throughout the section.

The repeat having been properly observed we move on into the Development; at once there is a surprise. The final cadence of the exposition has established E♭ major with no room for argument. When therefore the next notes we hear are these,

we are meant to think of them as being part of that key; by the laws of symmetry we might justifiably expect a comparable gesture to the one with which the symphony began:

Ex. 141.

Instead, Beethoven catches us unawares in two ways, first by eliminating the pause on the second bar so that we have a feeling of being tumbled forward, second by stretching the interval between the two phrases.

Ex. 142.

The resulting bare fifth, lacking either an E♮ or an E♭ as a decisive indicator, is a somewhat forbidding way to enter the sub-dominant key of F minor. Tentatively the music offers a reminder of what I described as the 'true' beginning, i.e. bars 6–21. The powerful D♮ from bar 126 (see above) continues to exert its influence, underlining the essential pathos of the material. For a time it even seems as though this poignant aspect is to be allowed more rein; the first evidence of this comes with the emergence of a new phrase, tinged with chromaticism.

Ex. 143.

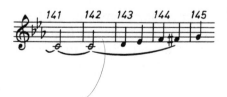

But even this is not allowed to proceed without a restless companion, a descending passage that not only mirrors its (Ex. 143's) ascent, but substantially extends a figure that had originally appeared in bars 14–19. Having found his way to G minor (a true G minor, not a mere dominant of C minor) Beethoven begins a slow climb to the central climax of the movement. The basic components are remarkably simple, breathless little phrases at the top, a continuous extension of the mirror pattern described above, and a remorseless ascent using the motto rhythm in the bass. The essentials can be clearly revealed in a mere three lines of score.

Ex. 144.

The elaborations on this simple framework are few, largely consisting of overlapping imitations of the violin phrases (top line) from the woodwind. Notice too the horn's insistent reiteration of the motto rhythm as well as the discreet initial drum-taps which suddenly break out into a thunderous barrage at bar 168. For the next few bars Beethoven discharges a salvo of shattering chords at us before embarking on a bold new treatment of the horn fanfare that had once so optimistically hailed the Second Subject. Instead of leading us to an oasis it now heads into a storm.

Ex. 145.

If I break off the example there, it is to draw attention to the two rising notes to be found in bars 180–181 or 188–189, for it is this ascending step (notes 2 and 3 from Ex. 133a on p. 130) which is about to be used in the most inventive way. It is the strange sequence of block harmonies that has already been quoted in Ex. 112a (pp. 106–7)). Gradually the chords seem to grow more distant both in tone and in tonality until an impasse is reached on this chord,

which is repeated seven times. As if impatient at this apparent indecision, there is a sudden violent outburst of great thematic interest, a fusion of the falling thirds that had begun the symphony and the minim extension from the horn fanfare.

Ex. 146.

It is the first time that there has been an attempt to harmonise the four-note pattern from which the entire movement has sprung, and bare though the harmonies may be, the effect is extraordinarily powerful. For seven more bars a quiet tolling of diminished sevenths keeps us in suspense before a ferocious reiteration of the interval Ab–F finally drops into the 'proper' place, G–Eb; we have reached the Recapitulation, a moment whose impact is intensified by the addition of full woodwind, brass and timpani to a statement originally made by strings alone. Furthermore the speculative harmonisation first introduced in Ex. 146 provides a new density to the motto theme, enlarging its stature still more.

As the Recapitulation gets under way new elements are introduced, each designed both to bring out the pathetic aspect and to reduce the force of the rhythm, countertunes on bassoon or oboe that have the effect of slowing the music's pulse somewhat. Most notable of these is the oboe-part which, at a point corresponding to the held violin note in bar 21 (see Ex. 135, p. 131), offers a moving cry from the heart which seems at first hearing to be a spontaneous invention. In fact is is wholly germane to the issue as the following sequence shows:

Violins (bars 261–3):

Transpose this down a third:

'Augment' by lengthening notes:

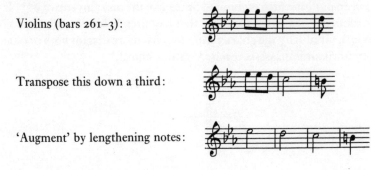

This phrase actually appears in the oboe-part just before the brief cadenza. It could be said to plant the idea of augmentation in the mind, an idea which duly flowers in a single adagio bar.[1]

This can readily be seen as an augmentation of the violin phrase shown above. When earlier I described this movement as a conflict between the 'cry for pity and the refusal to grant it', or between the pathetic and dynamic elements, I was preparing the way for moments such as the one we now find. According to the plan of the exposition the sustained G on the violins in bar 21 was followed by an angry outburst of the motto theme on the notes A♮–F (see p. 131). In this later instance in the recapitulation, such is the eloquence of the oboe's plea that the possible angry response is quelled; for once the melodic muse triumphs, if triumph is the proper word for music so permeated with implications of tragedy.

In due course we arrive at the fanfare-like link to the Second Subject; this time it presented a problem to Beethoven, for the horns, severely limited as to the notes they could actually play before the invention of valves, were unable to play the phrase in the 'new' key of C major.[2] Beethoven therefore had to give

---

[1] A suitable moment to perpetuate a favourite story concerning the late Sir Malcolm Sargent.

Sir M: (stopping the orchestra) 'Oboe, you're flat! Try it again . . .' (Oboe player does so) 'No, it won't do; oboe you're still flat!'

After being thus reprimanded a third time, the oboist held up his instrument and said loudly, 'D'you hear that, yer bugger, you're flat . . .'. Collapse of orchestra.

[2] Even as late as 1841 Schumann encountered a similar problem in the very opening bars of his First Symphony; he was rescued by Mendelssohn who suggested an alternative.

the theme to a pair of bassoons, who, high in their compass, were bound to seem a less than adequate substitute. In modern performances the heroic implications of the original thought are regarded as more worthy of preservation than the secondary matter of scoring; the phrase is invariably played by horns, to whose mechanical capabilities it can now safely be entrusted—so far as anything is ever 'safe' on a horn!

The progress of the Second Subject material proceeds according to convention for some seventy bars (307–374), at which point a final cadence into C major proves to be anything but final. In a passage that is driven by a positively demonic energy, the entire orchestra hammers away at the repeated-note motif, the sense of struggle increased by a disagreement between the strings and the rest about who should play what when. In furious frustration they break off, leaving a dramatic silence that is interrupted questioningly with an *inversion* of the opening pattern,

the first time that particular card has been played. To judge by the response it is not a popular move; an even more thunderous knocking batters our ears. This display of ill temper is suitably punished by being subjected to the restraint of school-room counterpoint, the only such passage in the movement. Using the fusion of motto theme and horn fanfare that appeared initially as Ex. 146, he introduces a new scale-like countersubject.

Ex. 147.

If it is a mite contrived it is at least ingeniously contrived, the minims of bars 399–401 being 'diminished' to crotchets in bars 407 onwards, while the quavers in bar 407 and subsequent bars are not only diminished further but inverted as well,

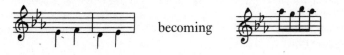

(I need hardly point out the relevance of this to notes 2, 3 and 4 of Ex. 133a on p. 130.) The sequence initiated at bar 407 continues for some way, leading to an upward-an-onward march of crotchets that is still largely concerned with falling thirds and rising tones—the essence of the motto theme. Trumpets and drums give an increasingly martial air to the music though one could scarcely describe it as a march. The scoring is strangely antiphonal, blocks of strings opposed to the woodwind choir. For a moment or two it even seems as if the pervasive rhythm has at last been jettisoned, crotchets having replaced the driving quavers for some thirty bars. Needless to say the force of the rhythm is not to be denied and it duly reappears more emphatically than ever.

Ex. 148.

As if exhausted by this frenzy, the violins give out a last whisper of the forlorn phrase that originally appeared as early as the sixth bar. A low sustained fifth on the two bottom strings of the cellos adds a touch of darkness and despair. For the last time the cry for pity is refused and the movement ends in a rain of blows.[1]

The instruction *Andante con moto* that applies to the second movement should serve as a reminder that it is a dance, not a dirge. Proof of this is to be found in the very first sketch which is specifically marked *Andante quasi menuetto*. The old-fashioned grace of the tune confirms that Beethoven's roots were still firmly fixed in the past however much his gaze might be directed towards more distant and adventurous horizons.

Ex. 149.

---

[1] Despite the impression of overwhelming intensity it is one of the most perfectly balanced movements Beethoven ever wrote, the Exposition being 124 bars in length, the Development 123 bars, the Recapitulation 126 and the Coda 129. Each bar lasts approximately two-thirds of a second at the main tempo!

Realising that this was altogether too plain for nineteenth-century needs he started to decorate it.

Ex. 149a.

This comes so near to the ultimate theme that it is surprising to find a later sketch that is further off the mark.

Ex. 149b.

The curious gruffness of this suggests that it is intended to be the start of a contrapuntal passage of sorts, perhaps on some such lines as these:

Ex. 149c.

In the end, by incorporating the dotted rhythms of Ex. 149 with the more graceful contours of Ex. 149a, he found the theme which was to serve as the basis for an elaborate set of orchestral variations—for that is the form the movement was to take. Its first presentation is sublimely simple, violas and cellos in unison with a few bass notes sketched in *pizzicato* by the double-basses.

Ex. 150.

The last segment of the tune, the 'horns of Elfland faintly blowing', so takes his fancy that he cannot resist the temptation to extend it lovingly.

Ex. 150a.

Instantly the strings take up the same extension and elaborate it still further.

Now while it is true that this movement is in variation form, it is somewhat unorthodox; indeed Tovey calls it unique. By using two quite separate themes as the basis for his variations as well as various unrelated episodes, Beethoven accomplishes a marriage of rondo and variation form. Some analysts even maintain that there are three main themes, though to my ears Ex. 150a and its subsequent embellishment are essentially a 'variation' on part of the 'theme', rather than being independent. Part of the confusion arises from Beethoven's insistence on Ab major as a common tonality from bars 1–26, thus leading us to think of a considerable span of music as one; in fact, the end of bar 22 sees the introduction of Theme II, a smoothly gliding woodwind tune whose accompaniment in triplet figuration (violas) tends to make us feel we are already moving into Variation I. The assumption is wrong; Theme II has a clear identity of its own, although, as we shall discover, Beethoven finds it harder than one might think wholly to shake off the influence of Theme I. Here is the start of Theme II.

Ex. 151.

After so confident a start, the violin entry at the end of bar 26 is disconcerting, particularly with alien A naturals hovering beneath. It is this fragment that strikes me as being a 'memory' of Theme I, a note of doubt as to the propriety of embarking on this new venture. (I should perhaps stress that when I use such terms to describe an event in music I am referring to subconscious rather than intellectual processes; Beethoven of all people would not have given a damn for propriety, but the sketchbooks constantly reveal the extreme caution he experienced before any final commitment to an idea.) The indisputable fact remains that those three tentative violin notes, three times repeated, *could* provide a way back to Theme I by this route:

Ex. 151a.

It is my belief that Beethoven, whether consciously aware of it or not, stood at this threshold before deciding resolutely to push on. The G♮ becomes an F♯, the F♯ leads to a G, and with a sudden blaze of *ff* we are pitched into C major. With all flags flying Theme II makes a new start, trumpets, horns and drums lending it a ceremonial air. The mood is short-lived; again the 'doubting' phrase makes its tentative entry, this time extending into a mysterious sequence of veiled harmonies which magically convey us back to A♭ major. Some 48 bars have passed since the beginning of the movement yet only now do we find the start of Variation I.

Perhaps using Ex. 149a as his rough model, Beethoven decorates the theme with a continuous stream of semiquavers, a technique he uses to markedly similar effect in the finale of the Sixth Symphony.

Ex. 152, Fifth Symphony

Ex. 152a, Sixth Symphony

The full span of the variation on Theme I completed we move on directly to a variation on Theme II. The new decorative element largely consists of fairly conventional arpeggio figuration in demisemiquavers, but again the onward progress of the music is twice halted by what I have called the 'doubting' phrase, this time accompanied by a faint tattoo on a single note to a rhythm that may or may not have some fleeting relationship to the first movement. Listening to this symphony one is liable to grasp a shade too readily at any repeated notes as being of some significance, especially when they are uttered as dramatically as these.

When we find such a figure played eleven times in all on various notes we can be forgiven for a spot of wishful thinking, though I doubt if it is intended to offer any conscious link with the preceding movement. It makes a disturbing undercurrent to the mysterious sequence of harmonies whose function has already been established earlier—how to return to the tonic without giving away one's destination.

Once the desirable goal of A♭ major has been thus attained, the second variation on Theme I follows; it might aptly be described as a variation on a variation since it is a doubly elaborate version of Ex. 152 considerably extended in length. An accumulation of throbbing chords erupts into two ascending scales of E♭ major; there is a long and dramatic pause. All thoughts of conventional variations are put aside as we embark on a journey into the unknown. Very quietly the strings play what in fact is a quite ordinary chord (a dominant seventh), but which, in this context, is given a strangely mysterious quality; eight times it is repeated before a solo clarinet begins a dialogue for wind instruments. It is most probably derived from Ex. 149b, the bassoon reply being an exact reproduction of the first eight notes thereof, though transposed up an octave. It develops into an extraordinary passage in thirds for flute, oboe and two clarinets, the patterns gliding in contrary motion so smoothly that the incidental dissonances pass almost unnoticed. A brief _crescendo_ ushers in a reappearance of Theme II, once more in C major; indeed, the firmness with which this key is established three times in this movement may be regarded in part as an aural preparation for the finale, a foretaste of triumphs to come. For the most part the slow movement is either in one of the two major keys A♭ and C or in no key at all—the 'doubting' sections. However, at one point, after curiously dithering on a little E♭ arpeggio for more than six bars, Beethoven decides to toy with the idea of going into A♭ minor, producing a less than strict variation on Theme I thereby. Almost as though accepting that there is no future in this he disperses the music with a few scales sent hither and thither before triumphantly reasserting Theme I in its most confident guise. The tender strains of Ex. 150a, later to be even more lovingly elaborated by the strings, seem to be drawing the movement to its close. Unexpectedly the pace quickens slightly while the bassoon reveals vaguely operatic aspirations, but the change of mood passes in a matter of moments. The last few phrases restore the calm of the opening, a calm that is saved from any suggestion of sentimentality by the surprising strength of the final bars.

Beethoven's original plan for this movement was far more conventional in layout, a Menuetto which would have incorporated Theme II as a Trio, complete with all the traditional repeats. In rejecting past custom he proved how assured he had become in the development of new forms whose inner logic would seem completely satisfying even though the listener might find it hard to put a label to it.

In all the nine symphonies there is not a Scherzo more individual than the one which now ensues. However lively or vigorous the other eight may be, they all acknowledge some indebtedness to the dance as a form, even if their ancestral minuet has been left far behind. In this symphony we find a movement that suggests an improvisation for orchestra; indeed it is well on the way towards the lyrical character that flowered so romantically in the first movement of the Piano Sonata in A, Op. 101. This assertion is sufficiently provocative to require some supporting evidence, something which can best be provided by a simple change of notation. Here are the opening bars of Op. 101 written in notes of double value, which is to say that

♩ ♪♩ ♪ becomes ♩ ♩ | ♩ ♩

The alteration is made purely for visual reasons and affects the actual sound not a whit.

Ex. 153.

Allowing for the different effect of a minor key, the similarity between this and bars 5–8 of the Scherzo from the Fifth Symphony is remarkable.

Ex. 153a.

Now I have said elsewhere[1] that Op. 101 is a sonata that comes very near to Schumann in idiom, both in its idyllic first movement and in the stirringly athletic march which serves as its highly unorthodox 'Scherzo'. If it were not for the fugue in the finale it would have to be considered as one of the most Romantic of all the sonatas; I stress the point since the Scherzo of the Fifth Symphony makes infinitely more sense if we see it as a prophecy of things to come rather than as an extension of past practice. Even Beethoven himself only

[1] *Talking about Sonatas*, Heinemann Educational Books, 1971.

came to realise this fully in the light of experience; originally the movement was intended to have the conventional pattern of repeats that we find in the Fourth, Sixth and Seventh Symphonies, the whole movement (including the Trio) being played twice. Thus it was played at the first performance, and it was some years before Beethoven decided that to continue to observe an outmoded convention was unjustified in a movement as unusual in character as this. In fact he does not even call it a scherzo, the movement simply being headed *Allegro*. (Incidentally, before we leave Op. 101 as a reference-point, it is worth mentioning that its opening theme reappears magically just before the finale, a structural feature sufficiently uncommon to justify a comparison to the reappearance of a theme from the Scherzo in the finale of this symphony.)

Although the opening of the movement, as we have seen, is derived from Mozart (see p. 127), it is anything but Mozartean in character. Dark and mysterious, it seems to grope its way forward, uncertain of its destination.

Ex. 154.

The music comes to a complete halt. The lower strings make a second start, even managing to make a little more progress—ten bars instead of eight. Once more there is a pause. In just such a way will an improviser seem to search for an idea. Realising that he is literally getting nowhere, Beethoven suddenly strikes out boldly in a completely new direction. The vague and nebulous shapes of the first eighteen bars give way to a rock-like theme, hammered out by horns in unison and reinforced with chunky chords from the strings.

Ex. 155.

On paper this looks pretty childish, but in performance the effect of the brassy-toned horns is electrifying. Inevitably we cannot help wondering if a relationship is intended between this harsh theme and the very opening notes of the symphony. Not only do the repetitions strike an echo; the fact that the horns are given the same G that began the symphony also nudges the memory. It is a question that will remain eternally open to debate, but since it would be cowardly to avoid the issue I will at least offer an opinion. In discussing the first movement I was at pains to separate the melodic and rhythmic aspects of the motto, considering it as a four-note *theme* propelled forward by a particularly dynamic *rhythm*. Now clearly Ex. 155 is in no way referring to the theme, since it stays firmly on one note; if it is harking back to the past it must therefore be recollecting the rhythm—in which case it recollects it wrongly. No musician with an ounce of feeling for rhythm could confuse

with

if Beethoven wanted to remind us of 'the ve-ry THÍNG' he would presumably do so, rather than fobbing us off 'THÍS is the JÓB'. It therefore seems more likely that the theme stands on its own, reflecting Beethoven's fondness for repeated notes[1] as a mode of emphasis rather than being a somewhat distorted allusion to the first movement.

There can be little doubt about the new theme's power, the more so when it is at once taken up by the full orchestra. Even so it suddenly falters, coming to rest on a chord whose waning strength dwindles to nothing. Again the ghostly opening phrase climbs out of the darkness, again the strings give their uncertain response. Having got himself into the relatively uncharted area of B♭ minor (one of the least used keys in music), he now sets out to find his way back to C minor. His route is ingenious, the path illuminated by a helpful beam from oboe and horns showing where the Dominant is. The safe arrival at the destination is the signal for the return of Ex. 155, the horn theme.

Again its resolution falters, again the cellos and basses offer us their strangely angular phrase; this time the 'response' (bars 5–8) is allowed to develop instead of stopping in its tracks. Gently prodded forward by reminders of the horn theme, the phrases reach out over a widening span. For the first time in the movement, quavers appear in the score, adding a more forward impulse to the music.

Ex. 156.

[1] Cf. Op. 18 No. 1, Op. 19, Op. 27 No. 2 Finale, Op. 53, 57, 58, 92, etc.

The four notes enclosed in the square bracket show that the cellos have still not forgotten the shape of their opening phrase,[1] though the gathering momentum of the music increasingly drives it out of mind. The horn theme reappears in blaring triumph for four bars, only to fall away surprisingly into a quiet cadence.

If the end of the last paragraph reads as something of an anticlimax it matches the music, for the lack of substance in the ending leaves us dissatisfied; a question hangs in the air—what can be going to happen? What happens is a (so-called) Trio section that so far as I know is without precedent, since it combines the scholarly pretensions of fugue with an almost impish sense of humour. Fired with a new resolve utterly unlike the apprehensive uncertainty they displayed at the start of the movement, the cellos and basses set off briskly in the key of C major, carrying a testimonial from Albrechtsberger certifying the composer's competence.

Ex. 157.

The little fugue bustles on its way for twenty bars, which are then repeated—not at all the 'done' thing in fugues. It is not that Beethoven needs a lesson in composition but that he is giving us one in how to listen. The closing tag of this section consists of four rising notes:

thrice repeated, it is clearly of some importance. The second time round we are more likely to perceive that the fugue subject contains a comparable group at two points.

[1] Cf. Ex. 154, bars 2–4.

This seemingly unimportant piece of information provides us with the vital clue that explains the relevance of the Trio. We are looking at a pattern in quavers; when and how did quavers first appear in the movement? Look at bar 116, Ex. 156, and observe the four *descending* quavers. Ten bars later Beethoven actually shows us how to invert them in case we are too foolish to know how to do it ourselves.

Notice that he has even put it into C major; admittedly it is only a small plant, but it proves itself capable of rapid growth, as the start of the Trio shows.

The same four-note pattern that ended the first section of the fugue is used to begin the next. Far from going according to academic precepts, the fugue suddenly falls apart, second violins and violas seizing on the pattern,

but not having the slightest idea of what to do with it. Lacking absolute conviction, the cellos and basses suggest that an F♮ might at least help to get everyone back into C major, though even they have a couple of false starts before finding a way out of the impasse.

Ex. 158.

Since there seems to be some danger that the cellos and basses may go on practising this three-finger exercise for all too long, the violas come to the rescue with the fugue subject. For a moment or two the counterpoint rolls along fluently enough, only to get seriously stuck at the apex of the tune which is repeated three times in the mistaken impression that it has become some sort of triumphal march.

Again the music falls apart; again the cellos and basses try to put it together, again the fugue begins, again . . . but no! At the very point when the listener begins to suffer the symptoms of *déja vu* a perky flute carries the fugue subject away and the music disintegrates into a few scattered drops of sound. Faced with such a situation what can one do but go back to the beginning and try again; with a brief pause for thought (just to make sure they are doing the right thing) that is precisely what the lower strings now do.

Ex. 159.

While it is interesting to note that the dotted minim C (bar 236) appears in an early sketch of this tune, the rests in bars 238–9 are a delightful additional touch of humour, leading to an even more fragmented version of the theme plucked from increasingly tentative strings. Very quietly, as if fearful of arousing the wrath of sleeping horns, various wind instruments play snippets of Ex. 155 over a virtually inaudible accompaniment. We seem to have been wafted from the concert-hall into the theatre for this is pure ballet-music, a ballet for elves and gnomes in forest glades, ready to play a mischievous trick upon some poor mortal. Suddenly—and it is truly an unforgettable moment— all movement is stilled save for the quiet beat of a drum. At first it echoes the rhythm of the horn theme, but soon it starts a continuous tapping, strangely sinister. In response to this hypnotic throb the violins initiate a weird dance, groping their way upwards step by cautious step.

Ex. 160.

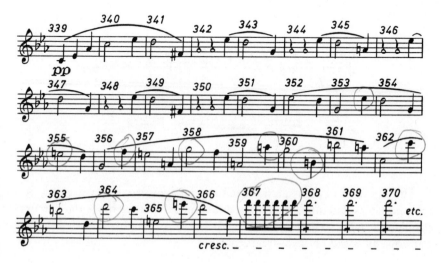

It was this passage that caused a child, seated beside Schumann at a concert, to whisper, 'I'm frightened', much to that composer's delight. The child understood the music intuitively, which could not be said for the contemporary Russian critic Oulibichef who likened it to the mewing of cats! It is an ascent from darkness into light, an ascent that has been hinted at from the very first bars of the movement, but which is only accomplished at the very last. Had Orpheus been able to resist temptation and lead his beloved Eurydice forth from the underworld, this music would have served as apt accompaniment to his journey, for it leads triumphantly to the radiance of day.

The sheer impact of the finale is increased by the addition of three trombones, a piccolo and a contra-bassoon; for three whole movements the players have been kept waiting, just as the percussion (to say nothing of the chorus and soloists!) are kept in reserve for the finale of the Ninth Symphony. The splendour of the sound was sufficient to make a veteran soldier spring to his feet at a Parisian performance crying '*C'est l'Empereur!*' While the specific appellation might not have pleased Beethoven, he would nevertheless have appreciated the sincere response to the ceremonial pomp of the music. He wrote a number of marches of one kind or another even though he sincerely believed in the brotherhood of men; perhaps loud music had a special appeal, being easier to hear. Certainly much of the previous movement must have been virtually inaudible to him and it is possible that the emergence of this blaze of sound out of what might be described as an 'aural fog' symbolised a sort of psychological victory over his infirmity. Harmonised in the most straightforward manner the theme proclaims the long-deferred tonality of C major with vigour and majesty.

Ex. 161.

The injection of some alert dotted rhythms ensures that the music is not allowed to develop into a trudge. In due course the heavy brass and percussion drop out, leaving strings and wind with a series of roughly accented four-note patterns, all based on scale-fragments.

Ex. 162.

Apart from the accents this seems to be something of a throwaway but it proves to have more thematic significance than at first appears. Horns and wind introduce a new theme (the one shown as Ex. 129a on p. 127, though here in C major) which is punctuated by massive chords from the first violins. The tune is extended further in the strings as they make a bid to break out of C major towards the dominant key of G, not forgetting to refer back to Ex. 162 once they have arrived there.

The reference is important because Beethoven is about to play a trick that is rather similar to the one discussed on p. 149. Just as the 'new' theme at the start of the Trio was found to be derived from a seemingly unimportant fragment that preceded it, so now we find a 'new theme'.

Ex. 163.

It will be seen that bars 47–48 are an inversion of bars 45–46; but if we think for a moment we will realise that it is the *first* part of the phrase which is strictly speaking the inversion, while the second half obligingly shows us how the trick was done. All those four-note groups in Ex. 162 (which seemed at the time to be jostling to find their right place) have now come into line and turned into this sprightly theme. Meanwhile, lurking unobtrusively in the bass is this apparently insignificant idea.

Ex. 163a.

[1] The similarity of shape to the material discussed on p. 150 is probably no more than a coincidence.

A less promising bit of material has seldom been seen but Beethoven was a master at using up the scraps; for the moment he gives no indication that it has any function other than to be a minimal bass to Ex. 163 (bars 47–48). A few vigorous scales sweep through the orchestra to prepare the way for the next event; it turns out to be another variant on the four-note pattern of Ex. 162, its rhythm changed, its notes lengthened.

Ex. 164.

It is worthwhile to pause briefly to consider the implications of this in terms of thematic growth. The very first theme of the movement contained this descent:

Almost immediately it was inverted at twice the speed,

an inversion which was extended sequentially three times.

This in turn was inverted and roughed up a little in Ex. 162, after which it was *again* inverted (which way up is 'right'?) and smoothed out into Ex. 163. The 'new' version, Ex. 164, echoes the *rhythm* of bars 2–3 of the movement even though it seems to have a completely individual turn of phrase. It is taken up enthusiastically by the full orchestra, having initially been greeted with quiet chortles of delight from the first violins. A double bar and a repeat sign tell us that the movement may safely be regarded as in sonata form though, as we shall discover, there is a substantial surprise in store.

The Development begins with a considerable amount of musical discussion concerning Ex. 163, with excursions into various keys including diversions into the minor. Suddenly Ex. 163a looms up with frightening importance, the contra-bassoon being used with notable effect to give an extra edge to the string tone. The phrase is taken over by the trombones, evoking an instant response from timpani. Despite the continuing triplet figure the whole mood of the music changes to something more serious.

Ex. 165.

The urgent repeated notes on trumpets and horns (bars 122–123 in Ex. 165) continue with increasing intensity, a signal as important in its way, though less theatrically contrived, as the famous trumpet call that announces the arrival of Florestan's reprieve in *Fidelio*. In this context their purpose is to remind us of the horn-theme from the third movement (Ex. 155) without being too obvious about it. A tremendous climax is built up, a preparation surely for an event of huge significance. There is a sudden break followed by a hollow ticking from the violins, seeming to mark the seconds as we wait with bated breath for the appearance of . . .

It is known that Beethoven planned to write an opera on *Macbeth* and I sometimes wonder whether he had Banquo's ghostly appearance at the feast in mind when he wrote the extraordinary passage which now literally stops the music in its tracks. The build-up has led us to expect the entrance of a king; instead, we are visited by a spectre, a hollow, macabre version of the horn-theme from the previous movement. To audiences of the day it must have seemed a uniquely daring stroke. Spohr, who didn't greatly care for the symphony, described it as 'so happy an idea that one cannot but envy the composer for it. The effect is ravishing'. In fact there is an obscure precedent in an early Haydn symphony (No. 46 in B), though the effect is so different as to nullify the comparison except from a purely formal viewpoint. The interruption lasts some fifty-four bars, not much in terms of time but making an impression out of all proportion to its duration.

The ghostly interlude is dispelled with the return of the opening march, the remainder of the movement proceeding on conventional sonata-form lines. One surprising piece of orchestration deserves comment where some tremendous *tutti* chords lead to a very exposed solo for the two bassoons.

The theme is not new, having been suggested as early as bar 35, but in this context one might have expected trombones to have been used to add majesty to the occasion, especially as the theme is subsequently extended for several pages. Gradually the tempo quickens until it breaks into a Presto, brilliantly contrived out of Ex. 164. The headlong rush towards the final cadence certainly detracts from the dignity of the march, and it is possible that Beethoven may have toyed in his mind with a similar image to the panic rush to get in out of the rain that terminates the Scherzo of the 'Pastoral' Symphony. To see a great procession break into a run would have tickled his humour; at any rate, for whatever reason, he felt the need to give us one of the most extended repetitions of the tonic in all music, more than forty bars of unadulterated C major. It may or may not be the food of love but he certainly gives us excess of it, and it has become a standard joke amongst musicians thus to prolong a final cadence. If the end may legitimately be regarded as a laughing matter, the beginning is anything but a jest, and it is hard to comprehend how the London Philharmonic, first reading it through in 1814, burst into gales of laughter, finding the idea of opening a symphony in such a way irresistibly comic. History has proved them wrong.

9

Interlude
Love and Nature

The subject of Inspiration is the source of much misunderstanding among those who are not creative themselves; they seek an explanation of the baffling phenomenon which enables man to compose music at all. Painting we can understand, since we have all experienced the desire to capture in more permanent form something that has caught our eye, whether it be a sunset, a flower, a landscape or a pretty face. Nor is there anything too esoteric about the concept of literature since, however exalted, it deals in words, the everyday currency of communication. We may not appreciate a novel by Thomas Mann or the poems of T. S. Eliot but we do not regard the language in which they are written as something so divorced from our own experience as to be incomprehensible; we are confident that if we were to make the effort we would 'understand', accepting without too much guilt that we are too lazy (or as we prefer to say 'too busy') to do so. Composition is a different matter, for while most of us can remember the *sound* of an orchestra, a quartet, a piano, or an operatic ensemble we do not in fact remember it in any great depth of detail; the idea of conjuring such sounds out of the mind alone in a silent studio seems like a form of magic, even though we may be able to hum a spontaneous tune as we go about some humdrum task. It is for this reason that we try to track down the elusive idea of Inspiration. How much easier it is to comprehend the art of composition if it is regarded as primarily descriptive, since we ourselves can hear the soughing of the wind, the beat of breakers on the shore, the song of birds or even the bustle of great cities. 'Don't you long to set that to music,' people have said to me from time to time, referring to what I would regard as a completely non-musical experience.

Needless to say I am not suggesting that descriptive music does not represent an important part of the repertoire; one must be grateful for such masterpieces as Debussy's 'La Mer', or 'Don Juan' as portrayed by Richard Strauss. It might even be said that the graphically pictorial nature of such compositions makes the concept of 'pure' music all the harder to understand. Yet the greater part of what is generally thought of as 'great' music exists independently without reference to anything but its own subject-matter. Music *is* about such seemingly boring things as key-relationships, rhythms, intervals, sequences, varying phrase-lengths, harmonic variation, sound texture and the like; in a word it is about Music. It is a truth people are reluctant to accept since inevitably is seems to dehumanise an art which appears to be concerned with a vivid depiction of human emotions. We know when music is sad, happy, exhilarating, restful, martial, seductive, urban or rural; there does exist what might be termed a vocabulary of association of which composers and listeners are both aware. Where the layman goes wrong is in his assumption that such a vocabulary will be used in a way that is comparable to the disposition of words in a language.

The idea of Inspiration has largely been fostered by romantic novelettes in women's magazines and by Hollywood film epics about either real or fictional artists—whether composer, writer or painter being immaterial. Inspiration of this type usually means the love of a good woman (in the case of the more impassioned artist a bad one), or a response to an outside event—storm, war, death, nature or whatever. Now while it is true that composers do write funeral pieces they seldom do so out of any sense of personal grief; the 'inspiration' is likely to be either the hope of an opportune performance or the promise of financial reward. Composers in love can write beautiful love-songs—but so can composers who are not. To dedicate a work to someone you love is a different matter, for it is a symbolic gift of part of oneself, the part which the composer values the most since it is the very justification of his existence.

In calling this chapter 'Love and Nature' I have deliberately picked on the two things most commonly believed to be the source of Inspiration; let us see to what extent the belief is valid. Of Beethoven's susceptibility to woman there can be no doubt; I have already quoted Ferdinand Ries' note to the effect that the composer was always glad to see women,

> especially beautiful, youthful faces, and usually when we walked past a rather attractive girl he would turn round, look at her again sharply through his glasses,[1] and laughed or grinned when he found that I had observed him. He was very frequently in love, but usually only for a very short time.

But much more revealing from a psychological point of view is an incident recounted by the Austrian dramatist and poet Grillparzer. Having described a squalid farmhouse not far from Beethoven's favourite country spot, Heiligenstadt, he mentions the farmer's daughter, a pretty though sluttish girl who worked hard in the fields, spreading muck from a cart or stacking and loading hay. Beethoven, it seems, was fascinated by her, never speaking to her,

---

[1] Strange that they never appear in the portraits.

but standing silently watching her at her labours. She would taunt him mockingly, doubtless having no idea who he was and believing him to be slightly touched, as most of the country-folk did. Thus abused, Beethoven would quickly walk away; but invariably the next time he saw her he would again stand as if bewitched. When her father found himself in court as the result of a drunken brawl, Beethoven even intervened on his behalf, though so offending the magistrate by his uncouth manners that he was nearly placed in the dock beside the offender. What seems to me significant about this story is that if Beethoven was as inclined to casual sexual encounters as has often been suggested he surely would not have behaved with such reticence towards a girl who should have been an easy conquest. On the other hand Ries also has a story to relate concerning an occasion when he called on Beethoven one evening for a lesson. To his surprise he found a beautiful girl in the room, seated on the same sofa as Beethoven. Tactfully, Ries started to make his departure, but Beethoven directed him to the piano, saying 'Play a little'. Ries had the impression that the girl was upset and that Beethoven had been over-familiar with her. Resolutely averting his gaze he began to play; after some time had elapsed a voice from the sofa commanded him to play 'some love music', then, after a while 'something sad', even, at one point 'something passionate'. After the girl had made a discreet and unobserved exit, Ries asked who she was and was astonished to find that Beethoven didn't know. She was, so he said, a lover of music who had appeared unbidden, begging the privilege of a few words with the Master. The two men hurried out into the street to follow her to her home but lost track of her in the darkness.

If one puts these two seemingly contradictory pieces of evidence together, the conclusion is that Beethoven was not averse to a sexual encounter providing that the woman made the first move. All witnesses agree that he was uncouth in manner and appearance, shabbily dressed (so much so that he was several times taken for a tramp) and totally lacking in the artificial veneer of gentility that society demanded. This, coupled with the embarrassment of deafness, must have made him feel awkward and inferior in his dealings with women. Fully realising that his commitment to music virtually precluded the possibility of a normal marriage,[1] he nevertheless yearned for affection.

In addition to the musical sketchbooks he left a number of notebooks and calendars in which he would write strange exhortations to himself. For example, as late as 1818 we find:

Only love, yes only love is capable of granting you a happy life. O God, let me find her at last, the woman who may strengthen me in virtue, who is permitted to be mine.

---

[1] 'I certainly could not marry . . .', letter to Wegeler, 1801.

Other entries from the years 1812–1813 indicate a tortured inner struggle:

> You must not be human, not for yourself, only for others; for you there can be
> no more happiness, except within, in your art. O God! Give me strength to
> conquer myself for nothing must bind me to this life. Behaving in this way with
> A. only leads to ruin.

(We will come to the identity of 'A' in due course, but the phrase 'nothing
must bind me to this life' must I think be taken as a dread of the responsibility
of marriage rather than the contemplation of suicide we found in the
Heiligenstadt Testament of 1802.) He continues:

> Oh terrible circumstances that do not suppress my feeling for domesticity but
> prevent its realisation! O God, God, look down upon this unhappy B., do not let
> it go on much longer like this.

This entry, dated May 1813, has led some commentators to assume that the
'terrible circumstance' that stood in the way of domestic bliss was venereal
disease though the evidence is slight and dubious. It seems more probable that
the barrier was self-imposed, presumably because he was instinctively aware of
his undesirable qualities as a husband. Certainly any wife would have had to
have been a saint to cope with him. When he was a dying man he was visited by
the pianist Hummel. 'You are a lucky fellow,' he said, 'you have a wife, she
looks after you, she loves you, but as for me—I'm a poor bachelor.' He then
sighed deeply, obviously feeling the burden of a decade or more of total
isolation from the world.

A number of women's names are to be found on the dedicatory pages of
Beethoven's works, naturally members of the aristocracy since it was they who
had the leisure to play or to listen to his music. But to assume romantic
entanglements on such evidence is rash indeed since most of them were
married.

'It is one of my first principles never to establish a relationship other than
pure friendship with another man's wife', wrote Beethoven in a letter to Marie
Bigot, she having interpreted a previous letter as showing some forwardness on
his part. Consequently it is unwise to accept at face value Beethoven's boasts of
love given and returned such as we find in a letter of 1810 to his close friend
Wegeler concerning the Countess Giulietta Guicciardi[1]—'a dear fascinating
girl who loves me and whom I love'. Asked about her relationship with
Beethoven many years later, she spoke of him without any trace of affection or
sentiment as the composer of 'some crazy music', though his playing, she said,
was 'heavenly'.

Like most teachers Beethoven conceived an infatuation for one of his pupils,

[1] The 'Moonlight' Sonata is dedicated to her.

a girl named Therese Malfatti, twenty years his junior. Even so, the relationship seems to have been quite innocent, though he was serious enough about it to have written to her father requesting permission to marry her. Sensibly the father turned him down as unsuitable in every way. It seems one more piece of evidence to prove that however much he may have been attracted to women, his inner self was terrified of involvement with them; in consequence he would invariably choose to fix his affections on someone who was unattainable, either because of rank, marital status or sheer unsuitability. Was he therefore sexually innocent? Not entirely it seems since one of his self-exhortations reads,

> Sensual enjoyment without the union of souls is and always will be bestial: after it there is no trace of exalted sentiment, rather one feels remorse.

Deliberate self-degradation through sex is a very common resort for those who have been deprived of love, and the implication that Beethoven had used sex as a form of punishment is strong.[1] Certainly his hapless childhood can have given him little inkling of what a loving relationship could really mean; it could even be argued that he did all he could to make himself physically unattractive in order to protect himself from the pain of rejection. While it is true that ugly and uncouth men are often surprisingly attractive to women, Beethoven's eccentricities were extreme. Even in the open streets of Vienna he would stride up and down for hours at a time singing and shouting like a drunkard, stopping every now and then to note down some idea that he snatched from the feverish tumult of his mind. Yet despite this seeming indifference to others, he could not bear to be overheard at work. To quote Grillparzer again:

> Our apartment faced the garden, while Beethoven had rented rooms facing the
> street. A communal passage leading to the stairs connected the two partitions.
> My brothers and I cared little for this extraordinary man—he had grown stouter
> in the meantime and walked about in untidy, even dirty clothes—when,
> grunting, he shot past us; but my mother, a passionate music-lover, from time to
> time when she heard him play yielded to the impulse to step out into the passage
> . . . and to listen with religious awe. This may have occurred a few times when
> suddenly Beethoven's door was opened, he himself stepped out, observed my
> mother, hurried back and immediately afterwards rushed down the stairs hat on
> head and out of the house. From that moment on he never touched the piano. In
> vain my mother assured him . . . that no one would ever eavesdrop on him again.
> . . . Beethoven remained unrelenting and left his piano untouched until at last
> autumn took us back to town.[2]

[1] At one time he actually lodged in a brothel.

[2] Grillparzer, 'Recollections of Beethoven', in *Letters, Journals & Conversations*, ed. Michael Hamburger, Thames & Hudson, 1951. (Text slightly modified.)

Such behaviour is neurotic to a degree bordering on psychosis since Grillparzer's mother would certainly have been a cultured and intelligent woman who would have made a congenial neighbour to any normal person.

We come now to the curious case of the three letters to the so-called Immortal Beloved, that mysterious romance that has so tantalised musical scholars over the years. After his death, three letters were discovered in Beethoven's desk; whoever first opened them must have sensed he had made a discovery of some importance for here, unquestionably, was documentary evidence of a deeply felt love.

July 6, Morning.

My angel, my all, my very self—Only a few words to-day; and those in pencil—your pencil. Till to-morrow I shall not know where I have to live: what shameful waste of time for such a matter! Why be so sorrowful when there is no other course? How is our love to exist but by sacrifices, and by not exacting everything? Can you help the fact that you are not wholly mine, and I not wholly yours? O God! Look at lovely nature and meet the inevitable by composure. Love wants to have everything, and quite right; thus I feel towards you, and you towards me: only you forget too easily that I have to live for myself and for you as well. If we were not absolutely one, you would feel your sorrow as little as I should.

My journey was fearful: there were not horses enough, and I did not get in till 4 o'clock yesterday morning. The post chose another road, a shocking one. At the last stage but one they warned me not to travel at night, and to beware of a certain wood: that only attracted me, but I was wrong—the carriage was bound to break down on this fearful road—a bottomless, rough country track—and but for my postillions I should have been left on the spot. Esterhazy had the same disaster on the ordinary road with his 8 horses that I had with my 4. However I had some enjoyment out of it, as I always have when I overcome a difficulty.

And now to go at once from these things to ourselves. I suppose, we shall see one another soon. I can't tell you now of all the reflections about my life, which I have been making in the last few days. If only our hearts were always close together, I should probably not make any of the kind. My heart is full of all it wants to say to you. Ah! There are times when I find that speech is absolutely no use. Cheer up.—Remain my true and only treasure, my all in all, as I am yours. As for other things we may let the Gods decree them and fix our lot.

Your faithful Ludwig.

Monday Evening, July 6.

You are in trouble my dearest creature! I have only just learnt that letters must leave here very early. Monday and Thursday are the only days on which the post goes to K. You are in trouble. Ah! Wherever I am, too, you are with me. With you to help me, I shall make it possible for us to live together. What a life! ! !—to be like this! ! !—without you—persecuted by the kindness of people

162

here and there, which I feel I do not care to deserve any more than I do deserve it,—the subservience of one man to another—it hurts me; and when I think of myself in relation to the universe what am I? and what is he whom we call greatest? and yet in that very thing lies the divine in man. I could cry when I think that perhaps you won't get any news of me till Saturday. However much you love me, my love is still stronger; but never conceal your thoughts from me. Good night. I am a patient and must go to bed. Oh God, so near and yet so far! Is not our love a truly heavenly structure, as firmly established as the firmament itself?

Good morning, July 7.

Even before I get up my thoughts are rushing to you, my immortal love—first joyful and then again sad—wondering if Fate will be good to us. I must live entirely with you or not at all; nay I have resolved to remain at a distance till I can fly into your arms, call myself quite at home with you, wrap my soul up in you, and send it into the realm of spirits. Yes, alas it must be so. You will be brave, all the more because you know my affection for you. No one else can ever possess my heart—never—never! O God, why must one be separated from that one loves best? And yet my life in W[1]., as things are, is a wretched sort of life. Your love has made me at once the happiest and most wretched of men. At my age I should need a certain uniformity and regularity of life—can this exist with our present relationship? Be calm! only by calm contemplation of our existence, can we achieve our object of living together. Be calm—love me. To-day— yesterday—how I have longed and wept for you! for you, for you, my life, my all—good-bye, oh, go on loving me—never misunderstand the most faithful heart of your lover.

Ever yours,
Ever mine,
Ever each other's.   L

Speculation as to the identity of the nameless lady was for a long time mostly guesswork, but in 1977 Maynard Solomon's massive book on Beethoven[2] gave a solution to the riddle, backed up by detective work so brilliant that Poirot himself could not have done better. It is one of the most intellectually dazzling and exciting pieces of deduction I have ever read, nor would I be so base as to copy it until it gains more general currency. To give the name, Antonie Brentano, will not spoil the excitement of the chase.

The one thing for which Maynard Solomon fails to find a convincing explanation is why the letters were found in Beethoven's desk. Did Antonie (the 'A.' of the note on p. 160) return them to him as documents too compromising for her to keep? That is certainly a possibility; however, I would offer one possible ironic twist to the whole tale. While I find Solomon's

[1]W—Wien, Vienna.   [2]Maynard Solomon, *Beethoven*, Cassell, 1977.

reconstruction of the events surrounding the letters wholly credible and convincing—in other words that Antonie Brentano was in the right place at the right time—I still find it hard to believe that the affair truly flared up into the brief passionate interlude that appears to have developed. Having regard to the extraordinary exorcism of the demon of despair represented by the *Heiligenstadt Testament* (also undelivered) and remembering the excessively dramatic language used in the notebooks (Thou mayest no longer be a man . . . Resignation, the most sincere resignation to thy fate . . . O hard struggle! . . . etc.), it seems to me quite possible that the letters were a way of acting out a fantasy. A composer by the very nature of his calling lives in the world of the imagination; perhaps the unexpected meeting that Solomon has so ingeniously reconstructed prompted a feeling of unattainable love so painful that Beethoven had to indulge in a few hours of make-believe alone in a strange hostelry. Some men will write poems to express love, others will carve the loved one's name on a tree, an enduring monument to what they may secretly accept to be a transient moment in their lives. Perhaps Beethoven wrote letters, distraught confused letters as they are, rambling through news of a journey to incoherent babblings. Certainly if his love for Antonie was ever consummated he remained silent about it thereafter. In May 1816 he wrote to Ries, 'I found only one [woman], whom I shall doubtless never possess'. In the same year he confessed to having been *hopelessly* in love for five years with someone 'a more intimate union with whom I would have considered the greatest happiness of my life'. While there is no doubt that Antonie Brentano had the most glowing admiration for Beethoven ('He walks godlike among the mortals . . . as a human being greater than as an artist . . .'), I suspect that he might have fought shy of actual physical involvement with her. If love was the potent inspirational force romantic writers would have us believe, how is it that Beethoven did not pour his heart out in a series of rhapsodic compositions for his beloved?[1] Not until 1823 did he dedicate a single work to Antonie Brentano, and then it was the 'Diabelli' variations, a work conspicuously lacking in the sort of personal tenderness that one might expect from even a recollected love-affair. It seems that if we wish to find the enduring and significant love of Beethoven's life we must forget about women and turn to Nature.

'Where are the trees?' cried Beethoven angrily on being offered lodgings in Baden; 'This house is no use to me. I love a tree more than a man.' He hated the city, his dislike of town-life being manifested in a restless and continuous urge to move house, so much so that at one time he was reputed to have several lodgings simultaneously. Every day, regardless of the weather, he would take a vigorous walk which, during the summer months when he was in the country, would sometimes last for twelve hours or more. The fashionable jogger of

[1] In fact the period 1812–1816 was one of his least productive.

today takes exercise to develop his body but Beethoven's walks were designed to exalt his spirit by communion with nature. 'I am only happy in the midst of untouched nature,' he told someone. And in his private notebook we find the following thoughts:

My only resolve to remain in the country. How easy to fulfil this in any place. Here I am no longer troubled by my wretched hearing. Does it not seem as though every tree said to me 'Holy, holy!' In the forest, enchantment! Who can express it all? Should all else fail, even in winter the country remains . . . Easy to find rooms at a peasant's, certainly cheap at that time. Sweet solitude of the forest! . . .

Almighty in the forest! I am happy, blissful in the forest: every tree speaks through you. O God, what splendour! In such a wooded scene in the heights there is calm, calm in which to serve Him.

There is an extraordinary contrast between the literal rapture of entries such as this and the more familiar cries of despair and exhortations to be courageous in adversity. In a letter to his pupil Therese Malfatti, the one he thought of marrying, he wrote,

How fortunate you are to be able to go to the country so early in the year! Not before the 8th shall I be able to enjoy this delight. I look forward to it with childish anticipation. How glad I shall be to wander among shrubs, forests, trees, herbs and rocks! No man can love the country as I do, for it is forests, trees and rocks that provide men with the resonance they desire.

A charming story is told of one of his visits to Gneixendorf where his brother Johann had a house with some land.[1] As usual Beethoven would spend the days walking through the fields, eliciting looks of amazement from the farmworkers as he sang and shouted on his way, conducting imaginary orchestras as he went. One day he passed three farm-lads who were shepherding two young bullocks towards a brick kiln. The animals took fright at the manic behaviour of the composer and ran off. With some difficulty they were recaptured only for the same thing to happen again.

His favourite country inn was called the Three Ravens, at Mödling on the outskirts of Vienna. There he would sit for hours at a time listening to a little village band of seven players whose repertory of Austrian folk-music was probably played by ear. He was to immortalise them in the Scherzo of the 'Pastoral' symphony, one of the few of his compositions which we can truly regard as being 'inspired' by extra-musical considerations. Even so Beethoven warned himself against the dangers of descriptive music when he wrote, 'All painting in instrumental music, if carried too far is a failure. The hearers should be able to discover the situation for themselves.' Let us attempt to do so.

---

[1] Having once described himself as 'land-owner', Johann must have smarted to receive a reply from Beethoven, 'brain-owner'.

10

Symphony No. 6 in F Major, Op. 68

Dedicated to Prince von Lobkowitz and Count von Razumovsky

Orchestra: 2 flutes; 1 piccolo; 2 oboes; 2 clarinets; 2 bassoons; 2 horns;
2 trumpets; 2 trombones; 2 timpani; strings

1. Allegro ma non troppo
2. Andante molto mosso
3. Allegro: leading to
4. Allegro: leading to
5. Allegretto

First performance: 22 December 1808

The first movement is described in the score as 'The cheerful impressions excited by arriving in the country'; the second is called 'By the stream'; the third is 'A happy get-together of peasants'; the fourth is 'Storm', and the fifth 'The Shepherds' Hymn, gratitude and thanksgiving after the storm'. The title 'Pastoral' was sanctioned by Beethoven, though in calling it a 'Pastoral Symphony, or a recollection of country life' he warned against a too literal interpretation with the phrase 'More an expression of feeling than a painting'.

Although this excursion into programme music was unusual for Beethoven, descriptive pieces had been in vogue for a considerable period. While it is extremely unlikely that he would have known such classic examples as 'The Battle of Marignan' or 'The Song of the Birds' by the sixteenth-century composer Jannequin, he had no doubt heard (and probably despised) a popular piano piece of the time called 'The Battle of Prague' by an obscure composer named Kotzwara. Liberally covered with explanatory comments such as 'flying bullets' or 'cries of the wounded', Kotzwara's music displayed such a childish naiveté that it is hard to understand its enormous popularity; it seems probable that Beethoven's admonition not to take the pictorial content of the 'Pastoral' Symphony too literally was prompted by the fear that listeners might approach it in a similar frame of mind to that induced by the wealth of descriptive works with which they were beguiled in numerous salon concerts. One work he certainly knew of by repute even if he had never heard it performed was a symphony by Justin Heinrich Knecht (1752–1817), 'The Musical Portrait of Nature'. Consisting of five movements, it had a plan remarkably similar to Beethoven's, including a first movement describing a beautiful sunlit countryside, a storm in the third movement, and a finale in which 'Nature raises her voice towards Heaven offering to the Creator . . . sweet and agreeable songs'. Sir George Grove made the intriguing discovery that this work was advertised on the cover of one of Beethoven's earliest published compositions, three sonatas written in his adolescence[1] and no longer generally known. The youthful composer must have read the detailed advertisement many times and it is quite compatible with what we know of his way of working that a seed thus planted may have flowered into a symphony more than twenty years later. Knecht, like Berlioz half a century later in the 'Fantastic' Symphony, wrote quite an extensive synopsis to describe in advance the content of each movement. Beethoven was sceptical about the need for any such literary prop; a notebook of 1807, referring to Op. 68 as both 'Sinfonia caracteristica' and 'Sinfonia pastorella', says:

> It is left to the listener to discover the situation . . . Every kind of painting loses by being carried too far in instrumental music . . . Anyone who has the faintest idea of rural life will have no need of descriptive titles to enable him to imagine for himself what the composer intends. Even without a description one will be able to recognise it all . . .

The only two symphonies of Beethoven to begin with a bare fifth are Nos. 6 and 9, yet such is the subtlety of the language of musical tonality that the effect of a seemingly comparable interval could scarcely be more different. In the Ninth, the fifth is based on the dominant, producing a feeling of suspense, of expectation; here in the Sixth Symphony, the interval is firmly based on the tonic and though it is only marked *p* and thinly scored, we are given a feeling of absolute security. It is the traditional drone bass of rustic music, the so-called Musette, of which the bagpipe is the classic exponent. Yet though its feet are clearly planted on the ground, the tune that immediately catches our ear floats as lightly as any ballerina. It is this that tells us that the music is concerned with Nature rather than Man, since when we do find mankind depicted in this symphony it is as a simple hobbledehoy, incapable of such ethereal grace as this.

---

[1] The 'Electoral' sonatas, WoO 47.

Ex. 166.

One is tempted to regard this as the start of the movement whereas it is more accurately the start of an Introduction; but whereas the Introductions to Symphonies 1, 2 and 4 are clearly defined by differences of tempo, here we have something not only germane to what follows but inseparable from it. Having made this first tentative essay at the main theme, Beethoven now experiments with it in ways so subtle as almost to defy analysis. Sunlight seems to be involved since there are a number of shadows and reflections, often slightly distorted as such phenomena usually are. For instance in the very next bar we find a 'shadow' of bar 1, when the second violins lend it a darker hue by transposing it down an octave and taking out the little point of light given by the *staccato* quaver.

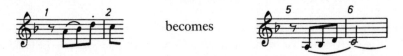

On the other hand bar 2 is fleetingly 'reflected' in bar 6, this fragment

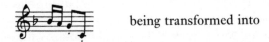 being transformed into

Meanwhile the violas introduce a rich new strand:

This in turn is 'reflected' in a free inversion in bars 9 and 10.

Ex. 167.

Yet this seemingly new theme appears on closer examination to be related to the very opening bars; again it is a 'shadow', shadows often being longer than the object from which they are reflected, and cast at an oblique angle. If we lengthen the opening notes and move them down one degree of the scale the relationship becomes apparent.

Ex. 167a.   Ex. 167b.

Now I do not wish to suggest that this imagery was consciously intended nor even that a relationship such as the one shown above was necessarily deliberate. One of the most notable characteristics of the entire first movement is its exploitation of repetition, the repetition of pattern that we find throughout nature. We do not need to count the leaves of an oak tree to be aware of their similarity, nor, when we see a meadow brightly caparisoned with buttercups and daisies, do we mistake one for the other. Beethoven is concerned to capture both the infinite similarity and the infinite variety of nature's patterns; therefore he gives us an unusual amount of repetition but also many subtle deviations. If there is one verb we are most likely to use in speaking of plant or animal life it is to *grow*; in this symphony we constantly find that one idea *grows* from another, and such relationships as I have just shown are examples of growth rather than development.

The first exploitation of repeated patterns occurs between bars 16–25, a section in which every bar in strings and horns is virtually identical yet different—identical in notes, but constantly changing in dynamic level. The only positive change of tone-colour comes with the addition of a pair of bassoons at the central point, duplicating a single phrase. Through the miracle of modern photographic techniques we can now watch a flower grow, emerge from its bud, blossom, wither and die, all in a matter of moments. Listening to this passage I cannot help wondering whether in some strange intuitive way Beethoven intended similarly to capture the phenomenon of emergent life; certainly the rhythmic pulse suggests a sort of dance of creation.

The first movement proper begins at bar 29 with the oboe stating a somewhat revised version of the initial phrase, a version which is taken up by clarinets and bassoons before being extended by strings and woodwind. The drone bass reappears, now more vital rhythmically than it was in the opening bars, and as the theme gathers strength flutes introduce a brief decorative figure which is certainly intended to be bird-song. This may also be true of the gentle repeated triplets which are a feature of the ensuing bridge-passage, possibly the cooing of wood-pigeons. Unsupported, the first violins toy with the first four notes of the symphony, trying them out on different degrees of the scale.

Ex. 168.

(It is a device which lends credence to my theory concerning the relationship between Ex. 167a and b.)

The Second Subject is surely unique, consisting as it does of three phrases that make not only a continuous melody but also a web of counterpoint, just as a 'round' does.

Ex. 169.

This can be read both horizontally (as one theme) and vertically, though its treatment is far from academic, the strings gradually enveloping it in a shimmering figure that suggests the rustle of foliage. It gives way to a lyrical dialogue between strings and wind that is certainly related, though distantly, to bar 2 of the symphony.

Ex. 170.

It is an admirable illustration of that process of growth I have already mentioned; compare the bracketed figures in bars 94 and 97–98 with bar 2, Ex. 166 and one can instantly see a relationship even though the themes seem to be quite different from each other; the original seed has literally flowered. Similarly the last 24 bars of the Exposition can all be traced to the first phrase of the symphony, being derived partly from the seminal pattern in bar 2, partly from the drone and partly from the melodic fragment in bar 1. After the distraught energy of the Fifth Symphony the mood of the music is extraordinarily relaxed, an unmistakable symbol of the inner peace that Beethoven found when alone in the country.

The contrast between the two works becomes particularly intriguing once we reach the Development. For as many as thirty-six bars at a time he will persist with one rhythm, moreover a rhythm that is always fitted to a similar shape.

The relationship to the second bar of the symphony hardly needs to be pointed out, but what is strange about the use of this rhythm is that its effect is static. In the Fifth Symphony the initial motif

never loses its dynamic force; even when halted in its tracks by an enforced pause one senses that it is straining at the leash, nor does its driving energy flag at any point in the movement. Here in the Sixth Symphony we find a similarly compact figure repeated just as relentlessly—or so it would seem as we first look at the printed page. The markedly different effect can be attributed to the very slow rate of harmonic change. For instance, starting from bar 151 we find twelve bars of Bb major followed by no less than twenty-four bars of D major. Long sustained notes in first or second violins shine like beams of sunlight through the texture; it is a marvellous symbol of the forest in which massive tree-trunks stand as immobile as pillars in a temple while their leaves dance in response to the wind's command. The score, like the forest, teems with life; yet the impression we gain is of a great stillness. From time to time we may hear a snatch of the opening theme, only to be lost again in the vastness of nature.

Now when we talk of descriptive music and the evocation of landscape we tend to think of Delius, Vaughan Williams or Sibelius. It would be absurd to deny that they are masters of musical pictorialism, as absurd as to suggest any common ground between them and Beethoven when it comes to the means by which their imagery is produced. The essential difference between the approach of such composers and Beethoven lies in the degree of priority given to descriptive impressionism. Whether it is Delius hearing the first cuckoo, Vaughan Williams observing a lark ascending or Sibelius listening to the howl of the northern tempest in Tapiola, each composer uses his skills to conjure up as vivid a tone-painting as he can. Beethoven specifically warns us against listening to the Pastoral as mere painting, 'Malerey' as he scornfully referred to it. Even though I have frequently had recourse to analogies drawn from the forest, it is time to stress that in this movement at least, he is more concerned with writing a symphony than we normally accept. It is in fact a perfect example of a classical symphony, perfect in form and extremely economical in material. The long passages of repeated figuration that I have described so lyrically may also be compared to the recurring arpeggios that form the central drama of the first movement of the 'Waldstein' Sonata, 'pure' music without any doubt for all its turbulence. The emotional effect may be very different but the classical structure is the same. Where else are we likely to find the constant repetition of a simple basic pattern? In the formal preludes of Bach which certainly have no descriptive intention, even though their majestic progress may remind us of wave following wave across the ocean. The unusual element in this symphony is not therefore the repetition of one rhythmic figure, a device which may be found in numerous movements by Beethoven, but the combination of compact repeated patterns with long sustained harmony that I have already mentioned. To an unsympathetic ear it may seem wearisome yet it is surely the composer's way of conveying the immensity of nature while at the same time preserving a severe and classical discipline.

Since it is an all too common failing not to be able to see the wood for the trees let us, in an endeavour to take the larger view, turn back to the opening pages of the symphony and in particular to the ten-fold repetition of a single phrase I have already discussed in (p. 169). Taken at face value it might be thought of as a series of cadences designed to establish C major.

Such an identification is mistaken since the persisting B flats establish a stronger gravitational pull, making it clear to any musically informed ear that this is a teasingly prolonged dominant that must ultimately resolve on to the tonic key of F major. Reduced to the bare harmonic implications bars 16–25 become this chord:

which, after three delicate phrases unsupported by harmony, duly arrives at its expected destination in bar 29.

As I have suggested, this is clearly not an Exposition but part of a subtly contrived Introduction. However it sets a precedent which is ingeniously followed in the Development. Having in effect 'sustained' such a chord for ten bars (even though vitalising it with the persistent rhythm), Beethoven adopts a precisely similar technique in the Development, the difference being that whereas bars 16–25 are poised on a dominant harmony with all the sense of expectation that implies, the comparable passages in bars 151–186 or 197–232 are always based on tonic harmony, even though the tonic may be temporary and alien. The dominant in the Introduction opens the way to the forest, the slight fidgeting with the harmony betraying an eagerness to get there; the long held tonic harmonies in the Development show that not only have we arrived but that we desire to linger there. The following chart should make the point clear.

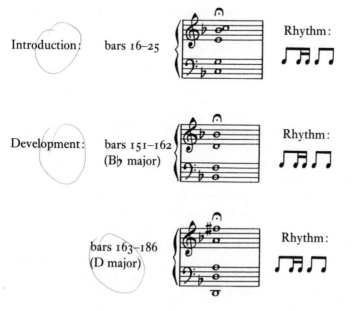

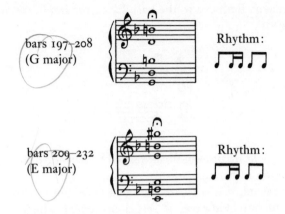

bars 197–208
(G major)

Rhythm:

bars 209–232
(E major)

Rhythm:

Notice that these abrupt changes of tonality, B♭ major–D major, G major–E major, are not modulations but tonal vistas whose static nature suggests Beethoven standing in contemplation of a landscape and then turning to take in another view. The procedure is sufficiently unorthodox to demand some such explanation. In fact the whole movement might be said to *breathe*; do we not speak of 'a breath of the country?' If we regard alternations of tonic and dominant harmony as comparable to breathing in and out, we find that an amazingly high proportion of the first movement proves to consist of inhalation and exhalation. Try taking a slow deep breath through bars 1–3 and then letting it out during the pause on bar 4 and you will see what I mean. The process can be continued at a more natural pace for page after page.

The only significant melodic development in the centre of the movement is a long extension of the phrase that first appeared in bars 9–12 (Ex. 167). Beginning in the shadows with low violas and cellos, it rises into the violins, making a brief excursion into G minor as it does so. More than 250 bars have passed, yet it is the first modulation into a minor key, an indication of the spiritual serenity that pervades the entire movement. The twinge of sadness is only momentary, soon to be contradicted by a glorious affirmation of the dominant of F in bars 263–274. Suddenly there is an unexpected diversion to the *sub*-dominant (B♭) which, having been held for four bars 'breathes out' on to the tonic, allowing the very opening phrase to reappear in second violins and violas. The first violins still have their gaze fixed upon the tree-tops, the original pause from bar 4 being now transformed into a trill that clearly evokes bird-song. A newly decorated version of the Introduction leads to the true Recapitulation at bar 312. From here, things proceed according to convention for some way, Beethoven feeling in too relaxed a mood to indulge in any violent surprises. Indeed the emphasis is on expansion, as his treatment of one phrase in particular shows. In the original exposition it had revealed a kinship to the all-pervading rhythm derived from bar 2.

Ex. 171.

As though really too indolent to be bothered with a rhythm as potentially energetic as this, the woodwind smooth it out into lazy triplets.

Ex. 172.

The infection spreads until the triplet rhythm predominates entirely, leading to a climax which is the most heartfelt passage in the whole movement. In essence it is childishly simple, a descending scale of an octave over a sustained dominant pedal-point in the bass, yet the effect is of true ecstasy. 'Oh God, what splendour!' (see p. 165).

Ex. 173.

Briefly the music teases us with alternations of B♭ and B♮ as shown in the last two bars, before Beethoven charmingly anticipates the arrival of the little village band we are to meet again in the Scherzo. The clarinettist is in fine fettle, displaying considerable virtuosity with his arpeggios; the bassoon player has a more limited range, a judgement that is only too clearly confirmed on later acquaintance. The sound of the clarinet recedes into the distance and we are left with the first violins playing the opening subject with a disarming simplicity. A single flute takes up the theme. Both versions terminate with a little five-note scale

which the clarinet and bassoon, doubtless warming up for the session at the tavern, neatly turn into a five-finger exercise. Suddenly, the game over, strings and wind seize upon this harmless fragment and firmly propel it towards the final cadence. It is a conclusion whose delicate wit still brings a smile of contentment to performers and listeners alike.

In 1803 Beethoven jotted down two ideas which were to be relevant to this symphony. One is particularly interesting in that it shows that despite the onset of deafness so harrowingly described the year before in the *Heiligenstadt Testament*, he was still listening intently to sounds that most of us would disregard. Words appear infrequently in the sketch-books, but here we find two phrases appended to music examples:

Ex. 174a.

Murmur of the streams: Andante molto

Beneath this we find a very similar phrase with the observation 'The wider the stream the deeper the note'.

Ex. 174b.

Compared to the brook in Schubert's '*Schöne Müllerin*', these waters would seem to run somewhat sluggishly; but the evidence is indisputable that these were the sounds Beethoven imagined he heard. Suitably modified they were to appear as the principal accompanying figure in the second movement of the 'Pastoral', the 'Scene by the Brook'.

Ex. 175.

Andante molto mosso

The stream must indeed be wide since the scoring is unusually dark in texture, two muted cellos being primarily responsible. They consistently add a deeper tone to the second violins and violas an octave above, while the remaining cellos simply reinforce the double-basses in an almost perfunctory bass part. Above this gently murmuring accompaniment the first violins (and then the wind) extend a meltingly beautiful tune whose initial phrases seem to be literally breathless at the beauty of the scene.

Ex. 176.

Clarinet and bassoon take over this limpid melody while the violins assume the role of a bird-chorus; then, as though tired of playing a subsidiary part, the violins extend the melodic line with a further two-bar phrase which in turn is taken over by the wind. At this point the music becomes a duet, the two lines interweaving in positively operatic fashion.

Ex. 177.

As in the first movement, we now find groups of six repeated chords, even more clearly suggesting doves or pigeons.[1] Certainly these are 'native wood-notes' though far from wild; the brief interruption leads us back to the first

---

[1] Shakespeare's 'Jug-jug' bird-call sounds remarkably similar.

theme, this time turned in new directions. The music flows as a continuous melodic line despite the occasional breathing spaces, while the accompanying figures keep up the gentle murmur of semiquavers almost without pause. Despite its length the movement is extremely concentrated in form, subscribing to the tenets of a fairly strict sonata-form design, complete with First and Second subjects, Development, Recapitulation and all. Listeners incapable of appreciating the sheer span of Beethoven's thought may get the impression that the movement rambles on without notable landmarks; if it is an understandable error, it is an error nonetheless. The truly unorthodox features are the continuity of the melodic line (which results in a blurring of the demarcation lines between First and Second Subject-matter) and the lack of contrast in the accompanying figures, a lack which is wholly explicable when we consider that their function is primarily descriptive.

The Second Subject group is ushered in with a glorious lyrical outburst:

Ex. 178.

Most composers would be happy enough to have thought of this alone, but Beethoven is profligate of melody in this movement and caps it with two more, of which the most irresistible is surely this.

Ex. 179.

Indeed Beethoven himself falls in love with the phrase for, having brought the exposition to a proper close with a cadential trill that should lead to the dominant, he cannot resist a diversion back to Ex. 179, adding a bewitching new counterpoint played *pizzicato* by the two solo cellists. This time the trill, emphasised by repetition, does lead to the dominant key of F, serving as a doorway to a true development section.

After briefly placing the 'brook' figure into the forefront once more he introduces a new theme which imperceptibly drifts into the unexpected key of G major. Oboe and flute begin a duet in which the oboe continues to explore the opening theme while the flute supplies decorative arpeggios. Once, while taking a walk through the countryside with his disciple Schindler, Beethoven paused and said, 'Here I composed the scene by the brook, and the yellowhammers up there, the quails, nightingales and cuckoos roundabout, composed with me'. Schindler, earnest and literal-minded, at once asked the composer whereabouts in the score the yellowhammers appeared, the other three species being clearly labelled on the final page. In reply Beethoven jotted down the flute arpeggio mentioned above:

Schindler's proper response should have been 'Hail to thee, blithe Spirit! Bird thou never wert . . .' since no bird known to man, least of all a yellowhammer, would be capable of such a phrase. If it was anything more than an unkind joke played on a gullible fellow, Beethoven's reply was simply an injunction to listen to the numerous sublimations of bird-song scattered throughout the movement. A flute is not a bird though it may aspire to imitate one; Beethoven's philosophy was surely to leave unto the flute those things that a flute can do better. In the same conversation he described the bird-calls at the end of the movement as a joke, and so they are, a caprice designed to delight naive souls. At any rate, what Tovey wittily calls 'Schindler's giraffe-throated yellowhammer' soon joins in an exquisite coloratura duet with the oboe, even the remotest suggestion of bird-song forgotten.

With an ingenious and unexpected twist of harmony the music shifts into the sub-dominant key of E♭ major. This time it is the clarinet that leads the way with the opening theme, elaborating it increasingly until it flowers into a miniature cadenza, complete with concluding trill. But the phrase does *not* conclude after all, drifting instead into the remote key of B major. Clarinet and bassoon exchange expressive versions of the 'brook' theme until at last, heralded by more sublimated bird-song from the violins, we arrive back at the Recapitulation (bar 91). The responsibility for carrying the main theme is given to a single flute, only marked *p* in spite of the teeming activity with which it is now surrounded. Here we find not only the murmur of the brook but delicately poised arpeggios (the 'giraffe-throated yellow hammers'!) and gently descending horn-calls. While one often hears of the dawn-chorus, it is not so generally noted that birds seem to sing in congregation towards the evening hour, a phenomenon that Beethoven appears to have heeded in this convergence of themes. Otherwise the recapitulation proceeds on predictable lines until the interpolation of two heartfelt sighs of contentment.

Ex. 180.

The music breaks off, and the little cadenza for woodwind, specifically labelled nightingale, quail and cuckoo, begins. As if nodding in approval of nature's aviary, the violins caress the lower phrase of Ex. 177 and then cease in turn as the bird-song begins once more. Four brief and expressive phrases draw on the veil of night and the movement ends.

A point that I have never seen made concerns the chronology of the movements in this symphony. The first movement is clearly morning, the second basks in the heat of the afternoon giving way to twilight with the audible appearance of the nightingale. The Scherzo logically follows as an evening piece, peasants being too busy during the day to indulge in such jollities, and the band being obviously already the worse for drink. The storm is consequently a night-storm whose fury abates with the arrival of a new day, probably a Sunday since its mood reflects the words 'Lord, we thank Thee' penned by Beethoven on the score. If this assumption is correct it is on a Saturday night that the *Lustiges Zusammensein* of the peasants now takes place.

Despite its amusing parody of a small village band, much of the third movement is scored with a delicacy that would not seem out of place in the most elegant and aristocratic surroundings. The opening phrase tiptoes its way in, unsupported by harmony.

Ex. 181.

Although played as a simple unison there are clear implications of a modulation here; bars 1–4 are unmistakably in F major, while bar 5 starts a drift towards the closely related key of D minor—they share the same key-signature. From there it is easy enough to make the transition to D *major*, a move which brings a complete change of character, a flowing melodic line in place of the light-footed steps of the opening.

Ex. 182.

dolce

While the transition into the key of D was accomplished smoothly enough, the ensuing return to F must have seemed abrupt and uncouth to listeners of the day; such changes of key are a feature of the movement, a feature already explored by Beethoven in the first movement. The transition between G major and E major shown in the last two chords of the chart on p. 174 is an exact equivalent to the F–D key-change in the scherzo.

The two phrases quoted above continue their interplay, passing through various keys and gathering strength as they go; by bar 53 F major has been regained, an achievement celebrated in *fortissimo* tones. A new theme is introduced, a there-and-back-again scale, rough-hewn with its heavy accents and the implied skirl of pipes.

Ex. 183.

High horns bellow their approval as scooping arpeggios in the strings suggest that the men are tossing a girl into the air; certainly there's a feeling of horse-play far removed from the delicacy of the opening. The strings take over the horns' motif, quietening things down so as to let the little band be heard. The humorous depiction of a group of musicians of rather limited capabilities is delightfully done, the oboe rhythmically insecure, the bassoon part mostly confined to the most rudimentary bass, the clarinet more accomplished than his colleagues and the horn filled with rash confidence as he aspires to dizzy and unaccustomed heights. An increase of tempo leads to a second dance-tune accompanied by droningly primitive harmonies. This, like the stream-music quoted in Ex. 174, appears in a sketchbook dated 1802, albeit in a slightly altered form.

Ex. 184.

Now it has been shown by scholars that several themes in this symphony are markedly similar to Croatian folk-melodies, notably the First Subject group from the opening movement, and the woodwind theme (Ex. 190a) from the finale. However, since the collection of folk-songs that was used as a source was not published until the late 1870s, it is hard to say which came first, the tunes or the symphony, since bastard versions of Beethoven's work could easily have circulated until, played incorrectly by ear, they became common property. All the same, themes such as Ex. 184 have an earthy ring about them and there is no reason why Beethoven should not have appropriated a few folk-songs if they served his purpose. What seems to me of greater interest is the way he introduces trumpets (their first notes in the whole symphony) into this central whirling dance. Like the other players in the village band they are strictly limited in technique, though the effectiveness of their entry is in no way diminished by the crudity of the actual notes. Due homage is paid to the conventions of form with a return to the opening material; the repetition of the *second* dance is more unusual, as is the end of the movement. Having stated the initial themes (Exx. 181/182) for the third time, Beethoven seems set upon a formal close. Instead, there is a sudden panic rush (*Presto*) as the peasants realise a storm is about to break. There is no time to observe the proprieties, just a scramble to get the chairs and tables indoors before the heavens open. With a quiet but ominous rumble from cellos and basses the storm makes its presence felt, the obvious cliché of timpani being subtly avoided at this stage. It is a true interruption though, not only of the preceding mood but also of the expected cadence to F major.

Ex. 185.

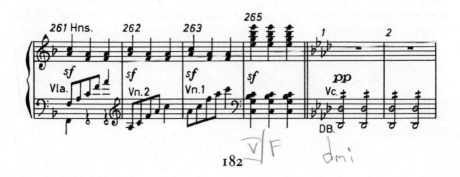

While it is clear that the *staccato* quavers in bars 3–4 represent the first drops of rain, their shape needs to be borne in mind against future events. The expressive little phrase in the first violins meanwhile suggests apprehensive glances towards the increasingly threatening sky. Suddenly the storm is upon us in all its fury, the roar of wind and rain being vividly depicted by the angry sound of cellos and basses not quite in synchronisation.

One could argue that the simpler bass part was dictated by considerations of practicality, but the fact is that the uneasy mixture of groups of five and four creates an admirable 'sound effect' in the theatrical sense; though the main harmonies in woodwind and brass are perfectly clear (largely diminished sevenths as one might expect), this churning bass gives a feeling of instability as though we are literally in danger of losing our balance.[1] Every now and then there is a flicker of lightning depicted by this figure;

---

[1] Berlioz was particularly taken by this effect.

the virtually simultaneous thunderclap tells us that the storm is directly overhead. A notable feature is the variation in dynamics from the extremes of *ff* to *pp*; storms are not constant in terms of sheer sound as Beethoven has correctly observed. Even so, the way in which he holds his forces in reserve is remarkable; the first reinforcement to the normal orchestra is the timpani, not used in the previous movements; in bar 82 he introduces the shrill note of the piccolo, but not until bar 106 does he allow himself the added weight of trombones, their impact being all the greater for being so long delayed. From time to time we are reminded of the 'rain' motif originally established by the second violins in bars 3–4 although never again is it unsupported once the storm has broken. We still have no inkling of the transformation that is ultimately due to take place, our attention being most obviously attracted by a massive descending scale in cellos and basses accompanied by a torrential downpour of arpeggios from the violins.

Ex. 186.

(The sequence is extended by a further seven bars.)

Accustomed as we are today to the huge resources of twentieth-century orchestral sound this may all seem a little too well-organised; it is worthwhile to quote Berlioz in order to convey the effect the music had on his admittedly impressionable mind.

> I despair of being able to give an idea of this prodigious movement . . . Listen!— listen to those rain-charged squalls of wind; to the dull grumblings of the basses; also to the keen whistling of the piccolo, which announces to us that a horrible tempest is about to break. The hurricane approaches and grows in force; an immense chromatic feature, starting from the heights . . . pursues its course until it gropes its way to the lowest orchestral depths. . . . Then the trombones burst forth, the thunder of the kettledrums becomes redoubled in violence, no longer merely rain and wind, but an awful cataclysm, the universal deluge—the end of the world.[1]

[1] Berlioz, *A Critical Study of Beethoven's Nine Symphonies*, trans. Edwin Evans, Wm. Reeves.

Even allowing for a characteristic hyperbole, this response indicates the stunning impact of this movement on contemporary ears.

The gradual recession of the storm is vividly described, the trombones only being used for a scant thirteen bars. For a second time we hear the sequence shown in Ex. 186, though now it is marked *sempre diminuendo*. An occasional clap of thunder still strikes fear into timid hearts but in time there is nothing but an almost inaudible rumble from the basses to tell us that somewhere far away the storm lingers on. Sweet and clear the oboe sings out this melody.

Ex. 187.

If we remember Beethoven's words, 'Even without a description one will be able to recognise it all', we should realise that this phrase is a musical rainbow, a glorious arc of melody derived directly from the original 'rain' motif of bar 3 (see Ex. 185). While the pattern of the third bar is thus transformed by augmentation ($\wp$ = $\wp$), the fourth bar is changed by extension, the initial suggestion of a scale

flowering at last into a ravishing flute passage that is unforgettable in its simplicity.

Ex. 188.

This effortless transition into the finale is markedly different from the laborious ascent from darkness to light we experienced in the Fifth Symphony, not only because the material on each side of the dividing double bar is more melodic in character, but also because there is no modulation involved. The Storm ends in C major; the Hymn of Thanksgiving begins in C major—or rather the introductory 'yodel' which ushers it in (bars 1–5 above) is in C. Gently, as the horn replies to the clarinet's call, the cellos insinuate into the harmony the same drone fifth with which the symphony began so that for a moment or two we hear a delicate blend of tonic and dominant.

Then, released from this last vestige of tension, the shepherds' song makes its first appearance.

Ex. 189.

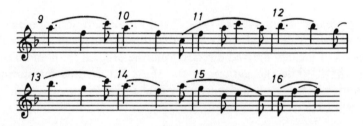

Although it seems that this is not an actual folk-song it has an authentic feel to it that gives it a markedly different quality from 'aristocratic' themes such as the slow movement of the Fifth Symphony. The theme is presented without any sort of decoration, quiet sustained chords in the woodwind giving a faint suggestion of an organ accompaniment, perhaps in a village church. But if this hymn begins in simple tones it is soon taken up in such a way as to leave such thoughts far behind since within a further eight bars the music is transformed into an ecstatic paean of joy that even the greatest cathedral could scarcely provide. The inclusion of the full brass section (including trombones) gives the theme a weight and majesty we would never have suspected from its first disarming appearance.

In form the movement combines elements of Rondo and Variations, the whole conceived on very spacious lines. After three repetitions of Ex. 189, each more elaborately scored than its predecessor, an important though subsidiary theme emerges:

Compared to the leisurely expansiveness of the shepherds' hymn it seems to have a strong forward impulse. Brief though it is, it is at once taken up enthusiastically by other sections of the orchestra, the phrase enclosed in the square bracket above being extended into an animated dialogue between the strings. As though feeling that he has strayed too far from the original subject, Beethoven brings things to a virtual halt, reintroducing the yodelling phrase that initiated the movement. In a matter of moments we are back with Ex. 189, now elegantly decorated with nodding arpeggios from the second violins. Just as it seems about to build into another great climax the introduction of some E♭s into the harmony produces a drift into the subdominant key of B♭. Clarinets and bassoons in truly pastoral mood introduce a new theme that ambles along in an easy-paced way that is only occasionally disturbed by the slight jolt of a *sforzando* accent—like a cartwheel giving a lurch as it surmounts a stone on the track.

Ex. 190.

From bar 86 onwards this theme bears such a close resemblance to a Croatian folk-song that one feels that Beethoven must have been quoting it.

Ex. 190a.   (Kuhac collection. Vol. III, No. 10)

There follows a section designed to lead us back to the initial shepherds' hymn; to begin with it is given in a rather crude version whose alternations of tonic and dominant give it a real touch of the country bumpkin.

Ex. 191.

Naturally enough, the pattern shown in bar 99 leads easily into the yodelling theme, thus opening the way for a return to the graceful hymn (Ex. 189), now lavishly ornamented by the first violins. Just as the theme itself was thrice repeated, growing in volume and richness of texture, so is this variation, passing first to the second violins and then to cellos and violas. Subsequent events tell us that Beethoven regards this not just as a variation but as the equivalent of a symphonic Recapitulation. Having built to a substantial climax (bars 162–165 corresponding structurally to bars 54–56), the music seems almost to dissolve as the first violins drift down through a sequence of F major arpeggios, gently steered towards the dominant seventh of C major by a marvellously placed B♮ in the second violins (bar 167). For a moment or two the harmony stays poised on the brink of a modulation into C but then thinks better of it and returns to F. The cellos, supported by bassoons, launch us into an extensive Coda, arguably the finest music of the whole symphony.

Up to this point Beethoven has eschewed modulation within the course of the main theme; now, by introducing delicately placed F sharps he seems to flirt with the idea of moving into G minor, a temptation he resists despite its appeal.

Ex. 192.

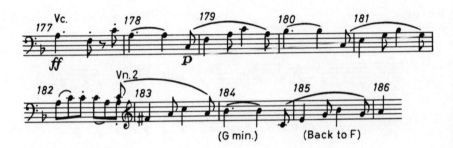

The ensuing passage reflects not only the 'Lord, we thank Thee' already mentioned, but the religious ecstasy generated in the composer's spirit by his contact with nature. Shimmering strings convey an impression of blazing sunlight, while the widespread arpeggios in cellos and basses suggest the trunks and branches of great trees reaching their arms heavenwards. 'Almighty in the forest! . . . every tree speaks through you . . .'

Ex. 193.

There is a sudden recession to *pp*; again the harmony hangs expectantly on the dominant seventh of C (see bars 194–95 above), again we are drawn back to F major. The cellos begin an elaborate variation of Ex. 192, soon to be joined by the other strings as the wind instruments take up the simple melody, unadorned. Once more the ecstatic passage shown in Ex. 193 sings out, this time considerably extended, the harmonies even richer. Gradually we experience a long descent, leading to one of the quietest and simplest statements of belief one could find anywhere. Here the Hymn of Thanksgiving truly becomes a prayer. 'A-men to that,' say wind and strings in turn. The music settles in a final chord; a last whisper of a breeze stirs through the strings as a muted horn sounds a distant, almost inaudible, curfew. 'Too sentimental!' says Beethoven, and slams the door with a peremptory gesture.

11

Interlude
The Creative Daemon

When we consider that composition was almost Beethoven's sole preoccupation for at least a third of his life, he seems to have been remarkably secretive about his method of work. Thayer, indefatigable researcher that he was, printed in good faith some letters from Bettina von Arnim to Goethe purporting to quote remarks made to her by Beethoven about the creative process. The language is so high-flown as to excite immediate suspicion and scholars today regard the letters as valueless fabrications. Virtually the only worthwhile statement appears to have been made to a young violinist called Louis Schlösser; even that was not written down until some fifty years had passed. Nevertheless it has the ring of truth, unlike Bettina's luridly romantic phraseology. According to Schlösser, Beethoven told him:

Once a theme has occurred to me, I can remember it for years. I alter much, rejecting and experimenting until I'm satisfied; the development begins in my head, whether in concentration [on idea], breadth [of treatment] or pitch, high or low. Since I know what I want, the basic idea never deserts me; it rises and grows. I hear and see the complete picture . . . there only remains the task of writing it down. Where the ideas come from I do not know; I do not seek them, directly or indirectly. I could grasp them in my hands, walking out of doors in the woods, in the middle of the night or in the early morning. A poet translates such moods into words: I turn them into sounds.

Most composers are driven by an inner force that they merely channel into various directions; the word Master, hallowed by usage in Europe (*Maestro, Meister, Maître*), is a misnomer, for they are not masters but slaves to the creative daemon. Regardless of health, poverty or social catastrophe, they continue to compose even when their music remains unperformed; one remembers Delius, blind and paralysed, Holst tormented by acute neuritis in his hands, Smetana maddened by an incessant high-pitched whistle in his ears, Chopin so weak with tuberculosis that he had to be carried up and down stairs, Handel blind or Mozart impoverished. Under such circumstances ordinary mortals would surely cry 'Enough' and end their servitude to so demanding a muse. We tend to think that such tenacity of purpose shows exceptional moral fibre yet that is not necessarily so; if one's brain teems with the music the only release is to find some way of letting it out. For Beethoven the process was long and painful; lacking the facility of a Mozart or Mendelssohn he often had to wrestle with the material. The sketchbooks, so often referred to already in this text, are mute evidence of this tortuous process.

We have already seen how unpromising many of his first ideas seem to be; one would have imagined that with maturity and experience he would have grown more selective before committing such trivia to paper, yet it seems not. A seed cupped in the palm of the hand gives no indication to the untrained eye that it will grow into a colourful flower; Beethoven's initial ideas are frequently no more than seeds, and only his eye sees any potential in them. Often disdaining such props as clefs or key-signatures, he scatters notes upon the page, only then assessing their worth. Perhaps the most surprising aspect of his very individual method of cultivation is that there is seldom any indication of harmony, not even the figured code used by musicians for centuries and still to be found in jazz guitar and piano parts today. For instance, there are three drafts of the finale to the Second Symphony. The first is barely recognisable and much of it is frankly shoddy; consisting of some fifty bars it is mostly a single line of notes, though occasionally a crude suggestion of a bass is to be found. Twice only do we find figures to indicate a shift of harmony. Turn to the second draft and we find that the opening flick and trill (see p. 54, Ex. 53) have been dispensed with, the sketch beginning with the agile figure still preserved in bars 3–6. This is instantly repeated without reference to the actual opening of the movement, even though the flick-and-trill figure has been used in the first draft and reappears later in the second. The music continues as a single unbroken line whether as a melody, a bass to an implied harmonic sequence, or even as an accompaniment to an unstated tune. It is the latter that seems the most meaningless to a casual glance:

Ex. 194.

Those who know the symphony well enough will be able to provide the woodwind melodies that pursue a smooth course against this urgent accompaniment (see Ex. 55, p. 55), yet it seems almost perverse of Beethoven thus to write an *accompaniment*—even going so far as to include two bars rest—without giving the slightest indication of the tune it was designed to support.[1]

The third draft is a single-line version of the entire finale, neither a violin part nor a cued-in score. Again it skips from treble to bass clefs, again it contains hardly a suggestion of harmony. Much of it is dead wood that was ruthlessly chopped away; from start to finish there is not a single indication of *p* or *f*, not a *crescendo* nor a *diminuendo*, not a hint of instrumentation.

Now while this may not seem all that unusual to an unmusical person, to a musician it is almost incomprehensible. The mind of a composer does not work this way; it is arguable whether melodies beget harmonies or vice versa but the two are inseparable. To conceive an entire movement as a single line is a denial of musical sense; one would not expect to gain much of an impression of a symphony from hearing just the first violin part on its own, and Beethoven has not even jotted down that. The sketch therefore must be seen as no more than a *reminder* of a much more substantial vision. Although the many alterations and developments that ensued later show that an element of trial and error was involved, it is clear that when Beethoven subsequently looked at such sketches they conveyed a great deal more than is shown on the page—harmonies, counterpoints and orchestration all being there by implication as an integral part of the picture.

Now as far as I am aware no other composer has ever worked in this way; moreover, when we take into account another aspect of Beethoven's genius it becomes harder than ever to comprehend. He was by all reports the most notable improviser of his day at a time when public improvisation was a great art. Stories are told of his extemporising for as much as an hour at a time; yet as reliable a witness as Czerny tells us that such improvisations were never formless, being clearly cast in the shape of a sonata movement, a rondo, a set of variations or some other acceptable form. So well-planned was the underlying scheme of these spontaneous performances that Beethoven boasted that he could instantly play the whole improvisation over again, which, on occasion, he proved he could do.

Without wishing to seem to be unduly sceptical, I have some doubts as to the real musical value of these extempore performances, impressive though they undoubtedly were to the listeners at the time. The nearest thing that we have to a transcript of such feats is to be found in the cadenzas to the piano concertos, the Piano Fantasia, Op. 77, and the long piano prelude to the Choral Fantasia

---

[1] For those wishing to compare Ex. 194 with the final version, see bars 52 et seq. last movement.

Op. 80 which we know him to have improvised on the spot at the first performance. None of these shows Beethoven at his best; there are moments in the cadenzas where he trots out pianistic clichés that are notably absent in the 'composed' passages of the concertos, while the two fantasias need considerable special pleading to bring conviction. Certainly they are not comparable in quality to the transcribed improvisations of Bach (in his Toccatas and Fantasias) or Mozart in the piano fantasies. Yet whatever the musical quality of Beethoven's improvisations may have been, they would certainly not have consisted of single unsupported lines; all keyboard players think harmonically; their hands naturally move to sequences of chords. With such a background, nurtured since boyhood days, the method of sketching down entire movements without having recourse to harmony seems almost inexplicable. One might expect it from Paganini or Wieniawski, starting from a violin solo to which some additional support could be added at leisure, but not from a truly symphonic mind such as Beethoven's. (Deafness had nothing to do with it; his method was the same before that nightmare loomed.)

Now it has often been the custom to divide Beethoven's output into three periods, no doubt for critical convenience. Elsewhere[1] I have tried to show that it is more revealing to pursue lines of development from early works to late. We have already seen relationships between Symphonies 4, 5 and 6, as well as the intriguing premonitions of the Ninth to be found in the Second. Here perhaps is a clue that may help to explain Beethoven's strange approach to composition. In many ways he was essentially conservative; his early works are not exceptional in boldness of harmony or rhythm nor adventurous in melody. The First Symphony creates no revolutionary scares apart from its mildly contentious opening. The formal discipline he imposes on even such impassioned movements as the opening Allegro of the Fifth Symphony or the finale of the Seventh is extraordinarily severe. Consider also that towards the end of his life he was increasingly drawn towards fugue, a form of intellectual control that had become virtually obsolete. It would seem then that he felt a definite need to exert strict control over his music; his inner daemon must be kept in check. How can we reconcile these contradictions, on the one hand a defiant rebel and a notable improviser (betokening supreme self-confidence), on the other a labouring craftsman seeking refuge in traditional forms (betraying insecurity)?

If we accept this dichotomy, enclosing the two opposing aspects within the mind of a single man, we may begin to understand something of his complex psychology. The phrase 'Man of Destiny' was not idly coined; it is an indisputable fact that there are men who genuinely feel that they are cast in

---

[1] See *Talking About Sonatas*, Chapters 4 and 6, Heinemann Educational Books, 1971.

such a role. (The fact that they too often turn out to be a Hitler, a Stalin or a Bonaparte is unfortunate but irrelevant.) All that we read of Beethoven's arrogance as a young man leads us to suppose that he could very well have regarded himself in such a light. We have seen though that early in his career he suffered a rebuff over both the Funeral and Coronation Cantatas, a blow which seems to have caused him to hold back from symphonic composition for ten years. Couple this loss of inner confidence with the onset of deafness and we find a man who may well have felt that Destiny was letting him down. However, he continues to compose piano sonatas and chamber music gaining in assurance and individuality as he does so. Being gifted with the genuine creative daemon that drives a man on remorselessly, he finds himself writing music that he scarcely knows how to handle. Standing on the threshold of a period when all the arts were to undergo a revolutionary period of liberation, his inner self strains at the leash, fired by limitless aspirations. The other self, the eighteenth-century man, goes altogether more cautiously, frightened by the sheer power that he feels within.

In effect, a great composer is a man possessed; to be thus possessed is not a comfortable experience. In Beethoven's case I believe it to have been profoundly disturbing. I suspect that all the tentative approaches to themes that we find in the sketchbooks are comparable to a nervous fiddling with the lock of Pandora's Box. He felt music burgeoning within him, but such music as he could barely grasp. Before he dared to let it out fully he had to contrive a mould; that I believe is the function of the single-line plan. That I also believe explains the paradox of the frantic haste with which many of the manuscripts appear to have been written despite the acknowledged labour of the preliminary workings. It was as though once the cast had been made, a flood of white-hot inspiration cascaded out to fill it.

Later in his life he was to grow discontented with the restraints of traditional forms; but for every new-found freedom there is usually a compensating assertion of old laws. The rhapsodic and lyrical first movement of the Piano Sonata in A major, Op. 101, is counter-balanced by the fugal finale; the unconventional alternations between *allegro* and *adagio* in the improvisational first movement of Op. 109 stand opposed by the strictly organised variations of the last; the eccentricities of the choral finale to the Ninth Symphony are heralded by a quasi-eighteenth-century use of recitative and (later) disciplined by a remarkably strict recourse to variation form.

Pursuing this line of thought a little further may help us to comprehend more fully the harping insistence on one rhythm or one chord that we find from time to time and which so irritates those who are unsympathetic to his music. There are those who can ride horses and there are those who are carried by them. If, as I suspect, Beethoven sometimes found himself in the position of a rider with both stirrups lost and a rein broken, one can scarcely blame him for hanging on with all the means at his disposal. To control so impetuous a muse calls for great strength, and it is the assertion of that strength that we find in the reiteration of one rhythm or the repetition of a harmony. 'I am in command' Beethoven seems to be saying as he hammers the point home. The daemon is tamed.

12

Symphony No. 7 in A Major, Op. 92

Dedicated to Moritz, Count Imperial von Fries

Orchestra; 2 flutes; 2 oboes; 2 clarinets; 2 bassoons; 2 horns; 2 trumpets; 2 timpani; strings

1. Poco sostenuto: leading to Vivace
2. Allegretto
3. Scherzo, Presto: Trio, Assai meno presto
4. Allegro con brio

First performance: 8 December 1813

After completing the 'Pastoral' Symphony Beethoven was to wait for more than three years before embarking on the Seventh. Begun in the latter months of 1811, the score was completed by May of the following year. Surprisingly enough the first performance did not materialise until some eighteen months had passed, an unusually long delay, possibly occasioned by his desire to visit England and the wish to reserve an important new work suitably to impress the natives. The symphony enjoyed a huge success at its première in Vienna, the slow movement being encored on the spot; its reception in Leipzig some years later was less happy, the general opinion being that he must have been drunk when he wrote the first and fourth movements. Weber, sixteen years Beethoven's junior, pronounced him ripe for the madhouse on the strength of one passage. By 1816 even the Viennese public had lost interest, greeting the Allegretto with a spatter of faint applause where once they had cheered. Nevertheless the period of the Seventh and Eighth Symphonies was the apogee of Beethoven's career in terms of both popular acclaim and financial reward.

Inevitably it was assumed at the time that the symphony was designed as a paean of victory celebrating Napoleon's downfall. (The so-called 'Battle' Symphony, largely composed by Johann Mälzel but orchestrated by

[1] More properly called 'Wellington's Victory', or the 'Battle of Vittoria'.

Beethoven, was given at the same concert.) The assumption was palpably ridiculous since, as we have seen, the work was completed by May 1812. The composer himself conducted, much to the amazement of Spohr who, playing in the orchestra amongst a host of celebrities, had a clear view.

Although much had been told me about his way of conducting, it nevertheless astounded me to the utmost degree. He was in the habit of giving dynamic indications to the orchestra by means of all sorts of peculiar movements of his body. When he wanted a *sforzando* he would vehemently throw out both his arms, which previously he had held crossed against his breast. For a *piano* he would crouch down, going down deeper as he wanted the sound to be softer. Then, at the beginning of a *crescendo* he would rise gradually and when the *forte* was reached he would leap into the air. . . . The execution was quite masterly despite Beethoven's uncertain and sometimes ludicrous conducting. It was evident that the poor deaf master was no longer able to hear the *pianos* in his music. This was particularly evident in a passage . . . where two pauses follow one another, the second being *pianissimo*. Beethoven had probably overlooked the second one, because he started off beating time again before the orchestra had even begun the second pause. Therefore, without realising it, he was ahead of the orchestra by as much as ten or twelve bars when it began to play the *pianissimo*. Beethoven . . . had crouched down under the music stand; at the *crescendo* which followed he became visible once more, making himself taller, and then leapt high in the air at the moment when he [thought] the *forte* should have begun. When it did not materialise, he looked about in terror, stared astonished at the orchestra (which was still playing *pianissimo*) and found his place only when the so-long-awaited *forte* began and became audible to him.[1]

This pathetic yet farcical scene is worth considering at more than its face value since it indicates the intensity of feeling Beethoven brought to his performances and the wide range of dynamics he clearly desired. Certainly Spohr was not exaggerating since there is an almost identical description of Beethoven conducting at another concert, the witness on this second occasion being a professional singer called Franz Wild. Despite his extreme eccentricity, Beethoven seems to have inspired admiration and respect amongst the players; they were ever ready to avert any disaster that appeared to be imminent, and there was usually a competent musician standing by ready tactfully to take over the direction of the music. The critics were not always as kind, and though the Allegretto invariably found favour, the finale was variously described as 'the acme of shapelessness', 'this absurd, untamed music', 'this delirium, in which there is no trace of melody or harmony, no single sound to fall gratefully upon the ear'.

In fact the symphony is almost wholly traditional in form even though it

---

[1] Quoted in Thayer, *Life of Beethoven*, Vol. II, p. 257.

might be said to lack a true slow movement. The slow Introduction, already used in Symphonies 1, 2 and 4, is admittedly substantially longer than those of its predecessors; the Scherzo with its five-part structure is designed on the same lines as that of No. 4 even though it is very different in spirit. Perhaps the one feature that stands out is the relentless drive of the rhythm; indeed Riezler in a memorable phrase described the work as 'the Victory of the Symphony over the tyranny of Rhythm'. Victories are not won without struggle or risk, the implication of Riezler's dictum being that although the obsessional use of rhythms threatens to swamp us, the sheer span of Beethoven's vision and his mastery of form win the day.

From the very first chord the music claims our attention; out of an explosive A major harmony played by the entire orchestra (including kettle-drum), there emerges a single line of melody played by a solo oboe. In bar 3 there is another abrupt but massive chord from the full orchestra—this time on the first inversion of the dominant. Two clarinets in unison now join the oboe so that where there was originally one connecting link there are now two. In bar 5 there is a third hammer-blow, releasing two horns followed by a flute, while the oboe and clarinet weave a more elaborate pattern. The gradual accumulation of the various strands, each with its individual tone-colour, suggests a literal gathering together of the available resources.

Ex. 195.

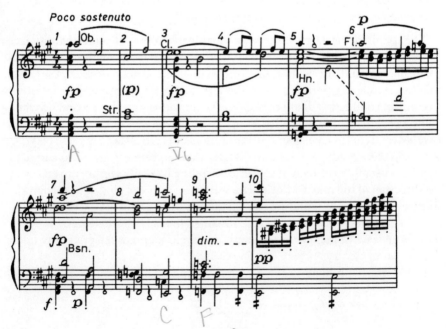

The passing reference to C major in the second half of bar 8 and to its sub-dominant (F) in bar 9 are premonitions of coming events. For the moment though our attention should be focussed on the rising scale that first appears so delicately in bar 10. By bar 15 it has been transformed into an awe-inspiring counterpoint to the initial theme as if from bar 1 onwards. At this point we find a dangerous miscalculation in the scoring, since the full wind including trumpets and horns hold a sustained A major chord *ff*, while the second violins alone are given the four minims originally played by the oboe in bars 1–2; as they are also menaced by the powerful rising scale in cellos and basses, the seconds are hard put to it to register the paramount importance of their theme, the *sf* marked against each note simply ensuring that they get E for Effort rather than A for Audibility. The first violins in the two subsequent bars have no such problem since their theme appears in a higher register.

At first it seems as though the passage from bar 15 onwards will be no more than a massively reinforced repetition of bars 1–10, but the lure of C major (of which we had a glimpse in bars 8–9) proves to be irresistible the second time round and by bar 23 this theoretically alien tonality is firmly established. So large is the scale of the Introduction—sixty-two bars of majestic 4/4—that it could almost be said to be a sonata-form movement of sorts; certainly this new theme, a grave march that would not seem out of place in Sarastro's temple in *The Magic Flute*, serves the function of a Second Subject.

Ex. 196.

First presented by the woodwind choir, it is soon taken over by the strings while a single oboe and bassoon start to nag at us with a reiterated G natural to this rhythm:

The true significance of this seemingly rather fussy gesture only becomes clear towards the end of the Introduction though it soon provokes a return to the bell-like minims from bars 1–2, now strongly reinforced by the full wind band and subjected to a positive hail of semiquavers from cellos and basses or second violins. If we were still in the world of the 'Pastoral' Symphony we might aptly interpret this as a rainstorm even though the literal-minded might argue that rain doesn't fall upwards. The clouds, if clouds they be, disperse, and once again the woodwind proffer us the subject quoted in Ex. 196, this time in F major (the other key predicted in the momentary reference in bar 9). Goaded by repeated semiquavers in the wind, the strings with great labour drag themselves out of this irrelevant key, searching for the dominant of A major, the 'home' or tonic key of the symphony which must be re-established before we can hope to begin the inevitable Allegro movement that is surely imminent. As though aware of the inherent tension of the situation, Beethoven starts to tease us. 'Nearly there,' he seems to say, having reached the vital E natural, and goes on to repeat the note over seventy times within the space of ten bars. The increasingly wide spacing of these repetitions confirms that he is toying with us in a way that is comparable even though not exactly similar to the game he played at the start of the finale of the First Symphony. At last the long-postponed release from the suspense comes as flute and oboe delicately spell out the rhythm which is to be the mainspring of the movement. Here is the crucial join:

Ex. 197.

The point made and a new momentum established, we can settle down happily to enjoy the First Subject as presented to us by a solo flute.

Ex. 198.

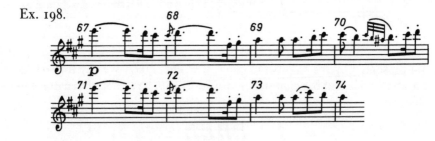

Berlioz has been chided by some commentators for calling this a 'Ronde des paysans'. They do him an injustice since that is not actually what he said. Attacking those who ridiculed the tune for its rustic simplicity, he went on to say with mild sarcasm that such a reproach would presumably not have been made had the composer (as in the 'Pastoral' Symphony) given it some such title as 'Peasants' Rondo'. Regretfully he accepts that here are those who are 'indisposed to welcome any idea presented to them in unaccustomed dress, unless they are told beforehand the reason for this anomaly'. In fact the second limb of the tune does have a strong family resemblance to an important motif from the 'Pastoral' as the following comparison shows.

Ex. 199a.

The dialogue treatment of the descending four-note fragment in bars 76–77 recalls a more extensive development of an almost identical phrase in the 'Pastoral' finale, here transposed into A for ease of comparison.

Ex. 199b.

Though I doubt if it is anything more than a coincidence it helps to establish the essentially 'outdoor' nature of both works.

In due course the first violins (with especially enthusiastic support from the first horn) take over an exuberant version of Ex. 198, substantially extending by the use of sequences the little dialogue shown in Ex. 199a. Before the arrival of the second subject group there are two brief excursions into foreign territory that deserve a mention, first to C sharp minor, and then to what looks on the page like E♭ tarred with the brush of A♭ minor. This is simply a convenient notation for what is in reality G♯ minor and its dominant, D♯. I only make the point since the sudden jump from flats to sharps makes the modulation seem more remote than it really is.

Ex. 200.

G♯ minor and E major are closely related, as this cadence shows:

Beethoven's sole reason for writing bars 116–118 in flats is to avoid the slightly daunting appearance created by the grammatically proper notation:

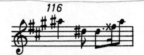

Whatever the means, it has enabled him to reach the first element of the second subject, the joyous tune to be found in bars 119–124 above. I identify it with some trepidation since Donald Tovey, with whom I would seldom dare to disagree, states categorically that the true Second Subject begins some bars later with this (surely less interesting) theme.

Ex. 201.

His reasoning strikes me as unduly pedantic since the dominant key of E is perfectly well established from bar 119 onwards (see Ex. 200). Despite his contention that harmony and phrasing only settle firmly in the new key at bar 130, the music has clearly been in E major for the preceding eleven bars. One should not have to wait until one can actually read the sign saying Victoria before realising that one has arrived at a terminus.

My doubts about Tovey's analysis seem confirmed by the fact that within seven bars Beethoven plunges us into the contradictory key of C major, a step which he immediately appears to regret since the music not only dies away to nothing but comes to a halt. There follows a wonderfully mysterious passage, poised on a tremulous diminished seventh, with a tiny wisp of a phrase being tossed from the lowest strings to an oboe and back again.[1] The deadlock is

---

[1] For those interested in the evolution of Beethoven's musical language it is intriguing to compare bars 142–145 of this movement with bars 108–112 of the slow movement of the Second Symphony; they could be said to symbolise the Romantic and Classical responses to a particular harmonic situation, the one mercurial and overtly dramatic in an almost operatic fashion, the other austere and controlled. Both are marvellously effective within their proper contexts.

broken with a long ascent to the biggest climax of the movement so far, a *fortissimo* re-assertion of the dominant in which cellos and basses have a phrase that bounds across two octaves.

Ex. 202.

Notice the stunning effect of the sudden shift of key in bar 156 coupled with the extreme change of dynamic from *ff* to *pp*. A brief reference to the First Subject (now in the dominant of course) initiates a Codetta whose most notable feature is the slap-happy scale with which it ends. The Leipzig critics who opined that Beethoven was drunk when he wrote this movement should at least be given credit for recognising an attack of hiccups.

Ex. 203.

The effect is sufficiently unusual as to justify the stunned two-bar silence. Having observed the repeat (rarely nowadays), the orchestra are collectively attacked with a somewhat briefer bout of musical eructation; there is another silence, pregnant with the unspoken question 'Where do we go from here?'

The answer is again C major, the key Beethoven used for the 'Second Subject' of the Introduction and which he had originally glimpsed as early as bar 8. Its importance in the Development is so great that it takes on the unorthodox character of a secondary dominant, unorthodox because it is so essentially hostile to the concept of A major. Having once established this tonality, in which he intends to stay for thirty bars, Beethoven begins a delightful development of the First Subject, a dancing scale-like extension which he treats almost like a round.

Ex. 204.

Roundabout and roundabout and roundabout it goes, emerging into a hugely aggrandised version of the bass from Ex. 202, extended in rhythm by incorporating tied notes stolen from the First Subject. It is a development important enough to be repeated in the 'proper' key of E, albeit not for long. After a brief slanging match between strings and woodwind there is a subtle modulation into F major, the other key of importance in the Introduction. In a section whose delicacy suggests Mendelssohn at his best, fragments of Ex. 204 are woven into a web of counterpoint. For some fourteen bars the dialogue is conducted in a whisper; then, unforgettably, it gathers strength, driving relentlessly towards the Recapitulation. It is a progress whose rhythm does not slacken once in forty-two bars, yet the triumphant arrival at the reprise lets us know that Beethoven has had his eye on that ultimate goal throughout.

In due course we come to the two pauses mentioned by Spohr in his description of Beethoven's conducting. Musically, the second pause serves an interesting function in that it modulates to the subdominant key of D, a tonality Beethoven has managed to avoid completely up to this point, in spite of its close relationship to the tonic. A gentle little scale on the oboe opens up this new vista and with it a host of new keys which are visited fleetingly. In other respects the Recapitulation is reasonably orthodox right up to the point where the hiccupping scale quoted in Ex. 203 reappears. Again there is a shocked silence, after which there is an abashed 'Pardon!' from the orchestra on the wildly inappropriate note A *flat*. The slapstick over, Beethoven leads us into an inspired Coda beginning in this hopelessly 'wrong' key. The transition back to A is masterly; although the ♩ ♪♪ rhythm continues without cessation the harmonies shift quite slowly in the woodwind, giving a sense of repose.

Ex. 205.

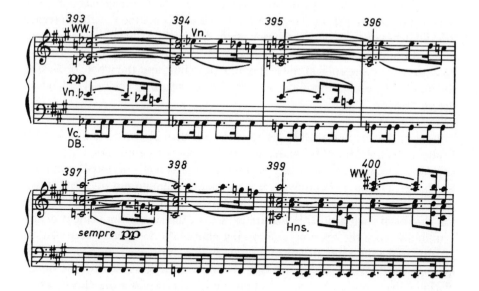

Now comes the passage to which the young Weber took such exception. Eleven times Beethoven repeats a disturbingly dissonant phrase in the bass,

the B sharps grinding against the clearly implied A major harmony above.[1] But if for B sharp we 'think' C natural it is possible to interpret the passage as a mixture of the tonic with the 'secondary dominant' as I have called it. Beethoven has a certain fondness for blending tonic and dominant harmony,

[1]This seemingly new theme may be regarded as a development of the First Subject, i.e.

becomes by transposition and rhythmic alteration

the famous horn entry in the Eroica for instance (see Ex. 77) or the coda of the first movement of the 'Les Adieux' Sonata, Op. 81a. C major has played so important a part in the movement as a whole that it is not too fanciful to regard this disturbing bass as a last reference to it. Meanwhile the violins are given a series of phrases each of which reaches up only to fall back again. At last they break free from the coils of the serpentine bass-line, and the whole orchestra, encouraged by jubilant fanfares from the horns, heads for the final cadence of the movement.

'But many that are first shall be last; and the last shall be first.' I cannot say that I fully understood the Biblical maxim until I realised its application to classical harmony, for in music, especially the music of such tonally oriented composers as Mozart, Haydn or Beethoven, it is frequently (though not invariably) true that the first chord of a movement is the same as the last and vice versa. Seldom has this been such a notable feature as it is in the second movement of this symphony since the opening and closing chords do not merely establish the tonality of A minor but also dictate a mood. The chord, sustained for two bars marked *forte diminuendo*, is sombre in colouring, being scored for oboes, clarinets, bassoons and horns. Technically it is known as a 6/4 chord, which simply means that its component notes are a sixth and a fourth above its bass; but a 6/4 chord has a curious sense of expectancy about it since it is not complete in itself. Though it lacks the tension of a sharp dissonance, tension there is nevertheless, a tension that is normally relieved in the following manner.

Beethoven's initial refusal to allow the wind to do this gives the chord a feeling of isolation that anticipates the bleak landscapes of Sibelius. While it is true that the strings do supply the expected resolution in bar 4, the movement ends as it began with the 6/4 chord repeated in the same sombre hue unresolved. It is a gesture far more striking and original than the opening chord of the First Symphony about which so much comment has been made.

Out of the dying echoes of this strangely plangent chord emerges a march of sorts—*not* a funeral march it should be noted, the tempo being Allegretto. In a conversation notebook of 1823 Schindler wrote questioningly 'so I am to mark the second movement of the A major symphony ♩ = 80 ?'[1] Evidence of this

[1] Instead of ♩ = 80

nature is frustrating since we do not know whether Beethoven replied Yes or No; however either marking would indicate a tempo with more forward impulse than we sometimes hear. The idea for the theme seems to have first come to Beethoven six years previously in a sketch for one of the Razumovsky quartets. Jotted down without indications of harmony it looks remarkably unattractive.

Ex. 206.

Give this to the average harmony student and he would be perplexed. It has a look of C major about it and one might be tempted to do something on these lines.

Ex. 207.

It is far from satisfying, though the substitution of F♯ for F♮ in the fifth bar would help matters—not entirely cheating since Beethoven often omitted accidentals in his sketches. Indeed the theme as it appears in the symphony does have an F♯, the stroke of genius being that it leads not to a chord of G, as it would in my hypothetical example, but to a 6/4 version of C.

Ex. 208.

It is worth pointing out that the slightly more accented dashes (as opposed to *staccato* dots) in bars 3, 5, 7 and 9 accord with Beethoven's manuscript. They give the theme something of an edge that it otherwise might lack.

Although the rhythm is all-pervading, the harmonic structure is rich, with wonderful chromaticisms that brush fleetingly against such alien tonalities as

B major, B minor and A major in addition to the C major shown in bar 10. The solemn tread continues for twenty-six bars;[1] there follows the moment that touches every heart, the emergence of the sustained counter-melody that the composer has clearly had in mind to illuminate these dark and shadowy harmonies.

Ex. 209.

The second limb of the tune (bars 35–42) is repeated, the measured tread of the march continuing throughout. Beethoven repeats this great stanza twice more, constantly enriching the texture; the effect, as of a grand procession passing, is enhanced by the *diminuendo* at the close. As the column 'disappears', clarinet and bassoon in unison introduce a new theme in A major. There is scarcely a commentator on this music who does not use the word 'sunlight' or its equivalent to describe this moment. The response came unprompted to me as a fifteen-year-old when I first heard the symphony and it seems to be a well-nigh universal reaction. It is indeed like a ray of sunshine stealing out of a grey sky, bringing with it both warmth and comfort. *Pizzicato* cellos and basses persist with the hypnotic rhythm of the march, but they are relegated to the background as this glorious new tune unfolds.

Ex. 210

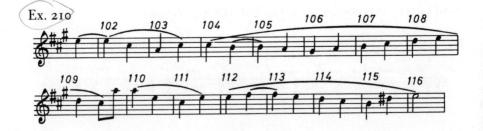

G naturals in the supporting harmony in bars 110–112 add a touch of poignancy, while the gently flowing triplets in the violins help to give a freedom

---

[1] Twenty-four if one omits the introductory chord.

of movement that might otherwise be lacking. The whole section is so full of felicities that to enumerate them would involve transcribing the entire forty bars or so; suffice it to say that Schubert himself could not excel its lyrical beauty. But if we are to visit the garden of Eden we must expect the Fall thereafter, and sure enough it comes with a great descending scale in triplets passing through nearly four octaves. It plunges us harshly back into A minor, the woodwind resuming Ex. 209 against a subdued but more restless accompaniment in the strings.

There follows a ghostly little fugue built on a subject derived by implication from a fragment of Ex. 208. Marked *sempre pp*, it is given an especially forlorn quality by having some notes a bare fifth apart displaced so that they fall between the beats. It is as though the players have literally lost touch with each other. As the wind instruments join in there is a gradual and intense *crescendo* spread over four bars. Once more (and it is only once) the eight-bar refrain returns with a stark ferocity that has not previously been suggested. The harsher mood is quickly dispelled as the clarinet again brings its radiant theme to disperse the threatening clouds.

In the coda to the movement, the initial theme is broken into fragments so that each two bars is allotted a different orchestration. The effect of disintegration must have seemed quite revolutionary at the time, though no more so than the unresolved woodwind chord with which the piece ends.

The movement proved to be so popular that it was sometimes taken out of context and inserted into the Second Symphony or even the Eighth. Its simple construction was easy to comprehend, its all-pervading rhythm gave it a continuity that more complex movements lacked. What perhaps was not fully appreciated was the sheer originality of the conception; it is a movement that has no parallel in music.

The Scherzo sets a new standard for vitality and humour, excelling all of its predecessors in its rhythmic vigour. The first inkling of the main tune that we find in the sketchbooks presents a very novel appearance, so much so that it has been suggested that it was originally intended for the first movement.

Ex. 211.

209

Only the first three bars of this proved to be of any further value; even they were to be subjected to changes of key, rhythm and register. Five pages later in the sketchbook we find this substantially altered version.

Ex. 211a.

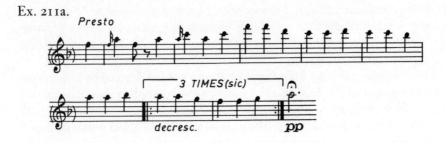

This is well on the way to the theme of the Scherzo as we know it, while the pause on the A suggests that Beethoven was already toying with the possibility of alternating between the two opposed tonalities of F and A. In the final version we find this unusual juxtaposition convincingly realised.

Ex. 212.

The repeat brings an instant plunge back to F major which, even to our twentieth-century ears, makes the alternation of keys seem quite violent.

Since the minim-crotchet figure in bars 14–16 is due to assume a much greater importance it is worthwhile to speculate a little about its origin. Denis Matthews, who has devoted much thought to the sketchbooks and whose musical intuition and scholarship give him formidable authority, has suggested that the figure stems from a sketch for the seldom played overture, Op. 115, 'Zur Namensfeier'. In all humility I venture to think there is a less arcane solution. Look again at Ex. 211 and in particular at the bracketed pair of notes in bar 7. In the eighth bar Beethoven has left a blank to make room for his viola entry; yet surely there can be little doubt as to what would have gone into the space. If, as we have seen in the previous chapter, he was capable of leaving two bars rest in a sketch knowing quite well what was going to be in them, a hiatus such as this should create no problem. By implication the lower line in bars 7–8 of Ex. 211 *must* logically be:

A simple change of notation and a concentration on the two bracketed pairs gives this,

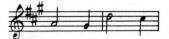

which is clearly relevant to the final version of the Scherzo. To spend so much time on a small detail would seem an academic indulgence were it not that this small pattern assumes immense importance in the ensuing section of the movement. After a brief game of 'Pass-the-parcel' in the strings (each section getting rid of the initial three-note figure as quickly as possible) the woodwind set up a veritable cooing on this figure

which they repeat *pianissimo* four times. The upper strings follow suit, whereupon cellos and bassoons gently suggest that since everyone else is clearly in the wrong key it's time to slide surreptitiously into the right one. 'Agreed!' is the communal shout, *ff*—the only trouble being that they've arrived at the dominant of C instead of F. The process is repeated, this time arriving at the dominant of B♭. Just as the sequence of events seems about to start yet another time, oboe and bassoon come to the rescue with a rather more refined version of the initial theme. The overlapping entry is another charming example of Beethoven's humour, the wind so eager to put things right that they don't allow the strings to finish their phrase.

Ex. 213.

The tune chatters along happily, some E naturals in a descending scale pattern smoothing the way back to the tonic key, F major. Crotchets dance, trills whirl as the music pursues its lively course; suddenly everything freezes on a long-held A, the pause originally foreseen in Ex. 211a, though now *ff* instead of *pp*. The entire section is repeated; the second time round, the pause has a *diminuendo* leading into the first Trio. It is in the unexpected key of D major, the sustained A now being treated as the dominant of D instead of the major third of F. Indeed the key scheme of the whole movement is based on the idea of harmonising the note A in three different ways.

The first part of the Scherzo is a struggle between 1 and 2, the Trio being a period of respite on 3.

The Trio is marked *Assai meno presto* (rather less hectic), an indication that surely means that it is still pretty fast though not very fast. All too often the knowledge that the melody is based on a pilgrim' hymn[1] causes conductors to adopt too slow a tempo. The tune is played with organ-like tones by woodwind and horns—very suitable for pilgrims—while the violins sustain a bagpipe drone that even has to be stoked up from time to time as the 'pipers' run short of breath. After the hectic scramble of the Scherzo, these long-held notes give a sense of great spaciousness. Notice the effectiveness of the second horn part, initially breathing at the same pace as his colleagues, but gradually growing more desperate and breathless until the whole orchestra is provoked into joining the refrain.

As is so often the case with Beethoven, ideas that start jokingly are transformed into sheer poetry. So it is with this horn phrase, its rude grumblings being turned to magic by the lower strings (bars 235-6).

[1] On the authority of the Abbé Stadler (1748–1833).

Ex. 214.

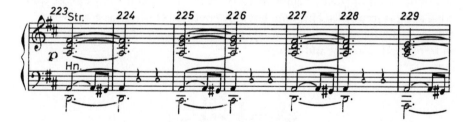

This return to the Scherzo material occupies the central position in the movement, the overall plan being Scherzo-Trio-Scherzo-Trio-Scherzo, with the briefest of references to the Trio tagged on in the final page. In score, the movement is fifty-seven pages long, 653 bars; compare the 214 bars of the Scherzo in the Second Symphony and it will give some idea of the changing scale of Beethoven's conception.

Of the finale it is often said that Wagner described it as the Apotheosis of the Dance whereas the remark was actually made about the entire symphony; 'the Dance in its highest condition; the happiest realisation of bodily movement in an ideal form'. Thus spoke the Master, reputedly carrying out his belief by improvising and himself dancing a balletic interpretation of the symphony to Liszt's piano accompaniment. The scene would be greeted with incredulous hilarity were it to appear in a film biography of either composer yet it seems that it happened.

The last movement should not be considered in isolation; remember that the Scherzo finishes in F major, and though the usual coughs and noises off will almost inevitably intervene, we should at least be aware of the lurch of a semitone when the finale begins on E. (Call it F *flat* and it brings home quite what a jolt is implied.) This note not only contradicts what has gone before; it also gives a false impression of what is going to happen. 'E major' it proclaims in terms both forceful and abrupt.

Needless to say it is *not* E major but the dominant of A, as the interpolation of D naturals into bar 3 confirms; however, the importance of the dominant has been resolutely established and the main theme of the movement is presented against a clanging background of dominant Es fit to rival the Anvil Chorus.

Ex. 215.

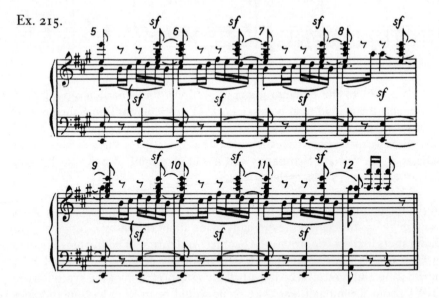

(Note in passing the sustained A in the first violins, held over into bar 9 regardless of the dominant harmony that surrounds it.) The pounding *sforzandi* give an impression of tremendous physical energy, while the use of the dominant as an anchor-note keeps the music in a state of suspense that skilfully prevents it from becoming bogged down. The second limb of the tune, while being equally accentuated, is more adventurous harmonically, introducing a few chromaticisms to add a touch of spice.

The origin of this theme is interesting. Beethoven had been commissioned by an Edinburgh music publisher called George Thomson to arrange a large number of folk-songs from Scotland, Ireland and Wales. While it was surely a waste of a great composer's time the commission was accepted for purely financial reasons, the work being spread over the years 1810–1815. Amongst the tunes Thomson sent was an Irish air, 'Nora Creina', whose lilting 6/4 rhythm seems harmless enough.

Ex. 215a.[1]

By putting it into 2/4 and turning the lazy triplets into whirling groups of semiquavers Beethoven transformed the character of the tune even though he preserved its melodic skeleton.

Soon a powerful new theme appears, horns, trumpets and drums giving it a martial air.

Ex. 216.

It is worth mentioning that this is basically a scale whereas the preliminary sketch took the form of an arpeggio.

Ex. 216a.

[1] Originally in F but transposed for ease of comparison.

215

Beethoven's decision to re-shape this was presumably dictated by a desire to create a homogeneity between Exx. 215 and 216 by building both from scale-segments. The supposition is reinforced by the next event, a theme of descending crotchets preceded by the circling figure from the opening tune.

Ex. 217.

This is clearly related to bar 5 by augmentation; compare bars 37–39 with bar 27 (Ex. 216) and the point is made.

Beethoven spins out Ex. 217 through four sequences before setting up a passage in a new rhythm—ten bars of ♩.♫♩ that leave us positively battered. Out of this ill-tempered display emerges the charming Second Subject scored with a delicacy fit for a ballerina. It approaches its unusual key (C♯ minor) through a somewhat oblique route.

Ex. 218.

The second-beat accents give a curiously gawky character to the tune; moreover the upper woodwind try to throw it off balance with disturbing little forays into D major. Increasingly this new tonality gains a hold as the timpani rumble away on a low A and the woodwind hold a long sustained dominant seventh above. Hop about as they will, the strings cannot escape the tremendous gravitational pull that this chord sets up; like it or not it appears that they are going to be dragged into D. In a real crisis send for a diminished seventh; with a sudden roar of sound Beethoven unleashes this multi-purpose chord creating a sense of chaotic disturbance. Battle is joined with the intention of regaining the tonality of C♯ minor. In a passage of remarkable intensity we find C♯s in the bass, D♯s in the top strings and wind, while B♯s collide with B♮s at the core of the harmony. If it didn't end with a good-natured return to the first bar of the movement one would take it to be serious. Naturally enough with the repetition observed the same quarrel blows up again; this time it is resolved by the somewhat brutal expedient of a violent modulation into the truly alien key of F major. It leads to one of the most remarkable passages in the whole symphony, a sort of trial of strength involving the rising sixth that originally appeared in bar 8 (see Ex. 215) and which is such a prominent feature of the main tune. The first tussle is quite brief, just two phrases; the second is more striking, upper and lower strings contradicting each other forcefully.

Ex. 219.

Notice how the conflict intensifies in bars 144–145 only to resolve into the whirling figures of the First Subject. The influence of the rising intervals in Ex. 219 continues to make itself felt however, and we soon find ourselves involved in an extraordinary section filled with rising anythings—minor thirds, major thirds, fourths, augmented intervals, even tones and semitones. With the accent invariably in the wrong part of the bar the effect borders on the grotesque, angular and uncouth. At last it settles down onto the dominant of the home key (E), though dissident D♯s continue to nudge it from beneath.

Just as we feel A major is in reach again, Beethoven sidesteps unexpectedly to F major, a move calculated to cause some consternation. The woodwind (who have had hardly a sniff at the First Subject) put a brave face on things by attempting to play it in the unfamiliar key of B♭ major—so far unvisited in this movement. It is a move that meets with somewhat grudging approval from the strings as they pass the concluding interval around.

Ex. 220.

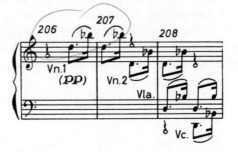

After another shot at the tune the wind suggest putting a B *natural* at the top of this rising interval, an idea taken up with considerably more enthusiasm by the strings since it opens the way back to a long overdue return home. The Recapitulation can begin, the tonality of A major securely re-established.

In a symphony with so massive an Introduction as the one we have here it is entirely proper to have a correspondingly lengthy Coda; indeed it is remarkable both for its span and its invention. It is sometimes difficult to define the precise moment where a coda begins; 'the point where the movement ought to end but doesn't' would be a cynical definition. The Diversion sign is either in bar 343 or bar 349, its exact location seeming to me to be of little importance.

What is important is to realise what immense stamina Beethoven shows in finding a wealth of new things to say in a movement of such intensity. Most noteworthy is an extraordinary grinding bass, reminding us a little of the twenty-two bar *ostinato* in the first movement (see p. 205). Descending through a somewhat irregular pattern of semitones, the cellos and basses gradually work their way down to a low E and D♯[1] where they stay for twenty-one bars, in Sir Henry Wood's immortal phrase 'sawing away regardless'. Meanwhile, against sustained wind chords, the strings incessantly repeat the whirling phrase from the First Subject, passing it from instrument to instrument until, having climbed progressively higher they rise to a climactic peak, ushering in a triumphant return of Ex. 216 (p. 215). Its scale-like shape

[1] The bottom D♯ was not available on the double bass of Beethoven's time; modern players with 5-string basses use the lower octave.

proves to be convenient, enabling the composer to develop it convincingly into a whole series of sweeping scales in contrary motion, not unlike the lowering and raising of the curtain at the end of a theatrical triumph. Triumph is indeed the word for this stunning peroration which must surely rank as one of Beethoven's most brilliantly conceived passages for orchestra. While he knew all about writing virtuoso music for the piano he was rather less adventurous in orchestral compositions, perhaps because of a series of unfortunate experiences. The quality of the music is not in question, merely his ability to exploit the orchestra as an instrument. His writing is sometimes awkward and one feels at times that the flight of his imagination is hampered by the limitations of instruments. Here, in the closing pages of this symphony, we find music that is basically easy to play but which *sounds* difficult; that is a skill he could learn from a lesser composer such as Cherubini, whom he genuinely admired, or, in later years, from Rossini.[1] Such writing may often be slick and facile; that is a criticism one could never make of Beethoven, for whom composition was so arduous a labour. The Seventh Symphony perhaps more than any of the others gives us a feeling of true spontaneity; the notes seem to fly off the page as we are borne along on a floodtide of inspired invention. Beethoven himself spoke of it fondly as 'one of my best works'. Who are we to dispute his judgement?

[1] Rossini was only twenty in 1812 and it is doubtful if Beethoven knew of his work, his early operas only having been performed in Italy.

13

Symphony No. 8 in F Major, Op. 93

No dedication

Orchestra: 2 flutes; 2 oboes; 2 clarinets; 2 bassoons; 2 horns; 2 trumpets; 2 timpani; strings

1. Allegro vivace e con brio
2. Allegretto scherzando
3. Tempo di menuetto
4. Allegro vivace

First performance: 27 February 1814

Despite Beethoven's high opinion of the Seventh Symphony, he was known on occasion to remark that the Eighth was the better work. It has been suggested that like many of his sayings this was not to be taken seriously. The symphony was undeniably overshadowed by its great predecessor. As the critic of the *Allgemeine musikalische Zeitung* wrote, 'The applause it received was not accompanied by the enthusiasm that distinguishes a work that has given universal delight; in short—as the Italian saying goes—it did not create a furore.' In all fairness the same writer went on to point out that the audience might have been suffering from a surfeit, and that were the symphony to be performed alone it would surely succeed. The concert was a typically marathon occasion beginning with the Seventh Symphony (not the first performance), continuing with 'an entirely new Italian terzetto' (Op. 116), then the Eighth Symphony, and finally 'Wellington's Victory'. The orchestra was unusually large; thirty-six violins, fourteen violas, twelve cellos, seventeen double-basses (!), with two contra-bassoons to augment the normal woodwind. Presumably it was the inclusion of the popular 'Battle' symphony that made such forces desirable though one can scarcely believe that the participation of a number of 'dilletanti' in the orchestra made for the polished precision required in the other works. Czerny tells us that after the concert, on his way home, Beethoven tried to buy some cherries from two girls in the street. They refused to take any money, saying that they had heard his 'beautiful music' in the concert-hall. Doubtless their spontaneous gesture of appreciation meant more to Beethoven than public applause—or the lack of it—since it seems he often recounted the incident. Although he referred to the Eighth as 'a little symphony', thereby distinguishing it from the 'grand Symphony in A', the affection Beethoven felt for it may well have been prompted by the comparative ease with which he wrote it. It appears to have caused him the least travail of all his major compositions; he started work on it as soon as he had completed the Seventh, doubtless still feeling exhilarated by the achievement. Within four months the Eighth had been committed to full score.

As with the Second Symphony, one would never guess from the musical content that it was written in a period of emotional disturbance. During the summer months of 1812, Beethoven's brother Johann, an apothecary by profession, acquired as housekeeper his lodger's sister, a pleasant and attractive young woman called Therese Obermeyer. Rumour soon spread with some justification that she looked after his needs as well by night as she did by day. Beethoven was furious, torn, I suspect, by secret envy of a state he had long desired. Impetuously he set off for Linz (where Johann was living) with the express purpose of breaking up what he regarded as an immoral affair. In the process he made both a fool and a nuisance of himself, endeavouring to enlist the aid of the Bishop, the civil authorities and even the police, from whom he ultimately obtained an order to evict Therese should the illicit relationship continue. Not surprisingly, Johann was exasperated by this unbrotherly interference; he was thirty-five and had no great respect for his uncouth and eccentric relative. On 8 November 1812, he put a stop to Beethoven's unpleasantness by marrying Therese, a step he was later to regret; in after years he blamed Beethoven for having forced him into a marriage he did not really want. This strangely bitter family row dragged on through the very period in which the cheerful Eighth Symphony was being composed, yet to judge from the music one would think that Beethoven was in an exceptionally good humour.

Although the symphony was composed with relative facility there are, needless to say, many preliminary sketches, most of them penned while he was still working on the Seventh. His first intention was to begin with two bars of repeated quaver chords to establish the tonality of F major, following this very conventional gesture with a strong theme.

Ex. 221.

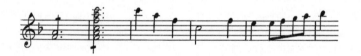

Second thoughts brought the elimination of the two introductory bars and a greatly improved modification to bar 3.

Thus the symphony begins, bringing us straight to the point without so much as a clearing of the throat. Of the preceding symphonies, only the 'Pastoral' begins without any preamble, although, as I have tried to show, a good case can be made for regarding its opening pages as an introduction of sorts, albeit skilfully disguised. To start a symphony is a formidable enterprise, but here one has the impression that Beethoven is so eager to begin that he cannot wait for even such brief preliminaries as we find in the 'Eroica' or the Fifth; yet at one time he contemplated a slow and majestic introduction in A leading to a recognisable version of the opening theme in D. Key played such an important part in Beethoven's conception that such an aberration is unusual; certainly to transpose the opening phrase (as we now know it) into D major changes its character to a marked degree.

An unusual feature of this symphony is that the opening material is projected as a twelve-bar theme instead of the more normal eight. Suppose we arrange the music in three units of four bars.

Ex. 222.

By conventional standards the 'proper' response to phrase 1 is to go straight to 3; the second phrase is an interloper. The point is made for us nearly 200 bars later at the start of the Recapitulation; the eight-bar norm is established, complete with the quite exceptional indication *fff*, making it not so much a new point of departure as an arrival at a central climax.

Before leaving the topic of the three initial phrases, I should draw attention to a fascinating theory put forward by Dr Lionel Pike in his stimulating book *Beethoven, Sibelius and the Profound Logic.*[1] Dr Pike produces cogent arguments to show that this symphony is based on numerology, the dominating figure being 3. He traces melodic formulae based on 3 notes, key-shifts to tonalities separated from each other by the interval of a third, triple repetitions of phrases or significant harmonies and so forth. Occasionally the evidence is somewhat rigged, as for instance when he hails F sharp minor as a special event simply because it has a key-signature of three sharps. (How many tonalities occur in the symphony that are *not* so endowed?) Nevertheless the entire exposition of this original theory is most convincingly presented. Intellectually it carries much more weight than the sort of analysis proffered by Schauffler[2] whose pursuit of what he calls 'germ-motives' leads him to relate almost any consecutive two or three notes to any other remotely comparable group regardless of musical probability. Any school of literary criticism that based its findings on the significance of the appearance of the words 'and', 'of', 'the', and 'but' within the context of a novel would lack credibility.

I mention these two very different books simply in order to underline the irresistible challenge that Beethoven's music continues to present over the years. No composer has provided a greater stimulus to enquiring minds, whether performers or commentators. The inevitable danger is that we can probe too far, tilling the soil so industriously that it becomes sterile. The sketchbooks in particular are a treasure-trove for the researcher, yet suppose they had none of them survived; might we not then accept the music more at its face-value? The Eighth Symphony speaks to us so directly that it seems gratuitous to subject it to the chilling process of analysis. Why then do we bother? Our best motive (and I must include myself in the ranks of the analysts) is to prevent the listener from taking this so familiar music for granted, to make people listen with the intensity the symphonies deserve. Though I may or may not agree with Dr Pike's thesis at least it compelled me to think anew about music I thought I had studied with some diligence. The point is made; let us return to the music.

The opening is disarmingly old-fashioned, almost as though Beethoven felt that he had pushed the frontiers of music too far. Knowing as we now do what was still to come we might also regard it as a reassuring look back over his shoulder before venturing on into the unknown. Both views are mistaken; the relevant word is 'disarming' since the solidly confident opening is destined to have its foundations undermined most wittily. For the first twenty-three bars Beethoven assures us with considerable force that the music is indisputably

---

[1] The Athlone Press, 1978.
[2] Robert Haven Schauffler, *Beethoven, the man who freed music*, Doubleday Doran, 1929.

positively undeniably without fear of contradiction in F major. The statement
is buttressed by references to those three pillars of righteous harmony, the
Tonic, the Dominant and the Subdominant. However, in bar 24 a dissident
element is introduced, A♭. In vain do the cellos and basses reiterate the tonic
note F, in vain do the violins proclaim the virtues of the subdominant;
grandiose as it is, the music grinds to a halt. It is as though an architect intent
upon building the Channel Bridge had landed up with Brighton Pier.

Ex. 223.

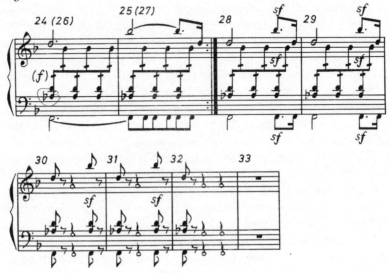

The deadlock is complete as the bar of silence indicates. Enter Pierrot,
deflating pomposity with an irreverent mime.

Ex. 224.

In case I should myself now be accused of irreverence let me quote the
eminently respectable Sir George Grove:

At this time of life (forty-two) [Beethoven's] love of fun and practical joking had
increased so much on him as to have become a habit; his letters are full of jokes;

he bursts into horse-laughs on every occasion; makes the vilest puns, and bestows the most execrable nicknames—and all this the most when he was most happy.[1]

Surely this is nearer to the mark than earnest excursions into numerology; for whatever reason Beethoven may have composed it seems to me unlikely that he would have done so to demonstrate a theory of numbers and their relation to music. Certainly the first movement could be said to have a plot; it can be expressed in the simplest of sentences—'I'll catch you out!' Time after time in this symphony we find carefully laid traps to gull the listener; we have just been caught by one; another lies ahead. There is a difference though; the joke that has just been played on us is pure slapstick; the joke to come is much more subtle.

By beginning in an old-fashioned way with an old-fashioned obsession with establishing tonality, Beethoven is asking us to expect that the game will be played according to old-fashioned rules. One of the most hallowed of conventions was that Second Subjects in sonata-form movements in major keys were invariably in the dominant. THUS SAITH THE LORD—which Lord nobody quite knows but he certainly said it . . . Therefore in this symphony of all symphonies, after so *honest* a beginning, we can be confident that the Second Subject will be in C major. But it isn't; it's in the unprecedented key of D, 'no relation to the key next door' as one might say. Accompanied with the greatest delicacy by *pizzicato* strings and a mincing bassoon the violins offer us this elegant tune seemingly unaware of the solecism they are committing; after four bars though they suddenly falter and, with a somewhat tortuous modulation, grope their way into the 'proper' key of C. Having reached this desirable goal by however devious means, they pick up the tempo and hand the tune over to the woodwind, now in the orthodox key.

Ex. 225.

[1] Grove, *Beethoven and his Nine Symphonies*, Novello, 1896.

The genesis of this tune is interesting; it first appears in the sketches as a possible continuation of the *First* Subject, an extension of the rising pattern of five note (E–B♭) in bars 3–4 (see Ex. 222, p. 222). Note that it is still in the tonic key (F), confirming that it was originally conceived as part of the first subject group. (Transposing it down a third will make the relationship to Ex. 225 doubly clear though it will not disguise the banality of the final bars.)

Ex. 225a.[1]

Compare this to Ex. 225 and we truly see the hand of a master at work.

Now I have said that when the woodwind take over the Second Subject (bar 45, Ex. 225) they do so in the proper key; not really thinking of the consequences they heedlessly copy the violins, producing a diversion away from the dominant that creates an instant feeling of insecurity. The harmony they have arrived at is the archetypal crisis chord, the diminished seventh. The wind sustain it as though terrified to let go, second violins tremble apprehensively, cellos, violas and first violins extend a huge rising arpeggio through nearly five octaves—a gesture copied by Brahms in both his Fourth Symphony and the Second Piano Concerto. Gradually the cloud created by this moment of indecision lifts as the 'lost' tonality of C major is regained. Congratulations all round . . .

This exuberant back-slapping is interrupted by a long and elegant phrase quite unlike anything that has gone before; it has the lilt of a waltz, the suggestion of a dance being enhanced by the graceful flowing counterpoint that supports it.

[1] I cannot resist drawing attention to a well-known Chopin waltz, Op. 18; suitably transposed it would read:

Ex. 226.

Notice the 'follow-my-leader' entries of bassoon and clarinet gliding so smoothly after the oboe tune, and then the characteristically boisterous interruption in bars 80–81. Disregarding such rudery, the elegant 'waltz' begins again, this time starting in the lower strings with the imitation coming from the higher wind. Some rousing affirmations of C major bring the Exposition to a close, one new figure being of particular importance.

Anyone buying such a fragment in the market-place might feel that it was scarcely worth having, even at a knock-down price; yet to a composer of Beethoven's resource such oddments are immensely valuable. One of the remarkable things about the construction of this movement is that the very first bar only appears once in the whole of the Exposition. It is possibly alluded to in a subtle way in the *a tempo* bar of Ex. 225, but otherwise it seems to have been entirely forgotten. As if to compensate for this Beethoven uses little else in the Development, little that is save for the fragment above. It is the violas who set the Development on its way with no fewer than eight quietly insistent repetitions of this new pattern. The violins provide gentle sustained harmonies (note the dominant seventh superimposed above the new tonic), while solo woodwind start a round-the-table discussion of bar 1.

Ex. 227.

This civilised conversation is violently interrupted by a thunderous roar of C major sustained for four bars and a beat. The violas resume pecking away at their octave C, the wind begin a comparable discourse; there is another crashing interruption, this time on the chord of Bb major. Now the cellos take up the little broken octave figure, moving from Bb to A as the harmonies above grow more remote and mysterious. The seemingly inevitable third interruption breaks in, bringing a veritable storm in its wake. The key is D minor, the atmosphere far from sympathetic to the theme.

Ex. 228.

Though surrounded by hostile chords in the wind and angry figuration in the violins, a fugue of sorts gets under way, the second violins entering with their version of Ex. 228 at the end of bar 151, the firsts responding in kind in bar 160. I describe it as a fugue of sorts since we are more aware of its harmonic strength than its contrapuntal ingenuity. Gradually the tension increases through some considerable dissonances until at last F major is regained in triumph. It is the cue for the Recapitulation, the opening theme being given to the bass instruments while a positive blaze of tonic harmony proclaims that the climb to this particular peak was well worth while. The woodwind settle down to relax after their exertions, offering us a pastoral version of the main theme that could comfortably be transplanted into the Sixth Symphony so rustic is its dress. As might be expected the Recapitulation proceeds in a lawful way so far as its little eccentricities allow; but once we reach the Coda Beethoven as is so often the case opens new and delightful vistas. A solo bassoon starts to play the octave game originally initiated by the violas (see Ex. 227). A cunning shift of tonality brings us into the unexpected key of Db major. Against the irregular tick-tocking of that octave pattern (now back in the violas) a clarinet introduces a blandly expansive version of the opening theme. The five-note scale with which it ends provides the strings with the material for a delightful game of tag.

Ex. 229.[1]

These delicate phrases duly build up into a *crescendo* culminating in the return of the main theme, harmonised somewhat disturbingly with dissonant D flats preventing a true definition of the tonic. Just as the impasse is resolved, the music comes to rest on a grand pause, clearing the way we would imagine for some portentous event. It is a false alarm; in fact at the first performance the movement ended almost at once by going directly to what we now know as the last eight[2] bars. Upon consideration Beethoven found this too abrupt a conclusion and inserted a further thirty-four bars largely concerned with

---

[1] cf. Piano Sonata Op. 2 No. 2. First movement, bars 181–188.
[2] Some would say six but eight makes better musical sense.

Ex. 226—though it becomes less waltz-like as it steers the course for home. The end is sheer delight, ten bars of receding F major chords, tucked away with a final whispered reminder of the very opening phrase.

The second movement is widely known to have some connection with the invention of the Metronome; let us try to establish the facts. We have already come across the name of Mälzel in connection with the 'Battle' Symphony (see p. 196). The son of an organ-builder, he inherited a real gift for music coupled with a talent for mechanical invention. His masterpiece was the so-called Panharmonicon, a mechanical orchestra that included flutes, clarinets, trumpets, violins, cellos, drums, cymbals and triangle, as well as wires struck by hammers that would have produced a cymbalom-like effect. The whole giant apparatus was a fore-runner of the cinema-organ of the thirties; it was to demonstrate its marvels that the proud inventor devised the 'Battle' Symphony, calling on Beethoven to orchestrate and adapt the music as he wished. Moved by the composer's plight, Mälzel devoted his ingenuity to devising ear-trumpets to aid his hearing; four were made in all. Mälzel's best known invention, the metronome, was actually pirated from a fellow-inventor called Winkel. In its original form it was named a Chronometer; a small lever activated by a cog-wheel beat against a little wooden anvil. It was during a visit to Amsterdam that Mälzel met up with Winkel who suggested that a weighted pendulum might prove more effective. Quick to see the possibilities of the idea, Mälzel took out a patent and, in 1816, founded a company in Paris to manufacture the improved device.

Beethoven took a keen interest in the development of Mälzel's invention, though he seems to have been thoroughly confused when attempting to use it. For two years the men were close friends until an inevitable dispute broke out over matters of copyright relating to 'Wellington's Victory'. In 1812, the year of the Eighth Symphony, they were still on the best of terms. One evening, at a supper party, Beethoven devised a canon as an affectionate tribute to his inventive friend.

The first three bars correspond to the opening bars of the *Allegretto Scherzando*, but scholars are very reluctant to say which came first. Schindler, not the most reliable of witnesses, declares that the canon came first and that the symphonic movement was developed from it. However he was not present at the famous party (he would have been a mere seventeen at the time); he got the story second-hand from Count Brunsvik. Thayer gives all the details in his exhaustive biography of Beethoven but refuses to commit himself to a final judgement; if anything he shows a preference for the idea that the symphony came first. It is a view with which I would agree for a purely musical reason. Even if we allow that the company was probably well primed with alcohol, it is frankly a very feeble canon to have come from a great composer's hand. The kindest explanation for the banality of the second three bars is that it was never intended to be a canon in the first place. While it seems perfectly feasible that the ticking semiquaver chords should represent the click-clack of the Chronometer's beat, the *melodic* part of the phrase (those notes in bars 1–3 other than the repeated Fs) is clearly a different conception; to integrate the two into a single line is a contradiction, as we see at once when we examine the orchestral score.

Ex. 230.

The canon is not a tune therefore, but a compromise between an accompaniment and a tune. It is not hard to imagine a scene in which Beethoven and Mälzel confide to the rest of the party that a movement of the new symphony is a compliment to the inventor. 'How does it go?' asks someone; giggling drunkenly Beethoven nudges Mälzel and says, 'Let's sing it for them'. They do so to general applause, Beethoven improvising the banal words; then, reaching for a pad, he scribbles down a second part and they try it out as a canon. This seems to me a far more convincing supposition than that Beethoven should remember a snatch of music whose second part is abysmal and perpetuate it in a symphony.

Leaving such speculation and turning to the music we find a movement that is full of humour. Haydn had hit upon a not dissimilar idea in his 'Clock' symphony, though needless to say the pulse is much slower. Beethoven's repeated chords give an impression of absolute regularity—an aural illusion since he wittily varies the placing of the melodic fragments that dance to the rhythm. Anyone who has ever tried playing to the beat of a metronome will know how hard it is to stay exactly in time. Beethoven reflects the dilemma enchantingly with sudden grabs at the beat or with misplaced accents. He even winds up the clockwork spring four times in the course of the movement with this startlingly descriptive gesture.

Here surely is not only the whirr of the mechanism in the swiftly repeated notes but even the rotation of the handle in the bass. Thematic quotation is hardly necessary in a movement so immediately accessible, but it is worth pointing out that the form is beautifully balanced, while any danger of bittiness is averted by the relatively slow pace of harmonic change. Two passages in parallel thirds deserve mention; they sound suspiciously like a mechanical organ—another aspect of Mälzel's inventive genius. As to the end of the movement, it is sheer Walt Disney. Clearly the machine breaks down; though shaken furiously it hardly stirs. Finally the whole thing disintegrates; wheels fly out, springs break, wires twang as, with a fearful whirring noise, the Chronometer expires.

The element of surprise so notably exploited in this symphony continues in the third movement; in the first place we expect a Scherzo—or possibly, since the previous Allegretto was marked *scherzando*, a genuine slow movement. A reversion to a Haydnesque menuetto might seem to be a retrogressive step, though certainly no more so than it was for Stravinsky to write his 'Dumbarton Oaks' concerto or 'Apollon Musagêtes'. The comparison seems valid since Stravinsky is not less himself for assuming superficially the manner of a bygone age, nor is Beethoven less himself for paying homage to a style for which he still preserved an affection though he had given ample proof that he could far outstrip its limitations if he so wished.

It appears that conductors in the latter part of the nineteenth century were so reluctant to accept the evidence of their own eyes that they would gallop through the movement at a rousing one-in-a-bar; yet surely the real purpose underlying the *sf* on each of the first six beats is to ensure that we can be in no doubt that we are listening to a steady 1-2-3, 1-2-3 rather than a more nimble 1 . . 1 . . Short of standing beside us and beating time himself, Beethoven could scarcely do more to indicate the tempo. Is it also possible that he was allowing the Mälzel joke to spill over into another movement, enough at any rate to establish a link of sorts?

Ex. 231

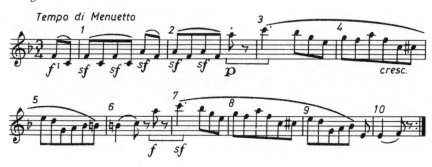

Beethoven makes a special feature of the lift-and-drop at the start of the tune (see brackets), giving it a very positive stance on trumpets and timpani or on unison wind; such references involve a modification so that the rising interval becomes a fourth or even a fifth though the relevance is clear. They also give him the justification for a rhythmic pun in the next part of the tune, in which the rising intervals, infected by an almost military spirit, are displaced in such a way as to throw the accent on to the second beat.

Ex. 232.

Just as it seems that this sequence is in danger of developing into a form of perpetual motion Beethoven decides to 'break it up' by displacing the accent in a different way, so that for a while anyone rash enough to attempt to dance a minuet to the music would find themselves doing so to an accompaniment in 2/4. Perplexed, the players themselves almost come to a halt until the bassoon

¹ *sf* in bassoon part.

gallantly resumes the main tune in the wittily prepared key of B♭, the sub-dominant. More jests follow, mostly based on a number of A-men cadences, some misleading, some distorted, some extended. Meanwhile horns and trumpets try to establish a parade-ground order.

The central Trio is most unusually orchestrated with a far more enterprising use of the horns than we normally find in Beethoven. When we recall the virtuoso horn parts in Leonore's magnificent recitative and aria 'Abscheu-licher! wo eilst du hin?' (*Fidelio*, Act I), it seems almost inexplicable that comparable demands were not made in the symphonies. Admittedly we do find some exuberant writing in the Seventh Symphony, though always reinforcing the main themes rather than stating them unaided. Here though the horns play a principal role in every sense, accompanied by an awkwardly written cello part that is altogether too wedded to the keyboard for a string-player's comfort. Despite this rather fussy accompaniment the tune is sweetly bland.

Ex. 233.

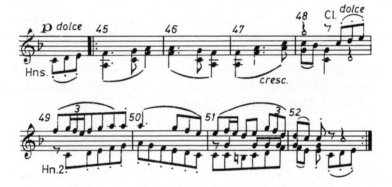

How subtly the clarinet varies and decorates the horn phrase, how elegantly in turn the second horn echoes the clarinet. As the theme expands further, more and more use is made of the initial figure of three quavers rising to a crotchet, both horn and clarinet gently interpolating it wherever possible against the tune, now in the violins. The modulations in this second portion of the Trio must surely have imprinted themselves on the young Schubert's heart so often did he exploit similar shifts of key. True chamber music in spirit, the Trio represents an oasis of calm before the hectic rush of the finale.

Marked *Allegro vivace* but usually played *Presto*, the last movement begins with a Mendelssohnian rustle, elusive as a will-o'-the-wisp. The basis of the opening theme is a three-note pattern beginning on the third and then the fourth degree of the scale. Presented in as bald terms as that it sounds far from promising.

Beethoven twitches this prosaic formula into life so that it fairly sizzles.

Ex. 234.[1]

I give a longer example than usual in order to emphasise the outrageous impropriety of that last roaring C♯. All that precedes it is so delicate in texture, so nimble and light-footed. In bars 15–16 the music is almost reduced to silence, *ppp* being a very rare indication in Beethoven. Having reached the threshold of inaudibility, he delivers this shattering blow, far outdoing Haydn's famous Surprise. Is it a comparable practical joke, serving no function except to shock? The answer is No; in its much more boisterous fashion it propounds a similar riddle to that offered by the mysterious D sharps soon after the beginning of the Violin Concerto. Inexplicable when they first appear, they prove to be harbingers of a later melody;[2] seeds that duly flower in such a way as to give us a feeling of relief as comprehension dawns. To understand the violent C♯ in Ex. 234 we need long memories, the solution to the problem being delayed for more than 350 bars. Meanwhile, having scared the wits out of the gentry, Beethoven invites the full orchestra to blast away with the opening

[1] Note the Scarlatti-like leap of 2½ octaves in bar 9.
[2] See my *Talking about Concertos*. Heinemann Educational Books, 1964.

theme, destroying its fragile image as ruthlessly as a tractor driving over a fairy ring. One point of orchestration deserves mention; for probably the first time in history the two timpani are tuned an octave apart, something Beethoven's predecessors would have regarded as wasteful since drums were never re-tuned during movements. Since orchestras seldom included more than two timpani before the time of Berlioz, to tune them to the same note (even allowing for the change of octave) amounted to the loss of half the harmonic potential offered by the drums. Despite his deafness Beethoven realised the immense gain in rhythmic buoyancy that a variation of pitch would bring. The experiment was so successful that he repeated it in the Scherzo of the Ninth to great effect, giving the timpani player a significant solo that is not merely a rhythm but part of a theme.

For some time the music hums along merrily until suddenly, without a hint of preparation, the Second Subject appears. The switch from G to A♭, a rise of a semitone, is accomplished so swiftly that we scarcely have time to grasp what has happened. It is comparable to (though not necessarily related to) the semitone ascent to the notorious C♯ in bar 17; here the dynamics are reversed so that the surprise note arrives softly out of a loud antecedent.

Ex. 235.

This presentation of the Second Subject in the 'wrong' key in the strings followed by a repetition in the 'right' key in the wind is a trick exactly comparable to the one played in the first movement (see Ex. 225, p. 225). The modulation that extricates the theme from A♭ major and lands it into the more orthodox C is sketched in in bars 56–58. Note also the span of the tune, so spacious after the breathless urgency of the First Subject.

After playing a game of Upstairs-Downstairs a couple of times (bars 68–84), Beethoven ends the Exposition unconventionally on the tonic instead of the dominant; though it is done with all the conviction he can muster it still sounds a little strange. There is a moment's silence. Not quite sure whether to make a repeat or not, and with the implied question 'Did you really mean to do that?' the violas make a timid attempt to get things started again. The violins raise a collective eyebrow, equally uncertain how to proceed. Even more timidly the violas suggest that a repeat would be in order, whereupon the violins launch into one—or so we are led to believe. The device is a brilliant one, exploiting the suspense of silences and false starts as well as toying with the conventions of form. We who listen are supposed to regard this as a conventional repeat; in fact it proves to be the start of the development. Yet again my proposition that the 'plot' of the symphony is 'I'll catch you out!' is confirmed.

The Development makes much play with the bracketed section of Ex. 234, bars 4–8. Treated sequentially and in contrary motion, it skips along in the rather solemn company of bell-like unisons in brass or wind. At one point Beethoven even finds himself unconsciously quoting the grinding D♯–E bass from the finale of the Seventh Symphony (bars 148–151), though to very different effect. Back comes the First Subject *ff* in the key of A; the question arises, how shall we get back to the tonic. Once more Beethoven has recourse to the rise of a semitone, the strings being stranded on E, bassoon and timpani reminding them *sotto voce* that they ought to be on F.

Skilfully disguised by the continuing drumbeat, a sustained tonic in the horns and a curiously impudent little phrase in the upper woodwind, the Recapitulation begins. Again the flow of the music is interrupted by the violent C♯, again Beethoven offers no explanation. As before, the Second Subject makes its entrance in the wrong key, as before the woodwind put things right. There are numerous new strokes of colour in the scoring which will be evident to any attentive listener; however, big surprises lie ahead. Following the previously ordained pattern the music comes to a halt, this time on a chord of B♭ major. Once again there is a silence broken by timid violas; somewhat incredulously the orchestra sets out to follow the previous plan, surely aware that at this stage it must be heading for disaster. First to realise this are the cellos and basses who violently call a halt.

Ex. 236.

The interruption is followed by a silence. Tentatively the strings try the same little pattern again, accompanied by even more hesitant woodwind. Cellos and basses cut them off angrily once more; there is another silence. The huge question 'What are we to do now?' hangs in the air.

A magnificent new development begins; while technically it may be called a Coda[1] it deserves a more important name so impressive are the new elements Beethoven brings before us. Curiously enough it has something in common with the Coda to the finale of the Seventh Symphony as the following comparison clearly shows:

Ex. 237. Symphony 7 (bar 349–   ).

Symphony 8 (bar 282).

(Read the upper example in the bass clef and the resemblance is really striking!)

Both symphonies make extensive use of this material, yet the effect is markedly different. In the Seventh one has the impression of a cauldron boiling over whereas here there is an uncanny feeling of calm. Certainly the rapid repeated-note figure continues its urgent tattoo but in so repressed a manner that it is dominated by the slowly wheeling minims. Inevitably we must wonder whether this is truly relevant to the matter in hand. Grove describes it as 'an entirely fresh idea', failing to spot the helpful clue Beethoven gives us. One of the most impressive treatments of this minim phrase is the way it is presented in contrary motion.

Ex. 238.

[1] Strictly speaking the Coda begins 15 bars earlier at bar 267, but dramatically speaking it starts here.

Thinking back a little, where else in this movement has contrary motion been exploited? Although not specifically quoting it at the time, I mentioned earlier that in the Development the bracketed section of Ex. 234 is treated in this way. Here is an example:

Ex. 239.

Smooth out the skipping rhythm and the secret is revealed:

Ex. 239a.

To compare this precisely with Ex. 238 it is necessary to switch the two strands round, but there can be no doubt as to the relationship.

Beethoven plays with these patterns for more than fifty bars, gradually increasing the volume and power of his utterance until at last the main theme bursts through once again in the contradictory key of D major—contradictory in that the salient note is F♯ in a symphony supposedly in F. Again it is the timpani that remind us of the proper tonality. Can there be another Recapitulation? It seems so; once more the strings set out with their Mendelssohnian theme, once more they die away to nothing, once more we find the outrageous wrong note at the end. At last, and we are now in bar 372, Beethoven finds the proper use for it. First it switches us into D♭ major—a cheat really, since it is done for the convenience of the woodwind rather than any musical purpose and may legitimately be regarded as C♯ major. Next there is a shift to C♯ minor, followed by three dogmatic assertions that he really means C♯ this time.

Ex. 240.

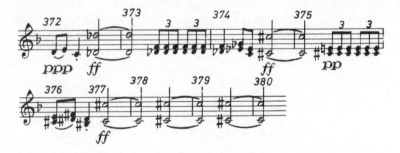

There is nothing for it but to accept the consequences of establishing this improbable new dominant; teeth gritted, the players plough on into the morass of F♯ minor — not at all the place to be in at this stage of the symphony. Then with a deft side-slip which never ceases to amaze they find their way back to F major and all that therein is. The end is surely in sight, but Beethoven finds time to explore the Second Subject fully once more. Just as we are getting ready to applaud there is another moment of silence. After a good party the best stories are often told on the doorstep; so it is now. On the brink of departure Beethoven thinks of a new joke.

Ex. 241.[1]

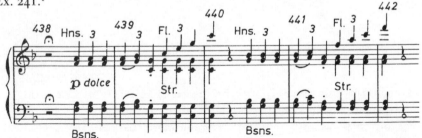

It is a deliciously silly phrase in its mock solemnity. Immediately there is a feeling of 'Must be off now' as the strings hurry onward; yet just as the happily drunk will linger for many a long minute exchanging interminable trivialities, so Beethoven is not done with us yet. With exquisite humour he tries out a number of versions of the F major chord, the strings buzzing anxiously as the woodwind search for a triad that refuses to materialise. (How can it when they are coupled in pairs? Triads need—'lesh think . . . *three* notes'.) The last

[1] For a serious treatment of a similar flute passage see the Second Symphony Larghetto: bars 264–271.

twenty-two bars are taken up with saying 'I really am going; not another word; no, I insist; don't bother to see me out; I'm on my way; yes; time to go now.' And he goes.

Before we turn to much more serious matters in the final chapter I feel I should justify what may seem a somewhat frivolous approach to what is unquestionably a masterpiece. Is it not absurd to propose that violas might make 'a timid suggestion', or that the woodwind 'put the strings right' by playing a tune in a different key? How can I say 'the players plough on into the morass of F♯ minor' when they have no choice but to play what is before them? It seems to me that there are two approaches to analysis; one is to apply the chilling hand of the anatomist, applying the correct labels according to musical terminology — 'here the subject is inverted in augmentation over a pedal-point on the mediant' etc.; the other is to describe what happens in less abstruse terms — 'the string chords increase in intensity as horns and trumpets pound out the all-pervasive rhythm'. I detest the first method and avoid it insofar as I can; inevitably I am often guilty of the second. However, both are merely descriptions of events and as such do not necessarily interpret what is happening.

Composition is a two-way process in which, though the composer may be the final arbiter, the material itself has a powerful say; dissonances demand resolution, rhythms need a predominating pulse and so on. To cite an elementary example, if one plays these notes,

the sense of dissatisfaction at the end is enormous. The phrase *wants* to go one step further; the need is inherent in the notes themselves regardless of who plays them or writes them down. In this sense music has a will of its own. Philosophers would agree that where there is will there must also be intelligence; music has intelligence of a sort though it is extremely elusive to define. For example it could be argued that music can be 'taught' to behave in a certain way; by repetition, a composer can establish a pattern ( ) which will become a habit; a deviation from that habit will then seem unnatural (unintelligent I venture to say) to the spirit of the music. Thus Beethoven's provocative C♯ seems unintelligent to that collective concept we think of as F major; but by repetition the music learns to accept it, absorbing it with the inevitable consequence that it will cause a shift of tonality.

If we start to enquire into the meaning of music we find that the easiest to explain is that which is descriptive of non-musical happenings — 'La Mer', 'On hearing the first cuckoo in spring', 'The Sorcerer's Apprentice'. A symphony such as this does not concern itself with such matters, yet the very word 'interpretation', universally used with regard to performance, suggests that all music must mean something. Increasingly I find that the most revealing way of interpreting in words an art that is properly constructed from sounds is to assume that the players and even the instruments themselves are not the composer's tools but his collaborators. Since music is dependant on performance, the composer's wishes are always at risk; strings can break, reeds crack, instruments can go out of tune, ensemble can come adrift, singers may faint. The ideal performance would come from a supremely gifted sight-reader, for a performance should be a voyage of discovery full of the wonder and delight that the unfamiliar should bring. It is this quality that I try to bring out with my fantasies about the violins 'raising a collective eyebrow' or the timpani 'reminding' the orchestra of the proper tonic.

Because it was a great charity occasion, the orchestra that gave the first performance of Beethoven's Seventh Symphony contained some of the greatest musicians of the day including Schuppanzigh, Spohr and Dragonetti; in the 'Battle' symphony the percussion was played by Meyerbeer, Hummel and Moscheles. Such men would have appreciated well enough the individual qualities that give the music its distinction. For them there was a First Time, that moment when music comes to life off the written page. For us the First Time experience is difficult to capture with any comparable intensity since we are usually introduced to Beethoven's music before we are knowledgeable enough to realise what is going on; what makes it worse is that the experience is increasingly likely to come to us through a machine, those great Pan-harmonicons of today, the radio and gramophone. It is partly to counter such mechanisation that I imbue instruments with intelligence. Is it so foolish to imagine that a violin has feelings? It certainly responds to good treatment, just as it whines hideously when mishandled. Furthermore a violin 'knows' that it cannot sound below a certain pitch; slacken its strings too much and it will refuse to play.

As for the finale, if I have approached it humourously I make no apology since it is clearly intended to be humorous. Old jokes are not always funny though — who laughs at Edwardian editions of *Punch* today? Beethoven would be the last to wish us to listen to such a work with reverence. (He would also be hurt and baffled by our refusal to applaud at the end of the first movements of concertos, but that is another matter.) Since I am dealing in words I am driven to have recourse to metaphor; do not misinterpret me by taking me to mean that the music at any point *describes* drunken farewells after a convivial evening. The world of music and the world of words exist on entirely different planes; at times we can find parallels that bring enlightenment since words are the medium of thought. To fuse these two worlds into one is an immense problem, a problem which we can see Beethoven struggling with in the final chapter.

14

Symphony No. 9 in D Minor, Op. 125

Dedicated to King Friedrich Wilhelm III of Prussia

Orchestra: piccolo; 2 flutes; 2 oboes; 2 clarinets; 2 bassoons; 1 contra-bassoon, 4 horns; 2 trumpets; 3 trombones; 2 timpani; triangle; cymbals; bass drum; strings

1. Allegro ma non troppo un poco maestoso
2. Molto vivace: Presto
3. Adagio molto e cantabile—Andante moderato
4. Presto

Bars 30–91
Allegro ma non troppo–Tempo I–Poco adagio–Vivace–Tempo I–Adagio cantabile—Tempo I—Allegro moderato—Tempo I—Allegro

Bar 92 Allegro assai

Bar 208
Presto. 29 bars (on the score this is counted as a new start)[1]
Allegro assai (but so is this!) (94 bars)
Allegro assai vivace, alla Marcia (264 bars)
Andante maestoso (32 bars)
Adagio ma non troppo, ma divoto (27 bars)
Allegro energico, sempre ben marcato (108 bars)
Allegro ma non tanto: poco adagio: Tempo I. Poco adagio—poco allegro, stringendo il tempo, sempre piu allegro (88 bars)
Prestissimo (65 bars)
Maestoso (4 bars)
Prestissimo (20 bars)

First performance: 7 May 1824

A single glance at the tempo indications above is enough to tell us that the fourth movement reveals a totally new conception. Frequent changes of tempo occur in a number of Beethoven's later works, both in the string quartets and the piano sonatas; that is to be expected since he was

---

[1] More recent editions prefer an unbroken sequence of bar numbers throughout.

beginning to feel a dissatisfaction with the normal constraints of sonata form. Thus in Op. 106 we find a number of fluctuations of tempo during the introduction to the final fugue; in Op. 109 the first movement alternates between a controlled *vivace* and an expressive *adagio*; in Op. 110 the third movement begins with a profoundly-felt recitative of the greatest freedom on whose first page alone Beethoven wrote no fewer than thirty-six actual *words* of instruction to the performer, so anxious was he to encourage flexibility of tempo and subtlety of expression. Such departures from a constant pulse present no insuperable problems to a soloist or a small chamber group such as a trio or quartet. However, for such variations of tempo to appear in a work for the largest available forces was quite unprecedented in the boldness of its challenge. Opera had not as yet developed the larger symphonic span of Verdi or Wagner; it was still at the stage when it was divided into sections of recitative-aria or recitative-ensemble. Admittedly Mozartean finales are often complex, involving a number of changes of pace; but Mozart would not have been thinking in terms of a large orchestra, chorus and soloists.

We have already seen that the idea of setting Schiller's 'Ode to Joy' had come to Beethoven as early as 1793, when a letter from his friend Fischenich to the poet's sister reveals the young composer's intention to set *Freude* verse by verse. I use the word *Freude* here since it has sometimes been contended that the ode was originally written to *Freiheit*, Freedom, rather than Joy. This would accord with Schiller's known political views, though fear of the censor may have caused the poet to substitute *Freude*, which scans equally well. Most present-day scholars express considerable doubts about this, although it has long been a staunchly held belief in Austria.

Nearly twenty years later, in 1811 or thereabouts, the first two lines of the poem appear in a sketchbook in a very indifferent setting.

Ex. 242.

It is fascinating to compare this clipped *staccato* conception with the smooth *legato* tune he was ultimately to use; they could hardly be more different from each other. Another sketch from the same period, showing material which was destined to be used in the Overture 'Zur Namensfeier' (Op. 115), suggests an equally abrupt treatment of the words. Indeed it seems that Beethoven at this stage was far from clear exactly how he was going to utilise the poem; even the words 'Overture Schiller' appear in a sketchbook, suggesting that he might have considered incorporating the poem into a symphonic tribute to the poet. Meanwhile, in 1812, as he was engaged on the Seventh and Eighth Symphonies, he notes his intention to write a 'Third Symphony in D minor', thus making a great triptych. This project seems to have been shelved for some years until, in 1818, he was taken with the idea of again composing a *pair* of symphonies, one to be purely instrumental (in D minor), the other to be choral in part, the voices entering either in the slow movement or the finale. He went so far as to write a brief résumé of this, giving it the curiously bi-lingual name 'Adagio Cantique'.

> Religious song in a symphony in the old modes (Lord God, we praise Thee, —Alleluja), either independently or to introduce a fugue. Perhaps the whole second symphony to be treated in this manner, the voices entering in the finale or as early as the Adagio. Orchestral violins etc. to be augmented tenfold in the final movement. Possibly repeat the Adagio in some way in the last movement. The text of the Adagio to be a Greek myth—Cantique Ecclesiastique. The allegro a festival to Bacchus.[1]

The emphasis on Greek or religious texts shows that this was a completely different concept from a setting of Schiller's Ode, while the clear suggestion that voices should be involved in at least two movements shows that a truly 'Choral' Symphony was in his mind. In the event the two ideas were fused together, the instrumental symphony in D minor and the 'Adagio Cantique' taking the vastly different shape that we know as the Ninth Symphony. Sketches of any real thematic significance are widely scattered over a number of years; first, in 1815, amongst ideas for a projected symphony in B♭ that never materialised, we find a fugue subject near enough to the theme of the Scherzo to be unquestionably relevant.

Ex. 242a.

By 1817 the symphony was beginning to become more than just a vague idea; the First Subject of the opening movement emerged from this disintegrated scale.

[1] He spelt it Bachus . . .

Ex. 242b.

A considerable gap ensued, during which the Missa Solemnis, the last three great piano sonatas and the Diabelli variations kept him fully occupied. In 1822 his thoughts returned to the symphony; he even jotted down a little memorandum of the principal themes so far as he had conceived them; notice that the Scherzo is quoted as beginning in the bass clef while the slow movement is a blank. The 'fourth movement' bears no relation to any part of the final version, while the fifth movement lacks either a clef or key-signature, as does the initial phrase.

Ex. 242c.

Not very conclusive evidence that one of the greatest symphonies ever written was in the process of evolution; one thing did emerge though, seemingly a sudden flash of inspiration.

Ex. 242d.

It is the first direct association between Schiller's poem and the thematic material that was painstakingly being assembled for the symphony. An alternative and much inferior version appears at about the same time, one we must be thankful that he rejected.

Ex. 242e.

Freude schöner Götter Funken Tochter aus E-ly-si-um.

The sketch is important despite its abysmal melody, since it suggests the lilting compound rhythm which appears in the latter part of the symphony; moreover it has attached to it a brief note, 'End of the symphony with Turkish music and full chorus'. Now so-called Turkish music, as lovers of Mozart will know, was an enormously popular example of a quasi-exotic art-form which (to be cynical) simply meant the use of percussion instruments such as the cymbals and the triangle. As we shall find, there is a memorable variation in the finale of the Ninth which audiences and critics of the time would unhesitatingly have described as a Turkish march, even though to our ears it carries not a trace of oriental influence.

The Adagio was the last movement to evolve, its central section appearing long before the opening theme. Although it seems so serene and effortless to us, Beethoven found great difficulty with this; here is the first version:

Ex. 242f.

The resemblance to the slow movement of the 'Pathétique' Sonata is quite striking, the more so if we combine bars 3–4 of the example above with the first two bars of this later sketch.

Ex. 242g.

Even at this stage, however, Beethoven was not wholly convinced that a choral finale was desirable, and in 1823 a sketch appears headed 'Finale instromentale' [sic]. It was not wholly wasted, being incorporated into the A minor string quartet, Op. 132. Having followed the birth-pangs this far it is time to make a diversion.

Mention has already been made of the Choral Fantasia, Op. 80, composed in December 1808.[1] In spite of a gap of some fifteen years between the completion of the two works, the Choral Fantasia is a significant pointer towards the Ninth Symphony. After the huge rambling cadenza for solo piano with which it begins, the cellos and basses begin a march-like phrase *pp*. They are interrupted by the pianist, who plays a profoundly expressive solo with a Mozartean flavour. It is marked *mezza voce* and has something of the style of a recitative.

Second violins and violas in turn present the same march-like theme that the lower strings had previously offered; again the soloist rejects their theme with a comparably eloquent reply. And now for two brief phrases the pianist is given a single unsupported melodic line punctuated by *pizzicato* chords that sound exactly like a keyboard-player accompanying a singer in a recitative. For a third time the strings propose the little march, for a third time it is rejected; then, after some terse but arresting fanfares from horns (echoed by oboes) the pianist produces a new and elegant theme, *dolce* and *legato*.

Ex. 243.

Beethoven had anticipated this theme almost exactly in a song called *Gegenliebe* not later than 1795, yet here surely is a melodic line that is well on the way towards the predominant theme of the 'Ode to Joy'. The smooth progression through adjacent notes of the scale, even the repetition of the four-note pattern in the last bars of Ex. 243, show an unmistakable relationship to that famous tune; it certainly bears a strong paternal likeness. In itself this might not be significant enough to be of much account, but let us consider some other factors. Once the pianist has proposed the theme it is made the

[1] The Op. number is misleading: it was written before the Emperor Concerto, Op. 73.

subject of a number of variations in which soloist and orchestra share. Then, against brilliant arpeggio figuration from the piano, we hear again the little fanfare from horns and oboes. It ushers in a sextet of solo voices who in their turn present a charming version of Ex. 243. This is taken up enthusiastically by full chorus and orchestra who together, after some considerable development, bring the work to a resounding conclusion.

Here in fact is a ground-plan remarkably similar to that of the finale of the Ninth Symphony. The long piano introduction might aptly be described, using the original meaning of the word, as the 'Symphony'. Cellos and basses offer a theme (as the orchestra does in the Ninth) which is rejected several times (as it is in the Ninth). The eloquent piano phrases quoted above show an instrument aspiring to the condition of the human voice—precisely what the lower strings attempt in the dramatic recitative passages that introduce the finale. After a period of puzzlement and contradiction the looked-for theme emerges, pure and simple in its character—again a moment that is exactly comparable. The theme is treated as a subject for variation (as is the theme of the Ninth), and then taken over by voices, first by soloists and later by the chorus. I need scarcely pursue the parallel any further; to a far greater degree than is generally realised the Choral Fantasia is an experimental version of the vast symphonic movement that was to follow fifteen years later. Needless to say there are many differences; it is the similarities that are worth exploring.

Now I am not suggesting that Beethoven wrote either work with the other in mind. We do not regard it as extraordinary if a great novelist in his maturity steals the plot or even a character or two from one of his early unsuccessful novels. Why then should not Beethoven have stolen the 'plot' of the Choral Fantasia when he found himself faced with a similar problem? In both works we find a drama of rejection and acceptance even if on a very different scale; even the awkward problem of the transition from instrumental to vocal music is solved in a comparable fashion. The pianist, in rejecting the march theme offered by cellos and basses, is analogous to the 'character', the baritone who rejects the earlier music and hails the new—'O friends, not these tones!'

Before we begin to explore the music we should take note of Beethoven's actual title; the work is *not* called a 'Choral Symphony' but 'Symphony No. 9 in D minor, with final chorus on Schiller's Ode to Joy'. In other words it was conceived first and foremost as an instrumental work, a true symphony. There are those, Vaughan Williams among them, who remain unconvinced by what all must accept as a gigantic work; they find the finale in every sense a strain. Others bow down before it, hailing it as the greatest of symphonies. Such judgements are subjective and legitimate; there is no divine or absolute law that ordains universal acceptance of a work of art. In the mid-nineteenth century many critics expressed bafflement or worse; Fanny Mendelssohn, on hearing her illustrious brother conduct it, wrote,

This gigantic Ninth Symphony which is so grand and in parts so abominable, as only the work of the greatest composer could be, was played as if by one man ... the music became comprehensible, and for the most part exquisitely beautiful. A gigantic tragedy, with a conclusion meant to be dithyrambic, but falling from its height into the opposite extreme—into burlesque.

Even the doubters though are compelled to admit that the symphony is truly epic in scale; its influence has been enormous. Tovey said that 'of all passages in a work of art, the first subject of the first movement has had the deepest and widest influence on later music ... [it] has been a radiating point for all subsequent experiments for enlarging the time-scale of music.'

The greatest art is often the simplest, or rather I should say, may give the impression of being the simplest. Having made some preparation for the complexities of the finale, let us now turn to the majestic simplicities of the first movement. I doubt whether in all music there is so profound a statement expressed in such fundamentally simple terms as we find here.

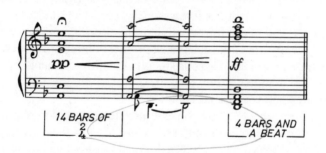

These are the bare essentials; bare indeed is the word, for one of the most immediately striking features of the symphony is the exposed fifth lacking the critical C♮ or C♯ to give it some positive definition. The title-page may tell us that the work is in D minor but it begins in a nebulous and mysterious land of No-key. As we have seen in all the preceding symphonies the proclamation of a tonal centre is a matter of prime importance in the opening bars. Even in the misty dawn of the Fourth Symphony the essential key-note is sounded first before doubts enshroud it. Here the suspense is prolonged with masterly skill so that when the final release into D minor does arrive its force is intensified to an extraordinary degree. (If you have a recording of the work try the experiment of turning the volume right off until bar 17 is reached; you should be able to see the actual moment as a black band on the disc. At the critical point, switch the volume up to normal; you will have an impressive opening theme for a symphony, but without those preliminary bars there will be a huge loss in tension.) Just as a tidal wave gathers its force invisibly, far out to sea, so this gigantic theme coils itself from a deceptively suppressed opening chord before unleashing its awesome ferocity upon us. Time and again we hear suggestions of its primal rhythm () though the first tentative strokes give no hint of the immense power it will ultimately generate.

Ex. 244.

So far as is possible this massive theme is played in unison; those instruments that cannot play all the notes (timpani, trumpets, two of the horns) lend all the support they can. The three hammer-blows from bars 21–22 are repeated, extending their tonal range to G minor. Back to D minor the great pendulum swings, martial notes from trumpet and drum eliciting a forlorn response from the woodwind before a swirling scale (how like but how different from that at the end of the Introduction to the Second Symphony!) brings us back to the *pp* bare fifth of the opening. The vital difference of course is that we now know the proper tonality; consequently the fifth is no longer poised upon the vaguest of dominants but securely founded on the tonic. The whole mysterious opening is repeated complete with the *crescendo* and the gradual contraction of the phrases. Now the first introductory bars were centred on A, the dominant of D minor; one might therefore suppose that this reprise, based on D, would also behave as if it were a dominant, exploding into G minor at its climax. Instead Beethoven resolves the tension with an equally tremendous statement of Ex. 244 in B♭ major (the so-called relative major of G minor, sharing the same key-signature). It is a master-stroke, presenting two contradictory aspects of the same mighty object, the North and South faces of the same mountain-peak. A rugged sequence begins, based on the terse semi-quaver figure from bar 19, or transpositions thereof. A sense of conflict is generated between strings and woodwind, culminating in another forceful theme in which the idea of opposition is sustained by an element of contrary motion.

Ex. 245.

(Notice how effectively and yet simply the chords in bars 66–67 establish a relationship to the main theme.) We are back in D minor for the moment, a clear indication that Ex. 245 is not the Second Subject. According to convention the Second Subject of any sonata-form movement in a minor key ought to appear in the relative major, in this case F. (Schubert, who cared little for convention, thought up a number of ingenious alternatives, but that is another matter.) By repeating his opening theme in the unexpected key of B♭ major—what I called the South face—Beethoven has established what might be described as a gravitational pull towards B♭; it is this key that he selects for his Second Subject, leading into it with a gentle theme in parallel thirds whose coincidental resemblance to the 'Song of Joy' has brought happy cries of 'Eureka!' from many a wishful-thinking analyst.

Ex. 246.

The Second Subject is shared between the woodwind, with an accompaniment made out of rather angular little groups of semiquavers in the strings.

Ex. 247.[1]

This theme is extended for some length, losing any pretence to serenity with uneasily paired semiquaver scale-passages and restless syncopations in the

---

[1] I am convinced that Brahms unconsciously copied this in the second subject of his Piano Concerto, Op. 15. The whole work is influenced by the Ninth Symphony.

horns. The mood is changed acutely by a particularly arresting rhythm:

Ex. 247a.

A bewitching modulation into the totally unexpected key of B major averts the crisis this might well have precipitated, even though it provokes a few muttered comments in violas and cellos; the violins meanwhile do their best to exert a calming influence.

An interesting passage follows; the timpani, not to be deprived of a spot of drama, start to foment trouble with constant reminders of the rhythm of Ex. 247a. Against this provocation, the first and second violins have a dialogue that is curiously reminiscent of an oft-repeated phrase in the Sixth Symphony:

Ex. 248

(Play the notes to this rhythm — ♪♪♫ — and the resemblance becomes striking.)

Considerable excitement is generated, with a swirl of demisemiquavers circling around, while cellos and basses take giant strides of a tenth with thumping accents off the beat. I have spoken before of the inner conflicts between contrasting musical elements and there could be few better examples than the subsequent passage (bars 138–150) in which the soothing gestures of the woodwind are ultimately ineffectual against the aggressive dotted rhythms which spring up in opposition to them. Suddenly the whole orchestra becomes as one,[1] converging on a great unison whose *ascending* arpeggio of B♭ major is the last great counterpoise to the descending D minor arpeggio of the opening theme. (cf. Ex. 244.)

Ex. 249.

[1] Apart from the violins who insist on leading the way.

Within the space of two bars this immense sound is totally repressed; the pitch shifts uneasily down a notch and the mysterious hum of the opening bars returns, re-forming itself on the identical bare fifth with which this impressive movement began. Is it no more than a conventional repeat that we are about to experience? Can music of this stature bow to the conventions of formal constraint? The answer of course is No; characteristically, Beethoven wants us to assume that orthodoxy is being observed the better to surprise us when he deviates from the expected course: as the Development gets under way we can hardly fail to notice the immense span of the music; although the melodic units are often no more than fragments two notes long,

the pace of harmonic change is extremely slow, eight or ten bars for each chord being quite normal. These chords, sustained in the wind, are kept vibrant by the pulsating repetitions in the strings which throb and hum like some giant dynamo. Gradually the allusions to the main theme (Ex. 244) grow more specific, the bassoon being the first to reassemble it coherently. Just as we think that the entire orchestra will take it up again, Beethoven changes his mind and introduces a distorted version of Ex. 249 instead. The outburst, strong though it is, is short-lived; with considerable pathos the woodwind introduce an expressive extension of a figure derived from the third bar of the main subject (Ex. 244, bar 19). The change of character is sufficient to make the music seem to falter in its progress.

Ex. 250.

As though affected by the plaintive woodwind phrases the violins (with violas lending shadowy support) introduce this modified version of the First Subject, revealing quite a different emotional potential. Such a yielding to sentiment cannot be tolerated for long and within a few bars a further distortion of Ex. 249 breaks in. Once more the woodwind counter this aggression with the forlorn little phrases of Ex. 250, this time in C minor; again the tempo hesitates, not surprisingly when we see what lies ahead. We are on the brink of the most fiercely intellectual part of the Development, a triple fugue whose main subject is based on bars 19–20 of Ex. 244.

Ex. 251.

Placed in opposition to this are two clearly defined ideas, the one a busy counterpoint —

Ex. 251a.

the other more of a rhythm than a theme.

Ex. 251b.

Soon the full orchestra becomes involved, goaded by trumpets and timpani. It is a matter of opinion whether one regards it as collaboration or conflict, but the effect is undeniably both powerful and turbulent.

Now much of the composer's art is dedicated to the idea of contrast, whether of tonality (as in what I called the North and South face) or of mood — pathos opposed to anger and so forth; but perhaps an even more potent device is the modification of themes so as to change their emotional significance. The preceding sections have shown us a plaintive derivation from Theme I (Ex. 250) and a stormy one (Ex. 251). Like characters in a play who by the pressure of circumstance affect each other's mood, these two elements work against each other. The angry violins become influenced by the pathos of Ex. 250, melting into a *cantabile* style that is quite new to them; but the strong syncopations of Ex. 251b leave a mark that cannot easily be erased, so that even as the violins touch our hearts with their tender dialogue, the cellos remain somewhat detached, still maintaining some of the tensions of a syncopated rhythm though the precise shape of the patterns in Ex. 251b seems to have been altered almost beyond recognition, a subtle fusion of elements from Ex. 251 *and* 251b.

Ex. 252.

Softly the Second Subject enters the scene, this time tinged with the melancholy implicit in A minor. Cellos and basses bring some consolation by turning the theme towards F major, a move that inevitably makes a return to the original tonic of D minor more practicable since the two keys are closely related. Any expectations that this will lead to an elaboration of the Second Subject are thwarted by a return to Ex. 252, also in F major and orchestrated in an entirely new way. An ominous shift to C♯ in the bass provokes an instant reaction as the music pivots towards D minor; a strongly reinforced unison passage in semiquavers leads inexorably towards that doom-laden key. I use the word 'inexorably' since, if the orchestra broke off abruptly on the final semiquaver of bar 300, not one in a thousand musicians would accurately predict the ensuing harmony. It is one of the supreme surprises of the entire repertoire; instead of the seemingly inevitable D minor, Beethoven introduces a powerful F♯ in the bass, thus creating a chord of D *major*. With a *fortissimo* blare from trumpets, horns and wind coupled to the resonant thunder of the timpani, the opening theme appears transformed. The ambiguity of that bare opening fifth is exploited to brilliant effect since the possibility of a major third,

257

however improbable, has always been there, though so far invariably denied. One might expect the emergence of a major key in this context to induce a feeling of optimism or even triumph, yet such is the character of the theme that it cannot do so. It is awe-inspiring in the same way that a vision of the avenging angel would be; one's eyes would be dazzled by his radiance though one's heart would quake with terror.

Now tremendous though this moment is, it is a fallacy to regard it as a recapitulation of the opening *Theme*; it is a recapitulation of the Introduction, vastly changed. Once the theme proper returns, the minor key is re-established, its terrible despair enhanced still further by the abortive attempt to establish a major tonality. The orchestration is fuller, new counterpoints being added such as the rising bass which counters the great descent of the First Subject. (It is presumably related, however distantly, to Ex. 249.) Yet though the treatment of the material is richer in detail it is even more concentrated in length, the Second Subject arriving almost before we are ready for it. Its reappearance enables Beethoven to relax a little in more ways than one, since for a while the Recapitulation proceeds according to the conventions of the day. When for the first time we hear the great ascending figure of Ex. 249 in D minor it not only tells us that this formality is over but warns us to pay heed to the Coda that follows. One of Beethoven's most significant contributions to symphonic form was his expansion of the Coda. As we might expect, this movement shows him to have a huge amount in reserve, so much so that (as in the 'Eroica') the Coda is comparable to an entire new development section. Most of all it emphasises the essentially tragic character of the movement, especially in its treatment of the First Subject. Stripped of any pretensions to heroism, its spirit seems almost broken.

Ex. 253.

While it is true that this builds in a substantial crescendo towards a *ff* climax, it is a climax not of triumph but despair. There is only one small glimmer of sunshine, an episode in D major initiated by the first horn. Improbably it seems to find some comfort in Ex. 251, though the second horn sounds a note of unease beneath.

Ex. 254.[1]

Although oboe, bassoon and flute join in this song of consolation it is to no avail; the strings in stark unison revert to D minor, growing frighteningly in intensity to the increasing agitation of the woodwind. At last the music seems to be on the point of disintegration, the flute lagging strangely behind; we have reached the Valley of the Shadow of Death. In what is possibly the most remarkable passage in this remarkable movement, Beethoven begins what is in effect a funeral march. Its foundation is a chromatic wailing in the bass above which brass and wind proclaim funereal fanfares.

Ex. 255.

With immense pomp and majesty this great phrase rises to its climax; it is a climax devoid of hope, for though the upper wind try desperately to establish F sharps (with their D major implications), the strings weigh them down with a huge arc-like phrase that covers a span of nearly two octaves.

Ex. 225a.

[1] Beethoven is fond of these grinding basses; but as an instance of the amazing flexibility of musical language compare this passage with the identical horn notes (G♯–A) in the Trio of Symphony No. 7, bars 441–466; bars 483–494; also see Ex. 214.

When at last the strings do attain the top D for which they seem to have been striving in vain, it is only a touch, for at once they are launched into the final massive statement of the opening theme. Confirming the key of D minor with a few last heroic gestures Beethoven ends the movement. In doing so he has unwittingly opened the door to an entire new world of musical experience. One might say with some truth that Mahler and Bruckner were born here, for certainly the influence of this immortal music extends as far.

We have seen (in Ex. 242a) that the seed of the Scherzo was planted in Beethoven's mind some years before the rest of the music began to take shape. From the start he had realised its contrapuntal possibilities, visualising it primarily as a fugue subject. Two years after its first fleeting appearance in the sketchbooks he noted an alternative, still clearly conceived as a fugue.

In the following year, 1818, he toyed briefly with a totally different concept, some rather conventional horn-calls such as might usher in a hunting-party. Even as late as 1823 he was still searching for the elusive phrase; in fact he had come somewhat adrift:

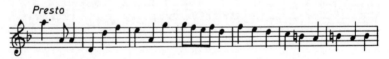

Light began to dawn with the elimination of the fussy little group of quavers in the fourth bar, an effete gesture that was out of place in this stark context. Having at last got the subject right, Beethoven devised a brilliantly arresting opening gesture, probably the most original exposition of the chord of D minor in all music.

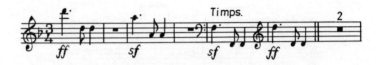

This splitting open of the D-F-A or D-A-F- triad is as ingenious as any of Stravinsky's neo-permutations of the common chord, yet it is no mere trick; coming as it does immediately after the last tremendous D minor arpeggio theme in the first movement, establishes a link that the ear acknowledges even though the mind may be unwilling to admit any thematic connection.

After two bars of stunned silence, necessary for rhythmical symmetry as well as for dramatic effect, the whispering fugue begins, *sempre pp*, the first note of each bar pricked out by woodwind, but the fugal exposition given to the strings.

Ex. 256.[1]

etc.

Last to enter in this five-part fugue are the double-basses, asserting a rare independence from the cellos. For no less than thirty-six bars the volume is kept under the tightest restraint, though the gradual addition of extra instruments gives an impression of sound accumulating in an uncanny way. Then a long sustained note in horns and clarinets gives the awaited signal for a *crescendo*; within a matter of seconds the whole orchestra is unleashed in an exuberant *fortissimo*, the drum marking the 'off-beat' bars in much the same way that we might clap hands in communal singing. Suddenly out of this swift and now energetic dance emerges a radiant theme whose harmonies made me gasp for breath the first time I heard them.

Ex. 257.

[1] Czerny declared that the movement was inspired by Beethoven one day finding that he could actually hear the cheeping of sparrows.

The subtle chromaticisms in bars 81 and 83 have an effect that cold print cannot convey even to the most educated eye, while the continually dancing octaves in the strings to the initial dotted rhythm prevent the least suggestion of stagnation that this chorale-like phrase might bring. Beethoven's own delight with this inspired idea may well be portrayed in the boisterous tune which follows:

Ex. 258.

As can be seen the strings are so drunk with the rhythm that they continue to repeat their octave Cs without regard to any harmonic collisions that may result. Suddenly, though, the exuberance is suppressed, as if an amiable schoolmaster had shouted 'Quiet!' to a crowd of children; for a few moments the conversation continues at a much subdued level as essential sentences are finished, then there is indeed total silence. It lasts for three whole bars, clearing the ears for the whispering repetition of the fugue.

The obligatory repeat once over there is a wittily stifled modulation to E♭ major, a move that brings another silence in its wake as Beethoven ponders where to go next. He embarks upon a maze of modulations, quitting each key as fast as he reaches it. The sequence is E♭ major, C minor, A♭ major, F minor, D♭ major, B♭ minor, G♭ major, E♭ minor, C♭ (=B) major, A♭ minor, E major, C♯ minor, A major—thirteen keys in thirteen bars! The last-mentioned seems like a good place to stop, being the dominant of D, the home key; but Beethoven is in a particularly capricious mood and whisks us upwards through a couple of bars of unison A♯s to B♭. Not surprisingly there is a brief pause to allow all concerned to take stock. A new section begins.

The indication *Ritmo di tre battute* tells us that he is now dealing with three-bar phrases instead of the twos and fours that he has used so far. The result is an intriguing compression of the theme, causing it to develop something of a limp.

Ex. 259.

Now it is the wind who lead the fugal dance, the strings who prick out the first beats—not all of them however; they only play on the second and third bars of each three-bar group. Their idleness in this respect is noticed by the timpanist who forcefully marks the 'missing' bars in the sequence with a further reminder of the octave theme. In due course, with a quite notable lurch to the rhythm, the normal four-bar phraseology is restored. At one point the strings try to calm things down with some quiet sustained harmonies, but the dancing octaves persist until, not to be denied, the initial subject returns at maximum strength. Structurally this passage (starting at bar 271 after four false attempts) is the equivalent of the Recapitulation in a sonata-form movement, a means of giving the audience a recognisable landmark. For a while the Scherzo continues to behave with the delusions of grandeur which come with the assumption that it is a sonata after all, until, suddenly losing confidence, it subsides into silence. Beethoven then expected this whole substantial section to be repeated, even though it is almost entirely dominated by one rhythm. Tovey remarks drily that it is 'an injunction not often followed in these days of hustle'.

Several false starts lead to a pause, giving the impression that nobody is quite sure where to go, even though the wind and brass disguise their hesitation by considerable huffing and puffing. The goal is sighted, and hurrying forward the orchestra precipitates us into the Trio. It involves an unusual change of pulse, the triple beat being adjusted so that two bars of 3/4 equal one bar of 2/2.

Ex. 260.

Such changes are child's play today but I have no doubt that the players at the time were perplexed by it.

I have already pointed out the interesting resemblance between the Trios of Symphonies No. 2 and No. 9.[1] Coincidence can be ruled out since in the middle of the sketches for 1818 we find what might be termed a go-between, neither one nor the other but clearly related to both.

[1] See pp. 52–53.

The Db major key-signature is inexplicable, but the fragment is labelled 'Symphony, 3rd movement'; its purpose is therefore not open to doubt. Rightly Beethoven decided that there had already been enough 3/4 in the movement; putting convention aside he chose to use duple time (*alla breve* 2/2), an exceptional decision. As if to herald this departure from normal practice there is a sudden blast from the bass-trombone — the first note he plays in the symphony! The first phrase it given to the woodwind (see Ex. 52a, p. 53); as a foil to this, with its *staccato* running bass in the bassoon-part, the strings are given a seductively smooth line. Anyone who regards the Ninth Symphony as forbidding or unapproachable should start here, for Beethoven seldom wrote a more beguiling passage than this entire section.

Ex. 261.

The whole conception is brilliant, exploiting the contrasts between *staccato* and *legato* as well as between the various orchestral families. One irresistible moment deserves mention when the oboist loses his way (or his head) and slips inadvertently into F major, only to make a somewhat tortuous return to the 'proper' key of D.

Ex. 262.

To extricate himself from this truly happy music and return to the more nervy character of the initial Scherzo Beethoven uses a single G minor chord (sustained as a pause) beneath a wistful phrase from the violins. He then whisks us back to the opening, dramatic introductory bars and all; the conventional reprise ensues until we reach the pause where there had been a hesitation previously—the one I described as huffing and puffing. At this point the players are diverted to the Coda, which is as compact and succinct as the remainder of the movement has been expansive and garrulous, twenty-eight bars out of a total of 559.[1]

It is an apt demonstration of Beethoven's enormous range as a composer that his work on the Diabelli Variations (1819–23) corresponds almost exactly in period to the time when he began developing his vision of the Ninth Symphony. The point is worth making since both the Adagio and the finale of the symphony are basically in variation form, yet their difference from the Diabelli variations is so marked that any comparison would be virtually impossible to pursue. The theme that Anton Diabelli gave to Beethoven was trite, cliché-ridden and extremely short. Starting from such basically trivial material Beethoven constructed a masterpiece that displayed all his prodigious powers of invention. The banality of the theme disappears as it is subjected to the piercing beam of the composer's intellect; the whole work is a virtuoso display of the art of composition which sets out to prove that it is not the material that matters so much as what a musician's genius can make out of it. In the Adagio of the Choral Symphony, and to a slightly lesser extent in the finale, the reverse is true. It is the material that is inspired, while the variations are decorative rather than inventive. (The doubts which Vaughan Williams expressed in a famous monograph were mostly founded on his instinctive distrust of the decorator's art.)

There are two clearly differentiated themes in this movement, both notable for their melodic span. The main tonal centres of the first movement are here reversed; instead of D and B♭ we find B♭ and D. One might dismiss this as of little importance were it not that the finale begins with a B♮ violently in opposition to a D minor chord, while the 'Song of Joy' is in D major with an elaborate variation in B♭ (the 'Turkish' march). It seems then that these two

[1] With all repeats nearly 1000 bars!

tonalities are like a great pendulum, countering to some extent the more normal tonic-dominant relationship.

At first hearing one takes the two-bar introduction to be little more than a series of sighs, expressive but restrained.

Ex. 263.

(Notice especially the effectiveness of the G♭ 'pressure-point' in bar 2, lending a more profound melancholy to the phrase than it otherwise would have.) Tempting though it is to look on this as the orchestral equivalent of a pianist playing a few gentle chords to get the feel of the keyboard, it is unwise thus to dismiss it, for here Beethoven plants a seed which is destined to flower into the second main melody of the movement. For the time being all we need to do is to respond to the beauty of the gesture and to store it in our minds for future reference. Gently the strings embark on Theme I, whose resemblance to the slow movement of the 'Pathétique' sonata has already been observed.[1] The tune is given a feeling of great spaciousness by the use of echoes, clarinets and bassoons expressing their approval of each string phrase by repeating the last few notes as if to say 'wasn't that lovely'.

Ex. 264.

[1] See Exx. 242f and 242g, p. 248.

The theme repays study not merely for its intrinsic beauty but because of the skilfully varied length of its phrases; the echoes, which could so easily degenerate into a pat formula, suddenly take on a life of their own in the last extended passage for wind, beneath which the strings place eloquently throbbing chords—a keyboard effect translated into orchestral terms.

Now the expected resolution of the final chord above would be G minor; instead we have an unprepared transition into D major. The music doesn't *modulate* into D, it *melts*, as Theme II makes its exquisite appearance. When the idea first came to him Beethoven visualised the tune in the key of A, but D gives it much greater richness. The initial version was also faster, a minuet of a relatively ordinary kind.

Ex. 265.

The banality of the ending was compounded by a continuation too trite to be worth quoting.

The stroke of genius that transformed this rather conventional tune into the sublime melody we find in the symphony seems so simple that one would scarcely credit the difference it makes; it was not just a matter of transposition but of eliminating the stresses on subsidiary beats. It is easier to see the effect by changing Beethoven's rather confusing notation to this:

Ex. 265a.

Written in this way we can see the lingering quality of bars 25–26 with the tune hanging motionless in the middle of the bar, as well as the added intensity that comes in bars 29–30 with the slightly more restless syncopations. The avoidance of the tonic note, D, at the start of bar 32 is a master-stroke. As the tune re-commences, the first violins add a descant, the theme having initially been given to second violins and violas in unison. Look again at this tune and see how each bar begins with a falling tone or semitone; at once the relevance of the two introductory bars of Ex. 263 becomes manifest. It is indeed a flowering which we could scarcely be expected to anticipate. Beethoven confirms the relationship with two notes that can easily pass unnoticed,

underlining the point with the descent G–F♮–E♭[1] in the flute part as he leads us back to B♭ major for Variation I on Theme I. Ingeniously it fuses elements of both themes since its elegantly decorated line makes several references to shapes derived from Theme II, for example:

Once again the woodwind nod approval at the end of each phrase although refraining from the sort of embroidery provided by the violins. The essential outlines are easy to follow. At precisely the same point as before, Theme II reappears, this time in the woodwind, the key being G major. I may well be wrong but I detect some significance in this with regard to the tonal balances I

[1] See bracketed phrase in Ex. 263.

have already mentioned. G major is the 'other' vital key in the finale; it is reserved for the great hymn-like entry of the men's voices, *Seid umschlungen Millionen, Diesen Kuss der ganzen Welt!*

Ex. 266.

Now a feature of Theme II that I have not mentioned so far is its bass, which rocks gently down to the dominant in a series of changing intervals. The first bar of this bass (transposed exactly from the original version of the theme) would be

which bears enough resemblance to the start of Ex. 266 to set my mind working. It is pure speculation, but here is a possible conjunction of ideas which at any rate makes musical sense.

Ex. 267.

The upper line is taken directly from the Adagio; the lower line has only to be compared to Ex. 266 to show its relevance. Now since Ex. 266 is also a counterpoint to the 'Song of Joy', albeit with some rhythmic alteration to both, a relationship of sorts can at least be imagined (though not proved) between Theme II of the Adagio and *both* the main themes of the finale. I must admit to finding this a more intriguing possibility than the one suggested by several other commentators who see Ex. 265a as a distant descendant of a theme from the Larghetto of the Second Symphony. It is true that both tunes have an *appoggiatura* on each first beat, but such embellishments are too common in certain types of expressive melody to have much weight as evidence. Let us leave these flights of fancy and return to Beethoven as he is and not as he might be.

The woodwind having enjoyed Theme II, the music modulates to E♭ major, again using a three-note descent that can be traced to the introductory two bars. Clarinets and bassoons appear to start a new variation on Theme I. In fact it is a strange interlude sixteen bars in length, so scored as to resemble nothing else in Beethoven's entire output. It is the horn-part in particular that strikes both eye and ear as outlandish. Why should the fourth horn-player be asked to play passages whose difficulty far exceeds anything else that Beethoven ever wrote? The apparent madness of the enterprise has a very acceptable explanation since it has been discovered that the player concerned in the original performance was the proud possessor of one of the earliest two-valved horns. Obligingly Beethoven gave him an opportunity to show what it could do. In the course of this diversion the music drifts into some remote keys so that when at last the tonic (B♭) is regained it is like an emergence into the light of day. The violins embark on the second variation on Theme I, so elaborate in ornamentation that it resembles an extract from a solo concerto. It would not be beyond the bounds of possibility that it was indeed played by a solo violin at the first performance, allowing for the minimal rehearsal-time available for so vast a work. Such may even have been Beethoven's intention, one scrap of evidence being the otherwise absurdly eccentric scoring in bar 121 where the violin part reads:

As the preparation for these lone chords is a little fanfare of the type that often heralds the entrance of a solo instrument, it is at least arguable that Beethoven was thinking in terms of a soloist versus the mass, even if the part is played by all the first violins. Considered simply as a musical gesture I feel that the essentially heroic quality of the moment would be better realised by a single player pitting his strength against odds. If Beethoven wanted a genuinely big sound at this point he could have used brass. Since nobody will ever have the courage to take so radical a step it must remain a provocative thought.

Throughout the elaborate variation that I have described, the woodwind maintain a steady course through Theme I, making only such modifications as are necessary for the newly prevailing triplet rhythm (12/8) to be accommodated. However, once the little fanfare already mentioned is reached (bars 121–2), the music does break away from the original plan. Where we might logically expect a return to Theme II we find a tiny outburst of militarism. Whatever its significance may be it makes little impression on the violins; with a notable display of calm they remind us of the interval of a descending fourth, derived needless to say from the first bar of Theme I. An ornate dialogue between strings and wind begins, near enough to the theme to sound relevant though not strictly speaking a variation. Again the little fanfare destroys the mood, again its effect is short-lived. There is a sudden shift to the unexpected key of Db major in a chorale-like episode of great beauty. Distantly the second violins echo a reminder of the trumpet-call; soon all is peaceful again as the horns lose the last traces of any martial character, joining the violins in a new theme.

Ex. 268.

A rich web of counterpoint develops, resolving itself at last through a brief violin cadenza to a gently throbbing chord of Bb major. Timpani softly remind us that they too can be treated as melodic instruments; there is a last ascent to establish an unclouded tonality of Bb and the movement is folded away. It is as well to savour the moment for our ears are about to be assaulted by the most ferocious passage Beethoven ever wrote.

Once he had decided to incorporate voices into the finale Beethoven had a difficult decision to make. Should he bring them straight in or would it be better to provide some sort of bridge from the preceding music? The whole conception was so novel that it needed careful consideration, and this at a time when even his creative drive was beginning to falter. In 1822 he confided to his friend Rochlitz, 'For some time past writing has not been easy for me. I sit and think, and think, and get it all settled; but it won't come on the paper and a great work troubles me enormously at the outset. Once I get into it it's all right.' In its entirety Schiller's poem was too long for Beethoven's purposes; he cut it and rearranged the order of verses with some skill, yet still felt there was a need to explain its inclusion. Schindler recounts that one day the composer had been striding restlessly round the room for some time when suddenly he exclaimed, 'I've got it, I've got it!' He jotted down the words 'Let us sing the song of the immortal Schiller', and explained that they were to be sung as a recitative by the basses, whereupon the Ode itself would be sung by a soprano soloist. It was a limp device but was a step in the right direction. Soon after he changed his idea for the text of the recitative to 'O friends, not these tones; let us sing something pleasanter, full of joy'. This was a crucial decision since the words 'not these tones' suggest the rejection of some alternative; as we shall see, rejection and acceptance are integral to the whole conception of the finale as we know it. Although the sketchbooks are sparse when it comes to words, Beethoven followed this idea up with a miniature scenario which reveals the 'plot' of the Introduction in down-to-earth terms. Leaving any attempt to poeticise till later he couched his argument in conversational prose.

> This is a day of jubilation, worth singing about . . . (Theme of first movement) O no, that won't do; I want something pleasanter . . . (Theme of the second movement) That is no better, merely rather more cheerful . . . (Theme of the third movement) That's also too tender. Must find something more rousing like the . . . I'll sing you something myself . . . (Theme of the fourth movement) That will do! Now I have found a way to express joy.

I find the picture of the deaf composer 'talking to himself' on paper in this way very touching. Although it may seem naive, the little drama achieves its effect since anyone with a musical ear can comprehend the purpose and meaning of the Introduction without guidance. Even so, Beethoven was still uncertain how to manage the transition from instrumental to vocal music. He once said that he hardly ever thought in terms of the human voice and it is certainly true that both *Fidelio* and the 'Missa Solemnis' cost him tremendous labour spread over a number of years.

Now since the prose sketch of a possible introduction could only be set as a recitative, at some point the vital idea must have come to him that of all vocal styles, recitative would most easily translate into instrumental terms. This may seem a paradox since recitatives are usually more interesting for their text than for their music. The point is that arias are to a certain extent interchangeable; a clarinettist could give a convincingly eloquent performance of 'Dove Sono'; cellists frequently play 'Après un rêve'. For an instrumentalist to play a recitative is less sensible, though it can be done, witness the central section of Bach's 'Chromatic Fantasia'. But recitatives conceived for the voice have a verbal inflection which prevents them from being 'pure' music; properly planned, it should be possible to write an instrumental recitative that would create a feeling of dissatisfaction or frustration that no singer was present. This was Beethoven's inspired solution to the problem; by making the cellos and basses play what was unmistakably vocal music—a 'verbal' recitative—he created an overwhelming need for singers to take over. In other words the voices answer not only his own artistic need but the *audience's*.

The other problem that had to be faced was the strophic construction of the poem, eight-line verses with four 'beats' to each line. Even when we sing a hymn with several verses we become bored with the repetition and like to have one verse with trebles only, one with the organist 'improving' on the harmonies and so on. For Beethoven to have attempted a continuously changing and developing setting of the poem could have led to a formless disaster; variations were the obvious solution, having both the virtue of formal restraint and the opportunity for providing contrasts.

The movement begins with a quite exceptional passage lasting a mere seven bars; described by some German commentators as a *Schreckensfanfare*, a 'horror' fanfare, I tend to think that Beethoven was thinking more of the title given by Haydn to the overture to his 'Creation', the 'Representation of Chaos'. Beethoven loved and admired the work and may well have taken a fancy to so graphic a phrase. Certainly his music is infinitely more chaotic than Haydn's, the blaring dissonance of the harmony being reinforced by a thunderous roll on the drums. There is a moment's silence; like an operatic hero suddenly appearing on stage, the lower strings declaim their first dramatic phrase, which Beethoven curiously describes as *Selon le caractère d'un recitative, mais in tempo*. (There are six such declamations in all which, at the first performance, were played as solos by Dragonetti, the famous double-bass virtuoso.[1]) This first phrase excites an even more ferocious outburst from the orchestra. A shorter recitative ensues, modulating to B♭; it is a key not kindly received by the orchestra who, with two brusque chords change direction. Suddenly, as though from a great distance, we hear the instantly recognisable hum from the very start of the symphony, complete with the descending two-note phrases in the violins. The harmony is somewhat more stable than it was originally, since a low C♯ gives us an assurance that it is the dominant of D minor. This retrospective glance lasts no more than eight bars before it is rejected emphatically with an impassioned recitative which I quote to give an impression of the style.

Ex. 269.

---

[1] Some support for my hypothesis that the violin 'cadenzas' in the slow movement might also have been played by a soloist.

The expressive change of pace and character in the last four bars gives a vivid suggestion of words, words still not precisely articulated but certainly on the verge of utterance. Quietly but briskly the orchestra offers eight bars of the Scherzo. There is a pause allowing us to take in the implications of the unexpected quotation. Again it is rejected; again the emphatic refusal is tempered by a closing *diminuendo* that leaves an unmistakable question hanging in the air. Gently the wind instruments propose two bars from the slow movement. They are not turned down so bluntly as the preceding offerings have been, but the frustration of the basses becomes evident towards the end of this fifth recitative. 'Surely you can do something better than mull over the past?' seems to be the implication. A 'choir' of woodwind (I choose the word deliberately) suggests two phrases circling smoothly in crotchets.

Ex. 270.

dolce

Before they can even reach the end of bar 80 they are interrupted by the basses, as though to say 'That's it!' Of course it isn't—quite; the phrases, being still poised on the dominant, lack the sense of arrival that is required. However, they show us the shape of the tune to come, and after a confirmation of their satisfaction from the basses, a massive A-men from wind, brass and timpani tells us that the recitative is ended.

Now clearly by his own confession Beethoven has seen this as a drama of sorts, the cellos and basses jointly playing the role of the central character, the orchestra being a surrogate stage chorus. His dramatic sense might seem to be at fault then when we find that the same cellos and basses who have been looking for a suitable tune (and rejecting several that were offered) are the first to disclose it. If they knew it all the time what was the fuss about? A producer's explanation in theoretical terms would be that at this point they, or the HE they represent is handed a manuscript with the searched-for theme on it. Quietly he hums it through as the onlookers listen with bated breath. As the full impact of its beauty begins to make itself felt, the surrounding chorus cannot resist the temptation to join in until everyone is singing with full voice. The analogy is not forced; this clearly is what happens during the next few pages. Only the actual human voices are lacking; their arrival is the *coup de théâtre* that Beethoven is keeping in reserve.

After such long and disturbing preliminaries, the appearance of the tune is doubly welcome, its smooth contours acting like balm.

Ex. 271.

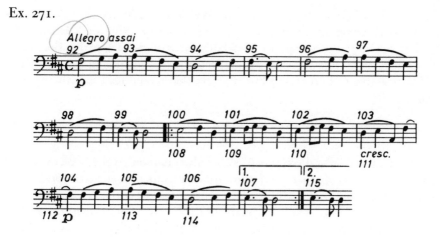

The gradual infiltration of other 'voices' after this first unison statement is done with masterly imagination. Violas join the cellos in a reprise of the tune an octave higher, while the basses add a bass-line whose sheer unpredictability gives the impression that it is being spontaneously improvised. Meantime a solo bassoon adds a counterpoint that has a similarly impromptu quality. (The second bassoon should play with the double-basses to add definition to the lower line, a point not made clear in most printed editions of the full score.) Not in a thousand attempts would a consortium of gifted musicians hit upon a harmonisation of this simple tune so original and effective as Beethoven's; it is a quite outstanding example of his individual genius.

In due course the violins join in, taking the tune up a further octave while the supporting parts flow in ever more liberated counterpoint. On the fourth repetition of the tune the full orchestra (less trombones) proclaims it in triumph, forming a veritable procession which breaks up into a happy but confused throng after the end cadence. Second violins and violas provide the bustle of the excited crowd while the upper wind extend the melody with the sort of

la - la - la - la

refrain that happy people might well sing spontaneously. (If the idea seems absurd, consider the uncanny way in which a crowd of thousands of football supporters will, without any apparent direction, go through a repertoire of songs such as 'You'll never walk alone', 'When the saints go marching in', 'Amazing Grace' or 'I'm forever blowing bubbles'.) Suddenly amid all the excitement there is a moment of stillness and a marked reduction in tone. There is an air of expectancy; something of import is about to happen.

What does happen is seen by many critics as a grave miscalculation, for Beethoven now repeats the opening paragraphs, substituting a solo baritone for the lower strings. With respect I would draw attention to a note that Beethoven wrote beneath his first sketch of the baritone's recitative; it is a further example of his attempts to find an explanatory text that would lead into the Schiller Ode.

> No, this chaos[1] reminds us of our despair. Today is a day of celebration; let it be celebrated with song *and dance* (My italics).

The last two words, disregarded as an embarrassment, seem to me to contain a potentially vital clue that goes far towards explaining the structure of this vast movement. Think back to the curious note about the 'Adagio Cantique' (see p. 246), remembering that it was planned to be a work on its own; think of its strange mixture of Greek and Roman myth, the final allegro to be a 'feast to Bacchus'. Consider also that in October 1814 there had been a huge Volksfest in the Prater in Vienna to celebrate the defeat of Napoleon; on such an occasion there would literally have been dancing in the streets, dancing that Beethoven would surely have witnessed. Is it not perfectly possible, even though the vision was never realised, that Beethoven had at the back of his mind the idea of what Wagner would have called a *Gesamtkunstwerk* combining music, song and dance? The variations in the choral part of the symphony are in dance rhythms for the most part, while the 'Turkish' march section seems to demand a staged procession just as positively as does the triumphal march from Aida. This grand march is followed by the one really static moment in the finale, the great 'cry to the millions' already quoted. Can one not imagine that having brought a chorus on stage during the march a producer would require them to stand packed in a strikingly posed group and address the audience, indeed the world, with this memorable exhortation? Concerts were often given in theatres; the facilities would have been available.

I fully realise that such speculation seems near to blasphemy, but if for a moment we accept such a possibility, the whole orchestral introduction to the last movement becomes an *overture*. The curtain rises as the orchestra briefly reminds us of the tremendous 'noises off' with which the 'overture' began. Enter the baritone soloist—or more probably he is 'found on'. Cast in the heroic mould of Siegfried he is the first musical incarnation of the Wagnerian hero. The first shouts of 'Freude' from the basses, somewhat ineffectual as a chorus entry in the concert-hall, would be immensely dramatic sung off-stage, while the chorus could enter during the subsequent sixteen bars. My purpose in putting forward this entire hypothesis is simply to offer an original defence for Beethoven's alleged miscalculation. It intrigues me for instance that Verdi

---

[1] 'Representation of Chaos'!

276

was much alienated by this part of the symphony; yet had he seen it as a theatrical conception he would surely have been the first to appreciate it. Although the very idea of a staged and choreographed version of the finale will probably seem repugnant to us, it is a very Germanic conception.[1]

After all his struggles to find a suitable *verbal* introduction to the Ode, Beethoven finally chose as economical a pair of phrases as he could:

> O friends, not these sounds; let us tune our voices more acceptably and more joyfully.

But though the words are few they are considerably expanded musically, the single syllable *Freu*—of *Freudenvollere*—being spread over four and a half bars and twenty-one notes. It makes for a perfect transition, the singer paying a reciprocal compliment to the orchestra; if the strings have aspired to the condition of the human voice, the voice responds by showing itself to be an instrument. The six recitatives of the strings are compressed to three while the final A-men cadence of the orchestra is deprived of its second chord, so eager are the wind to offer once again their delectable tune.

Two shouts of joy, *Freude!*, are heard from the basses. Significantly (so far as my theatrical hypothesis is concerned) they are accompanied not by horns and timpani as one might expect but by *pizzicato* strings—precisely the orchestration best suited to accompany off-stage singing. The solo baritone sings verse 1 to a gentle string accompaniment. (A few playful skips in the oboe part suggest that the soloist is accompanied by a happy child.) The last eight bars of the verse are repeated by the lower voices of the chorus, Beethoven, like a prudent general, clearly keeping his sopranos in reserve.

The second verse is sung by the solo quartet, the tune ingeniously divided between the voices so that to begin with the alto takes the first *six* bars, the soprano the remainder. As before the chorus repeats the final four lines of the verse, the orchestral accompaniment increasing in importance and complexity as the music continues on its way. It is now that the soloists are put to the cruellest test; beginning with the tenor and bass, Beethoven launches his singers into an ornate variation on the theme during which the soprano is expected to float her voice effortlessly to high As and Bs, as are the chorus sopranos later. So many complaints have been made about Beethoven's ill-treatment of sopranos that it is worth remarking that the pitch that he would have remembered from the days when he could hear was at least a full semitone flatter than what we have become used to. I have read of a performance given a semitone down in which the alleged difficulties all but vanished.

Once these daunting peaks have been tackled, the last line of the stanza, *und der Cherub steht vor Gott* is repeated again to a hymn-like phrase of great

---

[1] Since writing this I learn that the experiment has been tried in Austria.

majesty. Three times the word *Gott* is proclaimed on a top A, the third time with a sudden shift of harmony, opening the door to B♭ major. ('That key again', to paraphrase Shakespeare.) Out of the ensuing silence we hear in the far distance a drum, not timpani but a true bass drum, here being used for the first time in the symphonies if we discount the martial extravagances of 'Wellington's Victory'. At first we hear only the off-beats; but then, as triangle and cymbals add the clank of swords and the jingle of spurs, the rhythm falls into step and the 'Turkish' march variation begins.

Ex. 272.

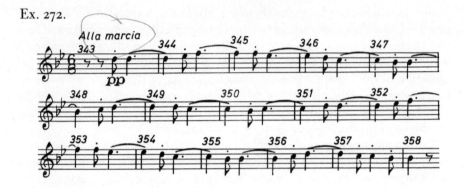

Apart from the change from duple to compound time the variation is remarkably straightforward. In his time Beethoven had written five marches for wind-band and the experience stood him in good stead here in his brilliant treatment of the orchestra. It may seem small-scale when compared to the 'March to the Scaffold'[1] which Berlioz was to write within the next decade, but its effectiveness within the context of an orchestral symphony is impressive. Against its steady tread the tenor sings of 'Brothers, hero-like to conquest flying'. The whole episode, complete with male-voice chorus, is totally operatic, as though the prisoners from *Fidelio* had enlisted in a great army of liberation. They appear to be an army of intellectuals since without for a moment losing the impetus of the march Beethoven embarks on a double fugue. The principal subject is a new variation on the 'Joy' theme.

Ex. 273.

[1] In the 'Symphonie Fantastique'.

The military character is maintained by the secondary subject whose rhythm is derived from the beginning of the march.

Ex. 273a.

It is typical of Beethoven's artistic integrity[1] that he should set himself this intellectual challenge at precisely the point where the music might degenerate into something dangerously trivial. After a thorny working out of the fugue subjects the music settles on to a giant octave F♯, a note which is stamped firmly home for eight bars before being isolated and allowed gradually to lose its intensity over a further four bars.

During the preceding passage all thought of the 'Joy' theme has tended to vanish from our minds. With unexpected gentleness the woodwind remind us of the first three rising notes:

Ex. 274.

Although they may be the right notes they are in the wrong key; some adjustment must be made. A tentative trial at B *minor* helps somewhat since it opens up three notes of the D major scale.

Ex. 274a.

[1] His integrity in other matters was dubious . . .

Bars 541–542 break the deadlock and D major is regained. For the first time the chorus comes in without preparation from the soloists; the impact is the greater as they re-introduce the 'Song of Joy' *fortissimo*, girt round with triplets from unison strings. Is this to be the final triumph? Just as we imagine the strings to be leading into a concluding coda, they modulate into G major, breaking off as though collectively astonished by the event. Again there is a silence. The 'Joy' theme seemingly put aside, tenors and basses in unison (with the massive support of bass trombone and the lower strings) launch the great Hymn of Brotherhood already shown in Ex. 266 (p. 269).

> O ye millions I embrace ye—
> Here's a joyful kiss for all!

The more sentimental writers on Beethoven regard this as a key-phrase in his life, seeing him as a near demi-god extending his love to all humanity. It is an image that is hard to equate with reality; he was bad-tempered, boorish, inconsiderate, self-centred and anti-social. However, the phrase is a magnificent one, occupying a position of immense importance in the symphony. Furthermore the two great upward extensions of a ninth and a sixth are clearly a symbol of arms extended in a huge gesture of embrace. The phrase is taken up by the sopranos, this time enriched by splendid harmonies in the other voices and decorative figures in the orchestra based on paired notes. All parts converge on a tremendous chord of the dominant. The male voices, this time with the support of two trombones, enunciate a new phrase:

Ex. 275.

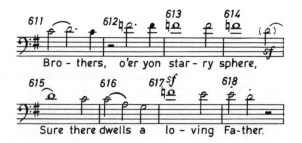

Bro - thers, o'er yon star - ry sphere,
Sure there dwells a lo - ving Fa-ther.

Again the great unison proclamation is taken up in full harmony by chorus and orchestra. A soft chord of G minor transforms the mood to one of quiet devotion. With scoring that suggests the tone of an organ Beethoven begins a very different type of hymn, the slower tempo lending it the dignity of a church ritual.

Ex. 276.

Adagio ma non troppo, ma divoto

The voices come in echoing this same phrase, but building it to a tremendous C major chord on the word *Welt* (World). It is a phrase that presents especial difficulties to translators owing to the very different sentence-constructions in German and English. The sentiment expressed is:

> Why fall prostrate ye millions? Oh World, dost feel the Creator's presence? Seek Him beyond the starry vault. Surely He dwells above the stars.

The immensity of the vision is matched by a wide range of dynamics from an awe-stricken *pp* to an exultant *ff* in the space of five bars. For a few moments the whole movement seems to stand still in contemplation of the stars, their pulsing light conveyed by throbbing chords in the wind. It is a moment of extraordinary magic considering how simple are the means employed. The chosen harmony is basically a dominant seventh, but it is made mysterious by the addition of a flattened ninth (B♭). The chord therefore hangs between the no-man's-land of a diminished seventh and the harmony most likely to lead us back to the original key of D major.

The moment of contemplation ends abruptly with the simultaneous return of the two principal themes, the 'Song of Joy' and the 'Hymn to Brotherhood'. The two are combined as a double fugue in a tour-de-force of counterpoint.

Ex. 277.

The music exists at three rhythmic levels, the measured two-in-a-bar beat of the lower line of Ex. 277, the lilting dance of the upper line, and a constant flow of quaver movement to add brilliance and impetus. The fugue is developed at length, culminating in a notorious climax where the sopranos are required to hold a top A *ff* for twelve bars. Were every singer except the basses to faint dead away in the following bar it would scarcely matter so abrupt is the contrast Beethoven now calls for. From the greatest possible sound from choir and orchestra including trombones, double-bassoon and timpani, he drops to the starkest *pianissimo*; there can be few more dramatic moments in all music.

Ex. 278.

Very quietly the wind keep a rhythmic pulse throbbing through the awe-struck silences that punctuate the voice-parts. First the basses, then tenors, altos and lastly the full choir have these strangely broken phrases, building to another climax on the dominant, A. The actual sequence of notes here is strange even though logical. It includes eleven of the twelve available notes, only B♮ being omitted.

As if to establish the firm foundation of universal brotherhood, these almost atonal phrases are followed by particularly strong affirmations of pure A major on the word *Brüder!* Once again though Beethoven defies expectation with a strangely wayward drift into G major. Despite a pause it is not a true modulation but a way of creating a further moment of suspense before the joyous dance of the Coda.

It is a moment to look back over some 250 pages of score, to remember the mysterious immensity of that opening paragraph, the stark unison of the great D minor theme that dominates the first movement, the nimble Scherzo with its ebullient Trio, the heart-stopping beauty of the two main themes of the slow movement, the drama of the beginning of the finale with its clangorous dissonance and impassioned recitatives, the emergence of the 'Song of Joy', the impact of voices, the intellectual power of fugue and double fugue. With so much behind him where can Beethoven lead us to give us a sense of finality? Few would anticipate the solution he offers. Remember that this finale despite its huge complexity is essentially a song of joy. Where do we turn when we seek the most untroubled happiness known to mankind? To children, or perhaps more truthfully to memories of childhood, when all days seemed golden and care was unknown. To say this of Beethoven (whose childhood was a nightmare) may seem cruelly ironic, yet there is a quality of childish innocence and infectious gaiety to be found in the music that now confronts us. It even applies to the 'Song of Joy' theme itself which is reduced to child-size by the process known as diminution.

Ex. 279.

(Again I am drawn towards the fancy that Beethoven visualised this as stage-music; how easily one can imagine a crowd of children running swiftly to their appointed places in this brief introduction.) The solo quartet now introduces a completely new theme whose innocent happiness recalls Mozart at this most beguiling. Tovey matches it to Papageno and Papagena which is as high a compliment as could be wished for; yet surely the clue lies in the word 'Elysium' for this is indeed such music as one might expect to hear in the Elysian fields.

Ex. 280.

Freu - de Tochter aus E - ly - si-um.

The music trips along in what I can only describe as a daze of happiness, even unfolding a canon so naive that it sounds like a children's game.

Ex. 281.

The chorus joins in in as unsophisticated a way as possible, all voices in unison. A marvellous climax ensues as they declare that 'all men should be brothers', a thought so ideal that it calls for a brief *adagio* as though to dwell upon its desirability; then the dance resumes. Again it arrives at an *adagio*, this time elaborated extensively into a cadenza for the four soloists. Skilfully Beethoven modulates into B major, a key calculated to refresh our ears after over-exposure to D since it cancels out most of the notes most vital to D major. The solo quartet weaves ecstatic patterns of counterpoint, culminating not only in a top B for the soprano but also in a surprise shift back to D.

Briskly, the orchestra starts a two-note phrase which those with long memories will recall echoes the baritone soloist's very first mention of the word *Freude*.[1] The pattern quickens, breaking into a headlong *prestissimo* in which the percussion join enthusiastically. It is easy to assume that we are in for nothing but a series of thumping repetitions of tonic and dominant harmony. In fact the music continues to avoid the obvious, shifting through several unexpected keys before suddenly coming to rest on a great dominant seventh.

[1] One wonders if César Franck unconsciously copied this section in the F♯ major *allegro* at the end of his Symphonic Variations.

It is virtually the chord with which we contemplated the stars some fifty pages previously, its one dissident note now removed; in this Elysium there are to be no such disturbing dissonances. Immense descending scales in the strings seem to draw curtains over the biggest stage in the world, the sopranos climb to a top A for the last time, the orchestra scampers to a finish, proclaiming the glory of D major to the last. It is the tonal goal of the entire symphony from the first groping elusive dominant to the ultimate triumphant affirmation of the joyous tonic.

Epilogue

From Grillparzer's Funeral Oration, 29 March 1827.

. . . The last Master of resounding song, the sweet lips that gave expression to the art of tones, the heir and successor of Handel's, of Bach's, of Haydn's and of Mozart's immortal fame has ended his life, and we stand weeping beside the tattered strings of the silent instrument.

Of the silent instrument! Let me call him so! For he was an artist, and all that he was he became only by virtue of his art. The thorns of life had wounded him deeply, and as the ship-wrecked cling to the shore, so he fled into thy arms, glorious sister alike of goodness and truth, consoler of the suffering, Art, whose origins are above. He held fast to thee, and even when the gate was closed through which thou hadst entered into him and hadst spoken to him . . . still he bore thy image in his heart, and when he died, still it lay upon his breast.

He was an artist, and who can bear comparison with him?

He was an artist, but he was a man, too, a man in every, in the highest sense. Because he shut himself off from the world they called him malevolent, and because he avoided sentiment they called him unfeeling. Oh, the man who knows himself to be hard does not flee! The finest points are those which are most easily blunted, bent or broken. Excessive sensibility recoils from sentiment. He fled the world because in the whole realm of his loving nature he could find no weapon with which to oppose it. He withdrew from men after he had given them everything and received nothing in return. He remained solitary because he could find no second I. But even unto his grave he preserved a human heart for all who are human, a paternal heart for those who were his kin, himself as a heritage for the whole world.

Thus he lived, thus he died, thus he shall live for ever.

Bibliography

The author acknowledges his indebtedness to the following volumes all of which to some extent cover similar ground.

Beethoven's Writings

The Letters of Beethoven, trans. Emily Anderson, Macmillan, 1961.

Beethoven: Letters Journals and Conversations, ed. Michael Hamburger, Thames and Hudson, 1951.

The Beethoven Companion, Faber, 1971.

Beethoven's Sketches, Paul Mies, Oxford University Press, 1929, Dover, 1974.

Two Beethoven Sketchbooks, Nottebohm, trans. Katz, Gollancz, 1979.

Music and Letters, Beethoven number, April, 1927.

Books on Beethoven

Martin Cooper, *Beethoven: The Last Decade*, Oxford University Press, 1970.

Sir George Grove, *Beethoven and his Nine Symphonies*, Novello, 1896.

Denis Matthews, 'Beethoven's Symphonies in Relation to the Sketches', *Journal of British Institute of Recorded Sound*, January 1970.

Pike, *Beethoven, Sibelius and the Profound Logic*, Athlone Press, 1978.

W. Riezler, *Beethoven*, M. C. Forrester, 1938.

H. C. Robbins Landon, *Beethoven*, Thames and Hudson, 1970.

Schauffler, *Beethoven: The Man who Freed Music*, Doubleday, Doran, 1929.

Maynard Solomon, *Beethoven*, Cassell, 1977.

J. W. N. Sullivan, *Beethoven*, Jonathan Cape, 1927.

Thayer, *Life of Beethoven*, Centaur Press, 1960.

D. F. Tovey, *Beethoven*, Oxford University Press, 1944.

General

The Symphony, Pelican Books, 1949.

Grove's Dictionary of Music and Musicians, Macmillan.

Charles Rosen, *The Classical Style*, Faber, 1971.

D. F. Tovey, *Essays in Musical Analysis*, Oxford University Press, 1935; *Essays and Lectures on Music*, Oxford University Press, 1949.

Index